A History of the Edmonton City Market, 1900–2000

For Harold Oppelt
with my best wishes — enjoy
reading it.

Kathryn Merrett

A History of the
EDMONTON CITY MARKET
1900–2000
Urban Values and Urban Culture

Kathryn Chase Merrett

UNIVERSITY OF
CALGARY
PRESS

University of Calgary Press
2500 University Drive NW
Calgary, Alberta
Canada T2N 1N4
www.uofcpress.com

National Library of Canada Cataloguing in Publication Data

Merrett, Kathryn Chase, 1944-
A history of the Edmonton City Market, 1900-2000

(Legacies shared book series, ISSN 1498-2358 ; 4)
Includes bibliographical references and index.
ISBN 1-55238-052-1

1. Farmers' markets--Alberta--Edmonton--History. I. Title. II. Series.
FC3696.4.M47 2001   381'.18'09712334   C2001-911014-6
F1079.5.E3M47 2001

 We acknowledge the financial support of the Government of Canada through the Book Publishing Industry Development Program (BPIDP) for our publishing activities.

The Canada Council for the Arts
Le Conseil des Arts du Canada

UNIVERSITY OF CALGARY LEARNING COMMONS

The author and publisher gratefully acknowledge the financial support of the following organizations and individuals towards the production of this book.
The Alberta Historical Resources Foundation
The Alberta Market Gardeners' Association
The Clifford E. Lee Foundation
The Honourable Anne McLellan, Minister of Justice and Attorney General of Canada and
    Member of parliament for Edmonton West
Mary and Julian Coward
Sheila and Jim Edwards
Sandy A. Mactaggart
Michael B. Morin
Barbara Poole
Tom and Betty Williams

Printed and bound in Canada by Houghton Boston.
∞ This book is printed on acid-free paper.

Cover: Oil painting by Ilona Kennedy (1998). The painting is based on a photograph of the main entrance to the 'old' Edmonton City Market which was taken by Jack Conway around 1962 and is in the collection of the CEA. Photograph for cover design by Ellis Brothers Photography Ltd.

Page and cover design and typesetting by Kristina Schuring.

Contents

Preface   vi

Acknowledgements   vii

Abbreviations   ix

List of Illustrations   x

Chapters   1. The Market and the City, I   1

2. A Castle in the Air, 1892-1916   19

3. Blue Sky Trading in Edmonton:
The Boom in the Bust, 1916-1939   49

4. The Market and the Civic Centre, 1940-1964   91

5. The 'New' City Market, 1965-2000   133

6. The Market and the City, II   171

Notes   191

References   List of Interviewees   223

Sources   224

Note on Primary Sources   224

Note on Secondary Sources   225

Works Consulted   226

Further Reading   228

Index   231

Preface

The Edmonton City Market, a well-known destination in Edmonton's downtown between 1900 and 1964, has barely managed to survive the post-1965 building boom which had the effect, if not the intention, of sucking life from the city centre. Those who remember the market in its original location knew the centre in a way that newcomers can only imagine — as a place where the rhythms of everyday life were not overwhelmed by the monotonous beat of workers entering their offices on Monday morning and leaving them on Friday afternoon. The public record confirms the impression conveyed to me in conversations with vendors and customers — that the market played a more important role in the evolution of the city than is readily apparent.

This book, which weaves together the stories of market vendors and customers with data obtained from public records, recounts the market's history in relation to changing urban values and an evolving urban culture. My purpose in writing it was twofold. Firstly, for those who have sold or shopped at the market and for anyone interested in Edmonton's history, I wanted to tell the story of the city market from its origins in 1900 to its hundredth birthday in the year 2000. I hope those who contributed their memories will understand their own pasts in a new way, seeing them as part of a larger story. Secondly, I have told the story of the city market to interest readers who have never shopped or sold there. When themes emerged from the history that resonated beyond the particular, I have not ignored them. On the contrary, I have incorporated them into the framework of the book. It has not been my purpose to constrain the details of my story within a specific theoretical framework. I have, however, tried to raise questions of theoretical interest for other scholars to investigate.

Acknowledgements

Without the support and co-operation of many groups and individuals, I could not have written this book. The Alberta Historical Resources Foundation (AHRF) generously supported the research when it awarded me a research grant in 1993. The Edmonton Downtown Development Corporation (EDDC), through the agency of Susan Wissink, Executive Director, supported the completion of the research and the commencement of the manuscript in 1999. Deanna Conrad and Shelley MacLaren, students employed by the EDDC in the summer of 1999, were able research assistants. The *Edmonton Journal* kindly allowed me to include reproductions of several advertisements and photographs directly from the pages of its printed copy.

Three organizations made it possible to test some of the ideas and arguments contained in this book. In January 1994, at the invitation of the Edmonton and District Historical Society, I gave a talk on the Edmonton City Market, advancing the thesis that the market's history sheds light on the attitudes and values that have shaped Edmonton's history as a corporate entity. In May 1995, I spoke at Edmonton's Bicentennial: Historical Reflections, a conference held at the Edmonton Convention Centre, suggesting that the many family-based businesses which had grown out of the Edmonton City Market raise questions about the relationship between farmers' markets and the local economy. Two years later, I was asked by the Alberta Farmers' Market Association to speak at its January 1998 meeting. Since the purpose of that meeting was to discuss the role played by farmers' markcts in the Albertan economy of the 1990s, I was able to provide historical context which was interesting to the assembled managers. I am grateful to those who were instrumental in my being invited to give these talks because they provided opportunities to put forward ideas from the research and to discuss them.

Offering their time, memories, interest, hospitality and, where possible, their photographs, were the many people interviewed, formally and casually, for this book. The first vendor to be interviewed, and the inspiration behind the oral history component of the research, was Mary Sernowski. With many stories to tell, and no reading or writing skills to tell them herself, she willingly offered herself as my first interviewee. Mary's story, and the stories of others — especially vendors and customers — influenced the conception of this book and helped to shape its contents. A list of the interviewees appears at the end of the book.

The majority of the archival research was carried out at the City of Edmonton Archives (CEA), where all the staff were courteous, helpful, and genuinely interested in the project. Special thanks go to archivist Bruce Ibsen and to June Honey, who was the mainstay at the reference desk during the initial phases of the research. Since then, Johwanna Alleyne, Kim Christie-Milley, Kathryn Ivany, Patrick Lamb, and Susan Stanton have maintained the high standards of knowledgeable service to be found at the CEA. Archivists and librarians at the City of Winnipeg Archives and Records Centre, the Edmonton and Calgary public libraries, the City of Calgary Archives and the Glenbow Archives (GA), Calgary all put themselves out on my behalf.

Kris Migos, president of the Edmonton Horticultural Society (formerly the Edmonton Horticultural and Vacant Lots Garden Association) kindly gave me access to the society's records and put me in touch with current society members who knew the old market building and had taken part in exhibitions there.

I would also like to acknowledge two former teachers. Carl Betke, from whom I took an evening course in Canadian history in the mid-1980s, sparked my interest in the discipline of history and has remained a mentor throughout my academic and professional career. Patricia Prestwich, who supervised my MA thesis at the University of Alberta, "*La France libre, 1940-1944: Resistance and Exile Journalism,*" combines an interest in oral history methodologies with a commitment to rigorous academic standards.

Bridging the gap between mentors and local historians is Michael Payne, who, as chief of research for Historic Sites and Archives Service, Alberta Community Development, has offered practical, professional, and personal advice whenever these were solicited.

Historians who have taken an interest in the project and flagged material I might otherwise have missed include David Leonard, Patricia Myers, Stephen Otto, Harry Sanders, and Don Wetherell, but many others have expressed interest. Patricia Myers was especially helpful when she offered the opinion that ideas and good intentions were never enough to finish a book.

Finally, I would like to acknowledge several special contributions: Betty Bre-Win for her seemingly bottomless memory and for all the newspaper articles she kept and all the photographs she collected; Barbara Budenz for the drawings that announce each chapter; Mary Coward for undertaking to read and comment on the early chapters and for maintaining an interest in the outcome; Simone Demers Collins, for her commitment to creating a regulatory framework for farmers' markets in Alberta and for her willingness to share information; Denis Hinse for reading several chapters and for representing the interests of vendors so capably; Ilona Kennedy for the oil painting that graces the cover; Gitta and Robert Lederer, owners of Grounds for Coffee, who love to talk about the history of the area and who were pleased to find the Edmonton City Market had a long history; and, especially, Robert Merrett who listened to me read each chapter when it was finished and who has been an unflagging supporter.

I do, of course, take full responsibility for the contents of this book.

Abbreviations

AMA	Alberta Motor Association
Bulletin	*Edmonton Bulletin*
CCA	City of Calgary Archives
CCF	Co-operative Commonwealth Federation
CEA	City of Edmonton Archives
CFRN	Sunwapta Broadcasting, radio station
CNR	Canadian National Railways
CPR	Canadian Pacific Railway
EDDC	Edmonton Downtown Development Corporation
GA	Glenbow Archives, Calgary
HBC	Hudson's Bay Company
IGA	Independent Grocers' Association
IODE	Imperial Order Daughters of the Empire
Journal	*Edmonton Journal*
Mail	*Toronto Mail*
MOH	Medical Officer of Health
PAA	Provincial Archives of Alberta, Edmonton
RCMP	Royal Canadian Mounted Police

List of Illustrations

1.1 Drawing: Market Square becomes the centre of Edmonton.

1.2 Mary Sernowski, June 1985.

1.3 Market Square, 1912.

1.4 Market Square, c. 1920.

1.5 Civic centre proposal, 1912 (looking south).

1.6 Winnipeg's first city hall and market, 1877.

1.7 Winnipeg's market building, 1889.

1.8 Sketch by Illingworth Holey Kerr of the Edmonton City Market in the 1940s.

2.1 Drawing: Routes to Market Square.

2.2 Firehall no. 1, Edmonton, 1908.

2.3 Cabbages in a garden plot, Edmonton, c. 1907.

2.4 Donald Ross.

2.5 Philip Heiminck, c. 1880.

2.6 Open air market, Market Square, Edmonton, c. 1910.

2.7 Weigh scale on Market Square, 1914.

2.8 Ernest Grierson, 1910.

2.9 Jasper Avenue looking east, 1 July 1901.

2.10 Civic centre proposal, 1912 (looking north).

2.11 Market Square, 1913.

2.12 Advertisement for the market from the *Edmonton Journal*, 13 November 1914.

2.13 Market building on 101st Street, 1919.

3.1 Drawing: Market Square in the 1930s.

3.2 The first market building on Market Square.

3.3 Post Office, Edmonton, 1910.

3.4 Civic Block, c. 1932.

3.5 McLeod Building, architect's drawing, 1914.

3.6 Allan and Ella McMann at the city market, c. 1925.

3.7 Market Square, c. 1937.

3.8 Fire Department Inspection on Market Square, c. 1926.

3.9 Aerial view of Market Square, 1929.

3.10 Lighting inside the market building at R. Hinse Poultry, c. 1958.

3.11 Crowd at Market Square, Edmonton, 24 May 1925.

3.12 South facade of market building, c. 1960.

3.13 Advertisements for Mrs. James Jones's fish store.

3.14 Louise and François Berger, 1926.

3.15 Advertisement for the Edmonton and District Market Gardeners and Florists' Association.

3.16 May Day parade starting from Market Square, 1937.

3.17 Unemployed men on Market Square, 5 July 1929.

3.18 Bre-Win's Meat Market, 1938.

4.1   Drawing: If not Market Square, where to put a new city market?

4.2   Joe Bre-Win outside Bre-Win's Meat Market in the 1950s.

4.3   Advertisement urging Edmontonians to grow a garden in 1942.

4.4   Patriotic auction sale on Market Square, 1943.

4.5   Betty Oppelt standing outside the market building, 1948.

4.6   Mary Oppelt at the city market, 1955.

4.7   Elliott's Fruit and Vegetables, c. 1950.

4.8   Dorothy Hurlbut in her garden at 78th Street and 128th Avenue, 1948.

4.9   Ardrossan Greenhouses, aerial view, c. 1970.

4.10 Greenhouse interior at Ardrossan Greenhouses.

4.11 Peter Lupul at the city market, 1955.

4.12 Customers at Lupul's Daily Meats, 1955.

4.13 Mary and Laurie Malcolm at the Natural Health Centre, c. 1955.

4.14 Testing a fire-fighting ladder on Market Square, 15 March 1948.

4.15 Advertisement for a model bungalow on Market Square.

4.16 Bagley and McManus Ins., 9944 - 101A Avenue on the southwest corner of Market Square.

4.17 Margaret Oppelt outside the city market.

4.18 Edmonton Horticultural and Vacant Lots Garden Association Prize List, 1943.

4.19 Mike Tremblay and Alexandra Belinsky, c. 1970.

4.20 Rummage sale held at the market, 7 November 1963.

4.21 Concept for the Civic Centre, 1962.

4.22 Edmonton Motors Building, also known as the Pay'n Save.

5.1   Drawing: The market on 97th Street.

5.2   'New' market building, 1979.

5.3   Interior, city market, 1975.

5.4   Advertisements from the *Edmonton Journal*, 9 April 1965.

5.5   Mary Gordulic talking to a customer at the city market, 14 April 1980.

5.6   Stalwart market vendors gathered for a photograph in September 1994.

5.7   Lisa Frenzel at the city market, 1995

5.8   The city market in September 1978.

5.9   Kuhlmann's stall at the city market, May 1979.

5.10   Dorothee (Kuhlmann) Hauf selling at the Kuhlmann's market stall, 1996.

5.11   Children in front of poultry stall at the city market, 11 August 1964.

5.12   Customers at the market, 21 September 1978.

5.13   Val Lampa and one of his staff, Prince Rupert Fish Market, August 1976.

5.14   Mary Malcolm, Natural Health Centre at the market on 97th Street.

5.15   Betty Bre-Win with a class from Alex Taylor School at Betty's Fruit Basket, 1978.

5.16   Mischa Koopmans selling at the Eyot Creek stall at the city market, 1996.

5.17   W. W. Arcade Hardware Store in the Goodridge Block one block south of the market, 1976.

5.18   Otto Holzbauer and Ann Tong at the city market, 1997.

5.19   Old Towne Market Site.

5.20   Old Towne Market concept plan, Kasian Kennedy, 1992.

5.21   Leslie and Ron Prins, vendors at the city market, 1999.

6.1   Drawing: Farmers' markets in and around Edmonton.

6.2   Sod turning for city market shed, Calgary, 1908.

6.3   Calgary Public Market, n.d.

6.4   Robert Simonet in his greenhouse, c. 1965.

6.5   The Thiel family just after their arrival in Canada, 1954.

6.6   Rudolf Thiel's homemade greenhouse, c. 1960.

6.7   Thiel's Greenhouses, Bruderheim, c. 1990.

6.8   Farming in the Belmont Area, 1936.

6.9   Hinse chickens ready to go to the market, c. 1955.

6.10   Flore Hinse selling chicken at the city market, c. 1955.

6.11   Denis Hinse selling at the city market, c. 1955.

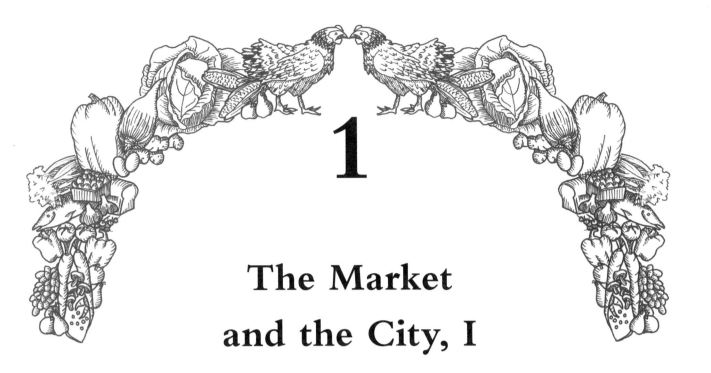

The Market
and the City, I

On 30 June 1932, when the Great Depression had bitten the luxuries out of most spending diets and was nibbling into the necessities for many, an article appeared in the *Edmonton Journal* proposing to readers that a Saturday morning spent at the Edmonton City Market would more than compensate for an exotic foreign holiday. A little imagination, the reporter suggested, and the market-goer could as easily be in Baghdad, Cairo, or Montreal, as in Edmonton. Edmonton, the reporter wrote, "is almost exclusively a Saturday market but for that one day at least it affords Edmontonians an opportunity to romanticize, if they are so inclined, and to make themselves think ... they are somewhere else, wandering through alleys and crowded streets lined with booths, like travelers in far lands tell about."

Why would Edmontonians have wanted to be roaming alleys and crowded streets lined with booths in Baghdad or Cairo? If they did have such cravings, how could a morning spent at the Edmonton City Market possibly satisfy them? What lay behind the *Journal* writer's representation of Edmonton's then well-patronized market as exotic?

The opposite of exotic, if exoticism implies what is foreign, produce markets are the incarnation of the local, bringing producer and consumer together to transact business in locally grown turnips or homemade raspberry jam. Yet, although they draw on a small geographic area, markets bring together individuals who would otherwise have no connection with one another. The small commercial exchanges which take place there have economic and social dimensions. They bring the countryside — its people and products — to the city, giving urbanites direct and sensuous contact with the land around them. Markets are colourful, noisy, sometimes smelly; they overload the senses. They materialize like magic at dawn and evaporate into thin air

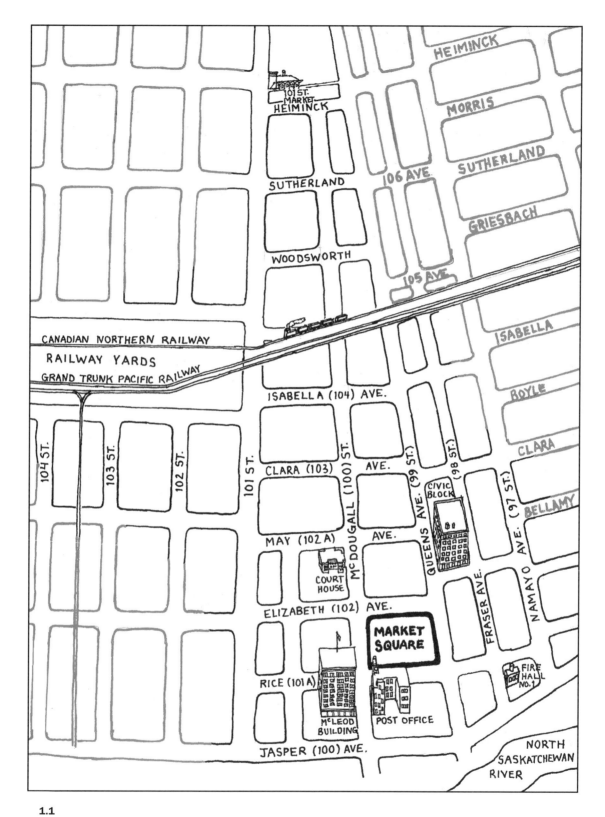

1.1

1900-1916: Market Square becomes the centre of downtown Edmonton. Drawing by Barbara Budenz

2

before dusk only to be reconstituted at the next appointed time. They create addicts out of vendors and customers, attracting local characters whose personal histories combine to create a picture not just of an institution but of a place and its distinctive culture.

Anna Triska, who came to Edmonton from Vienna in 1910 and became an egg vendor at the market from 1916 until her death in 1963, was one such local character. Anna would have been at her stall in 1932 when the *Journal* writer strolled by, transported by his experience. Years later, in March 1962, another *Journal* reporter described her as "a little old white-haired lady in a print dress caught at the neck with an old-fashioned brooch, sitting with hands folded, humming softly and watching the passing parade."[1]

One of Anna's daughters, Mrs. Frieda Powell, may have been helping her mother in the late 1940s or early 1950s when Mary Svekla began shopping regularly at the city market. Mary and her husband, who moved to Edmonton from a farm near Vegreville in 1947 to improve their material circumstances, craved the fresh farm-raised chicken they had once supplied for themselves. Their first day at the market, they

1.2

On 14 June 1985, this photograph of Mary Sernowski appeared in the *Edmonton Journal*. Mary was never more "at home" than when she presided over a stall at the market. She sold there in June 1998, just a few months before she died on 4 August that year. Courtesy of the *Edmonton Journal*

bought a chicken from a Mrs. Powell and managed to get a good price because of a joke Mary's husband made. In August 1993, Mary still crooned with laughter as she recounted the experience that turned her into a regular market customer:

> My husband saw that she had all those chickens. He said, "Mrs. Powell, I want this chicken — how much?" She says, "A dollar fifty." He says, "But they are dead!" You know he joked; he was such a joker. "You know, they're dead. I'll give you a dollar for one." She said, "OK — give me a dollar." So, I'll never forget. We had such a laugh over it. She said, "OK give me your dollar."[2]

About twenty years after Anna Triska began selling at the market, a young farm wife from St. Albert began going there to sell her home-grown produce, especially carrots and potatoes. Mary (known as Baba) Sernowski, born in 1907 near

Lvov at the eastern edge of what was then the Austro-Hungarian Empire, had survived a traumatic childhood and several hard years as an indentured farm labourer before coming to Canada. Life as a farm worker in Alberta was difficult and unrewarding, and even marriage to Peter Sernowski did not give her a role she could throw herself into. Sometime around 1940, two Belgian neighbours urged Mary to sell at the city market, and from that point on she was hooked.[3]

At the market, Mary presented herself as a strong, independent-minded person with unorthodox opinions and tender sensibilities. She joked with friends and acquaintances that the market was her bingo, her hotel, and her church rolled into one. Delivering the remark so as to provoke laughter, offence, or admiration, Mary shrewdly assessed the reactions of her interlocutors so she could decide where to place them in her personal pantheon of friends. A favourite subject of *Edmonton Journal* photographers, Mary's tiny frame was never apparent in images dominated by a smile, crinkly eyes, and strong hands — the tools she relied on to take her where she wanted to be, the Edmonton City Market. Anna Triska, Mary Svekla, and Mary Sernowski — none of these women were, or could ever have been, in Baghdad or Cairo, but their bit parts in the weekly Saturday events at the Edmonton City Market contributed to its particular colour and texture.

There is no universal formula for exoticism to be applied like lipstick or implemented like an architect's plan. The Edmonton City Market, which seemed rich and exciting to the 1932 reporter, was no more than a thirty-two-year-old institution in a sixteen-year-old building and no less than a regular coming together and splitting apart of thousands of people speaking several languages, representing many traditions and customs, and selling a variety of products with a range of styles and motives. If the scent that emanated from this brew every week was heady and exotic, the pot ingredients were unadulteratedly local.

When, in December 1900, the Edmonton Town Council opened its first public market, promoting the local was not an end in itself. Quite the opposite, the market's main advocate, Philip Heiminck, argued in a letter to the *Edmonton Bulletin* that "a town especially of the size of ours without a market has little right to demand even the title of a village that aspires to prosperity."[4] Heiminck may have had in mind models based on his upbringing in Simcoe, Ontario, or perhaps he was thinking of the combined city hall and market building constructed in Winnipeg shortly after it became a city in 1873.

Heiminck wanted Edmonton to be an important place, and all important places, in his view, had public markets. But his notion, conveyed in the same letter, that a market has a geographical dimension as "the fixed centre for trade not only for the city housekeeper, but for ranchers, farmers and traders," a temporal dimension or "a fixed hour at which we are able to find a selection of the choicest products of our fair country," and a politico-economic dimension as the agent for "the development of our export trade and the abolishment of ranky butter," points to another model he would not have known about — the Greek *agora*. Contemporary classical archaeologists' success in uncovering and restoring the *agora*, the centre of classical Athens, has brought to view the centrality of the marketplace in the development of Greek culture.

The *agora*, or Greek marketplace, has been called the predecessor of the great *piazzas* and squares found in European capitals: "Administrative, legislative, judicial, commercial, social, and religious activities all took place in and around the area and made the *agora* the heart of an ancient city." Scholars' descriptions of how the *agora* functioned over centuries of Greek classical civilization touch on themes which are still relevant. For example, the evolution of the market in Greek civilization from temporary booths and stalls scattered about the square to its accommodation in a long colonnaded building (*stoa*) which has been described as "the ancient predecessor of the modern shopping mall," provides a perspective on contemporary discussions about the relation of architectural form to function.[5]

The years in and around 1914 in Edmonton saw the matter of marketplace accommodation become first a civic issue and then a minifiasco which can better be understood with reference to the Greek model. A passing understanding of the *agora* helps to explain why an expensive new market building, opened in Edmonton in November 1914, was never used for its intended purpose and why a cheap substitute was not only heavily patronized but became a familiar and a much loved landmark.

When Edmonton's public market opened in December 1900, there was no talk of a market building to shelter vendors and customers. Over time, temporary shelters appeared at strategic points on Market Square but most farmers sold directly from their 'rigs' or wagons, parking them so that they opened out towards the sidewalks.

In 1913, Edmonton's council took action on a plan to move the market from the city centre to the northeast corner of 101st Street and 107th Avenue — north of the main civic, cultural and business centre of the city (see fig. 1.1). A committee was struck to study markets in other centres, and the new city architect, Allan Merrick Jeffers, whose recent designs had included the Alberta Legislature Building, worked hard to produce a plan which committee members and Edmonton City Council would approve. In 1914, council decided to proceed with the $100,000 project, and by November of that year the new facility was open. That it was rejected from the start — boycotted by vendors and customers alike — was something of a mystery — not to speak of an aggravation — to those who had brought it into being.[6]

1.3

In 1912, vendors placed their stalls near the sidewalks for the ease of customers. CEA, EA-10-714

By January 1915, the former market location on Rice Street was back in business and the next year council finally agreed to provide basic shelter on the old site. In retrospect, it is clear that for vendors and customers a market was not simply a building. For fourteen years prior to the attempted move, the Edmonton City Market had been an integral part of the centre, linked to a host of civic, business, and commercial institutions. Market Square had become Edmonton's *agora*, surrounded by the main Post Office with its landmark clock, the Civic Block, which housed Edmonton's council and administration, the McLeod Building owned by businessman K. A. (Kenny) McLeod who vigorously opposed the market's move to 101st Street, and by a host of small complementary enterprises, many of which had sprung up to cater to the needs of vendors and customers.

The uncovering and restoration of the *agora* in Athens showed that, for the classical Greeks, the terms "civic centre" and "marketplace" were not separable — one implied the other. The long, open, colonnaded *stoa*, developed as early as the fifth century B.C. in Greece to accommodate trading and regulatory functions, would not have been patronized had it been located in a remote

1.4

By 1920, most selling took place inside the new market building, although Saturday overflow took up portions of the square. This photograph looks south and west, offering views of the Post Office and the McLeod Building in the background. The main entrance to the market was on Rice Street, opposite the Post Office. CEA, EA-10-207

part of the city. Empty of furnishings and fittings, it could be reinvented daily, adapting to myriad seasonal, ceremonial, political, or even religious influences. Edmonton's attempt to build a finely appointed market away from the civic centre failed because Edmontonians had come to experience the market as *agora* and they obviously preferred this model to the alternative offered them in 1914.

Beginning in 1916, when the city spent about $3,800 from its budget to build a shed-like building intended to house the market temporarily, and ending in 1965, when the market was relocated to 97th Street, the Edmonton City Market flourished at the geographic, even the spiritual, centre of civic life.[7] Market Square, crammed to its edges on Saturdays by the vehicles of vendors and customers and, in the summer, by temporary stalls set up to accommodate the overflow, was often used on nonmarket days as a parade martialling ground, an open space to test fire-fighting equipment or demonstrate the newest model home, a drill space or a casual meeting area for loafers and city aldermen alike. The few permanently assigned retail stalls built into the market building were always in demand, regarded by vendors like Peter Lupul, who bought a butcher business there in 1950, as a choice location. Indeed, Lupul tailored his business to the customers whose patronage he most avidly courted — the politicians and professionals who worked in and around the centre. For this butcher, as for others, the city market was not only located at the heart of the city but also was what kept that heart ticking.[8] Yet, as the one-hundred-year history of the Edmonton City Market amply illustrates, Edmonton's councils never endorsed this idea or secured it as part of a civic vision. Hence, the notion of market as *agora* was threatened from the start.

If the Athenian *agora* is a somewhat abstruse model, one that would not have been known to the 1932 *Journal* reporter or to his readers, twentieth-century European markets, many with roots going back to the Middle Ages, probably informed the opinions of both promoters and detractors of the Rice Street site. Those who favoured the Rice Street site might have agreed with Howard Saalman, a medieval historian, that "public buildings may be a public necessity, but in contrast to public spaces, they are not always fully accessible or penetrable."[9] Saalman's view that the activity of the marketplace was the key to understanding how a medieval city operated prompts speculation as to how the first few generations of Edmontonians reconciled their desire for the sociable commerce of the marketplace with their desire to build a city that would impress visitors and newcomers through the elegance of its physical layout and buildings. Canadian cities, too new to reflect the building patterns and technologies of centuries past, generally emulated European styles of architecture and urban planning which had long since left the medieval period behind.

For sixty-five years, while the Edmonton City Market presided at the centre, its advocates often recalled European models to support arguments for keeping it there. In September 1962, Mrs. J. I. Johnston wrote to the *Edmonton Journal* that "many large cities have retained a niche for their markets close to the main thoroughfares because the city fathers have realised that they bring life and gaiety to the all too solemn bricks and mortar."[10] Letters written to the *Journal* in 1962 to persuade the city not to close the market portrayed it as fresh, rich, sensuous, and friendly — a celebration of local products in an atmosphere that brought vitality to the centre. And one Saturday in early September of that year, Walter Oppelt, secretary of the stallholders' committee, reported that more than six thousand shoppers had signed a petition to keep the market as part of the city centre.[11]

Arguments for eliminating the market as a feature of the civic centre reflected a different set of urban values — a respect for order, rationality, and wealth as it had been manifested in major centres around the world. Around the time that Edmonton's first civic centre plan was being prepared (1912), two chapters of The Imperial Order Daughters of the Empire (IODE) wrote to the mayor and council arguing that the market be eliminated from the centre and that a new city hall be built in its place: "we wish our city to be not only wealthy but healthy & beautiful as well."[12] This desire for beauty and order at the centre lay behind the regulation, introduced by council in 1911, that horses on Market Square be restricted to eating oats from nosebags so that bits of hay were not blown around on respectable businesses.[13]

The IODE's ideas about what constituted a city and how it should evolve were not extreme or out of step with their time. In fact, they were consistent with theories frequently drawn on by city planners in the period leading up to the displacement of the market in 1965. Although the city's first formal commitment to town planning was in 1929, when it established a town planning commission, the province had passed a town planning act in 1913, and well before that proponents of urban reform (who held that well-designed urban spaces promoted healthy living) and of the City Beautiful movement (who promoted the incorporation of gardens and green spaces into urban plans) influenced urban design. In 1912, when the design firm of Morell and Nichols presented Edmonton with its first civic centre plan and relegated the market to a peripheral location, they claimed that their main object had been "to prevent or remedy the physical or moral evils and losses which accompany the growth of any city or town in a haphazard way."[14] Subsequent designs upheld this philosophy and either marginalized the city market or eliminated it altogether. In 1926, when Mabel Dean wrote to Alderman Findlay to complain that horses were forbidden hay or green feed in Market Square, arguing that it was cruel to deprive the horses belonging to farmers who had run out of grain, she was hardly equipped to take on planning orthodoxies that continued to acquire status well into the latter half of the century.[15]

If Edmonton's elected representatives began to question the fitness of the town centre as a market location soon after it opened, one is tempted to wonder why they bought the site in the first place. There is no evidence that council discussed siting criteria. Rather it was simply assumed the site would be central. An unarticulated convention that markets were centrally located, next to or near the town hall, must have led to the labelling of one of the town's first standing committees, the Town Hall and Market Committee. Most town and city councils in Canada struck such committees, probably conforming to norms appropriated from British and other European cultures. The argument has been made that town squares built in North American cities were based on models remembered from Europe but not always used for the same purposes as their European originals.[16] In Edmonton's case, if the choice of location for a market originated in a desire to imitate what had been done before, as soon as the market opened for

· PROPOSED · CIVIC · CENTER · LOOKING · SOVTH ·
CITY · OF · EDMONTON · ALBERTA · CANADA ·
· MORELL · AND · NICHOLS ·   · LANDSCAPE · ARCHITECTS ·
· MINNEAPOLIS · MINNESOTA ·

1.5

This drawing shows how Morell and Nichols, authors of Edmonton's first civic centre proposal (1912), would have re-developed Market Square. The view, looking south towards Jasper Avenue and the Saskatchewan River, shows an imposing city hall on the site then occupied by the market. CEA, EA-362-67

business a new logic began to emerge, and that logic, proceeding from the local, was not always compatible with council's more grandiose plans for the city.

Many of Edmonton's founding settlers, those who came just before and soon after 1900, drew on their experience of other Canadian or American cities when they formed and expressed opinions about how they wanted Edmonton to develop. These North American cities probably had public markets, most of them near, or linked to, the town or city hall and run by the civic government. No wonder Philip Heiminck was categorical in his view that any place calling itself urban had to have a market.[17] Variations in the cost, style, and siting of public markets prevailed, but, however elaborate or humble and wherever situated, they were a prominent feature of civic life in nineteenth-century Ontario.

In their book on courthouses and town halls in nineteenth-century Ontario, Marion MacRae and Anthony Adamson inadvertently offer a clue as to why the Edmonton City Market was never treated by its city parent as a full member of the civic family:

> In the third quarter of the nineteenth century, the market in Ontario towns of any size was still a social as well as a commercial affair. The wares displayed for sale had become more interesting as the trains brought manufactured goods and out-of-season produce into Ontario's heartland. News was exchanged at the market, political problems sifted and bargains of many kinds struck around the counters, both inside and outside the town hall.[18]

Sentences one and three above certainly describe the nineteenth century, but they could also refer to any market from the time of Christ to the dawn of the third millennium. Sentence two, on the other hand, is more time specific. It suggests that, by the third quarter of the nineteenth century, railways had introduced a new dynamic into food shopping, making it possible for fresh produce, as well as dry goods, to travel distances to market. Edmonton in 1900 was still not accessible by rail, and the town council was far more interested in securing a rail link than it was in establishing a market. By 1900, to some progressive minds, a public market could have seemed either redundant or positively regressive, an admission of backwardness and an inability to bring in luxury foods from faraway places. To put this point another way, Edmonton was founded as a twentieth-century city at a time when food marketing was about to be revolutionized by transportation technology.

By contrast, the tradition of public markets linked to town halls had long been established in urban centres east of what is now the Ontario/Manitoba border when railways began to revolutionize the food production and distribution system. St. John, New Brunswick, which became a city by Royal Charter in 1785, set up a market immediately, the mayor serving as market clerk. Indeed, the mayor's salary came partly from the fees he charged producers for the right to sell in the city. Today, St. John boasts the oldest centrally located public market building which has operated continuously since 1876.[19]

In Ontario, from where a large number of Edmonton's early settlers came, incorporation began in the 1830s, and the town hall/market tradition emerged at the same time. The procedures by which sites were selected, land acquired, buildings designed, and decisions made regarding the colocation of facilities, established precedents which western cities like Winnipeg and Edmonton would later draw on and even imitate. Hamilton, for instance, received a rudimentary form of incorporation in 1833 and set about immediately to establish a market shelter. A couple of years later, when more elaborate facilities were aspired to, the city accepted a gift of land from a local citizen. When, shortly after the town hall and market building had been completed, the donor went bankrupt, leaving in doubt the legal status of the building, Hamiltonians apparently continued to patronize the market and to attend concerts in the hall above it. But it was not until 1849, three years after full incorporation, that the city was allowed to buy the land — thus securing its hall and market.[20]

The story of Hamilton's first hall and market contains features which marked the development of similar facilities across Ontario — the eagerness of citizens to donate land for civic buildings, the urgency with which town or city officials moved to build a hall and a market shelter despite their lack of capital, the preference for durable materials like brick and stone, and the tendency to go to architectural competitions to obtain the most striking designs.

Toronto's long market tradition, which precedes the incorporation of that city in 1834, is rich both in local content and in features which bear comparison with Edmonton's evolution as a market city. In 1803, long before incorporation and while Toronto was still known as York, a market square was established south of King Street and supplied with a wooden shed as shelter. This shed was moved in the early 1830s to make way for a new hall and market commissioned by the home district magistrates in anticipation of incorporation. When Toronto finally achieved city status, it inherited this building, built on the 1803 site and designed in 1831 by James Cooper.[21] The Cooper building, which became known as Toronto's first city hall and market, "ran from King to Front Street, with the town assembly hall occupying the position of honour in the pedimented centre of the King Street facade." Underneath the council chamber were three arches through which pedestrians entered "a large paved market courtyard." Shops lined the east and west sides of the market so that the square, filled with wagons and temporary stalls, was completely surrounded by buildings.[22]

Historian Stephen A. Otto has speculated that Cooper's design for what became Toronto's first city hall and market may have been modelled on British prototypes such as the new Covent Garden Market in London, England, completed in 1830 and designed by Charles Fowler. Toronto's first official market facility differed from most of its contemporaries whose squares spilled out around them. According to Otto, "never again in the history of Toronto perhaps would so many diverse uses be found together, and the classical ideal of the *agora* come so near to being realized, as in this City Hall and Market."[23] Cooper's building was replaced by 1850 as part of the redevelopment of the block for St. Lawrence Hall — site of today's North St. Lawrence Market. Throughout its almost two-century existence, Toronto's public market, unlike Edmonton's, has never lacked for accommodation.

Points of comparison and contrast between the market traditions in Toronto and Edmonton suggest the power of the local to elaborate itself differently, resulting in distinctive renderings in each city. While Toronto's market predated incorporation, Edmonton had been incorporated eight years before it established its first public market. Unlike Toronto, Edmonton's town hall was never attached to the Edmonton City Market; its first hall consisted of a council chamber and a clerk's office built into Fire Hall no. 1 in 1893, east of the site chosen in 1900 for a market. In 1912, when the city built a substitute for a city hall which it called the Civic Block, the site chosen was kitty-corner to the bustling Market Square, a choice which was not colocation so much as a strategic position from which to launch a future displacement. Although Edmonton's market site may, like Toronto's, have evolved from an unofficial to an official site, no grandiose building schemes were ever proposed or executed on the Rice Street site in Edmonton, as they were in Toronto. While Edmonton's somewhat shabby Market Square grew into a lively civic space which linked together otherwise disparate elements of the downtown, Toronto's market enclosed its multiple functions in a purpose-designed building. Thus emerged two very different models for endowing local commerce with civic status.

The early development and untimely demise of Winnipeg's public market contrasts strongly with the late-developing/late-blooming pattern that is Edmonton's most striking feature. As soon as Winnipeg was incorporated as a city (1873), its market committee, chaired by Alexander Logan, moved to select the best site for a combined town hall and market building. From among the several sites offered as "free gifts" by citizens, the committee chose the one it judged to be "most central and accessible to the greater number of

1.6

Winnipeg's first city hall (opened 1877) was built with an attached market, visible at the back of this photograph. The entire building collapsed a few years after it opened. Western Canada Pictorial Index, A0050-01515

the inhabitants of the City." The entire project was, as they say today, "fast-tracked," and haste brought with it inevitable waste. Although the Winnipeg market must have been in operation by April, 1875, for that was when the first by-law establishing public markets was passed, the architect was fired that May; a few years later, the entire facility began to fall down. In 1886, a new city hall was opened on the same site, and by 1889-90 a new and elaborate free-standing market, designed by George Browne Jr., was opened alongside it.[24] This was one of the market buildings, along with the Toronto market, for which A. M. Jeffers was instructed to obtain the plans at the 15 May 1913 special market committee meeting in Edmonton.

While Winnipeg fell readily into the orthodox pattern followed by Ontario towns and cities — building a combined city hall and market as quickly as possible after incorporation — Edmonton's dawdle-and-delay approach suggests that successive councils distrusted the purely local, looking to define their urban centre in relation to something grander. This tactic had ironic consequences. Early in the twentieth century, Winnipeg's centre slipped a little west and south of its original location, drawn by growth and development in these directions. Even the Hudson's Bay Store reinforced the shift by opening a new store on

1.7

The building in the foreground was designed as Winnipeg's public market by George Browne Jr. (1889). In the background, to the right, is the Winnipeg City Hall, designed in Victorian Gothic style by the firm of Barber and Barber (1886). Western Canada Pictorial Index, A0178-05578

Portage Avenue several blocks south of Main in 1906. After the 1919 Winnipeg General Strike, civic leaders in that city closed the market, judging it to be unnecessary and simply a forum for political unrest; it was, after all, a place where workers could congregate, talk, and even plot. By 1919, Winnipeg's civic values were firmly based on its economic prospects as a transportation hub and as a centre for business and finance. Although other produce markets were set up in Winnipeg, the public market was converted, symbolically in retrospect, to civic offices.[25] Edmonton, on the other hand, having failed to displace its market through legitimate city processes, was stuck with a remarkably vital institution flourishing on the very site that had been long dedicated as a city centre.

Over the years, depending on the state of the economy and political preoccupations of the time, the Edmonton City Market was either the jewel or the thorn in the civic crown. In 1900, its necessity was questioned as often as it was affirmed. In 1912 and again in 1925, the market's popularity on its central site was a major obstacle for councils preoccupied with reconstructing Edmonton's civic centre in a new image. However, in the late 1920s and throughout the 1930s, as we have already seen through the eyes of an *Edmonton Journal* reporter, it was one of the few institutions to flourish at a time when money and jobs

1.8

After a trip to Edmonton in the 1940s, Illingworth Holey Kerr returned to his home in Calgary with several sketches which he intended to convert to paintings. This one, depicting the inside of the city market building, includes notes scribbled directly on the drawing to help the artist remember the colours and textures he intended to capture. Upside down in the left corner he wrote, "swell town." Author's collection. Courtesy of the Canadian Art gallery for I. Kerr Estate.

were in short supply. Until the end of World War II in 1945, the market was as popular with politicians as it was with the general public. No wonder it was one of a few sites chosen in the 1940s by the Alberta artist Illingworth Kerr as a possible subject for a painting when he visited Alberta's capital from his home in Calgary.[26]

In July 1946, Commissioner J. Hodgson was given an opportunity to boast about the then forty-six-year-old market when he responded to a request for information sent by his counterpart in Red Deer. Emphasizing the significance of historical context, he wrote, "the majority of our present stall holders grew up with the market, ... are loyal to our public market idea and are the backbone of our success." He cited the market's central location and its financial viability as key factors in its success and longevity, explaining that while revenue each year amounted to about $14,000, costs amounted only to $8,000 or $9,000, thus leaving the city a modest profit. Hodgson's letter probably documents the most favourable attitude towards the market ever expressed by a city official, a recognition that its persistence as a civic institution was linked to historical factors.[27]

The postwar boom in the economy, reinforced in Edmonton by the discovery of oil in Leduc in 1947, brought inevitable pressures on the market site and inspired visions of civic centre sugar-plums in the minds of local politicians. Although the market continued for two decades after 1945 to transform the city centre on Saturdays into the magical, perhaps even exotic, experience which had provoked the *Journal* reporter to rhapsodize in 1932, its value as civic stock declined steadily. The move two blocks east to 97th Street in 1965 was represented as a continuation, but the vendors who relocated knew immediately that civic blood was no longer flowing through the veins of their institution. The consequences were inevitable.

This book is the story of how the Edmonton City Market came to dominate the city centre for sixty-five years and of how it reached centenarian status despite its displacement from the centre. The plot revolves around a conflict of values, never openly confronted in civic discourse but important nonetheless. Those who patronized and supported the Edmonton City Market stood on one side of the debate, upholding the role played by local agriculture and its products in defining Edmonton's urban culture. On the other side were those who would have erased all reference to the local in their definition of Edmonton as a city. For these people, the market was at best an anachronism and at worst a blight and an embarrassment.

For the most part, the story of the city market's first hundred years is pieced together from the stories of hundreds of people, most of them either vendors or patrons whose simple transactions are carried out verbally and never documented. Behind these apparently simple transactions between buyer and seller in any marketplace, including local produce markets, lie a complex tangle of networks and relationships. Sort out this tangle, separate the threads, and you will feel you are revealing the pattern of a particular culture, in this case, the culture of the city we know as Edmonton.

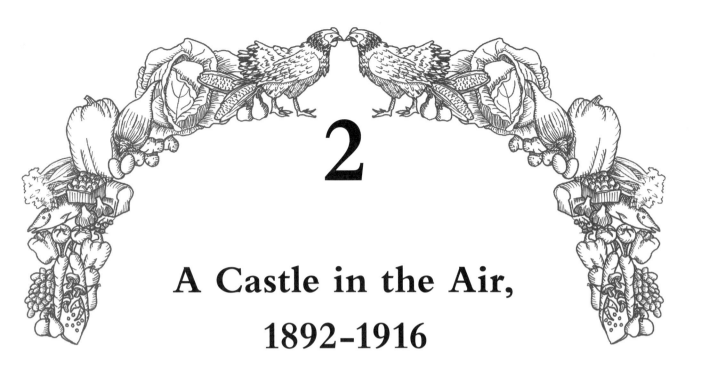

2

A Castle in the Air,
1892–1916

When Edmonton became a town in 1892, its first council might have acted quickly to build a combined town hall and marketplace. It did not. To serve the town's modest needs, a meeting chamber and clerk's office were included in the design of Edmonton's Fire Hall no. 1 (1893).[1] As for a market, council initiated a site search in 1893 but quickly dropped the project on the recommendation of its Town Hall and Market Committee.[2] In 1895, however, the market project reappeared on the civic agenda and remained there until, in December 1900, the Edmonton Public Market was finally opened.

The indecision, delay, and half-hearted civic action which characterized the seven-year search for a market site in Edmonton had unforeseen consequences. In a move which subsequently backfired, council placed the market on a site coveted for another purpose, only to have it take root and begin to flourish. Like a bad weed, the market defied the city's subsequent efforts to uproot it. Not until 1916 did the city call a temporary halt to its campaign to move the market by caving in to public demands to build a shelter there. By that time, the market's presence on a site earmarked for a civic centre had acquired a heightened meaning. In many Edmontonians' minds, the Edmonton City Market stood for the presence of the country in the city, the notion that Edmonton's urban identity should not be separated from its agricultural context.

Beginning in 1870, when Rupert's Land was transferred from the Hudson's Bay Company to Canada,[3] the Edmonton settlement came increasingly to define itself in relation to its potential as a centre of mixed agriculture. Notes appearing in the *Edmonton Bulletin* from time to time provided jaunty updates — as if they were weather reports — on the status of local gardens:

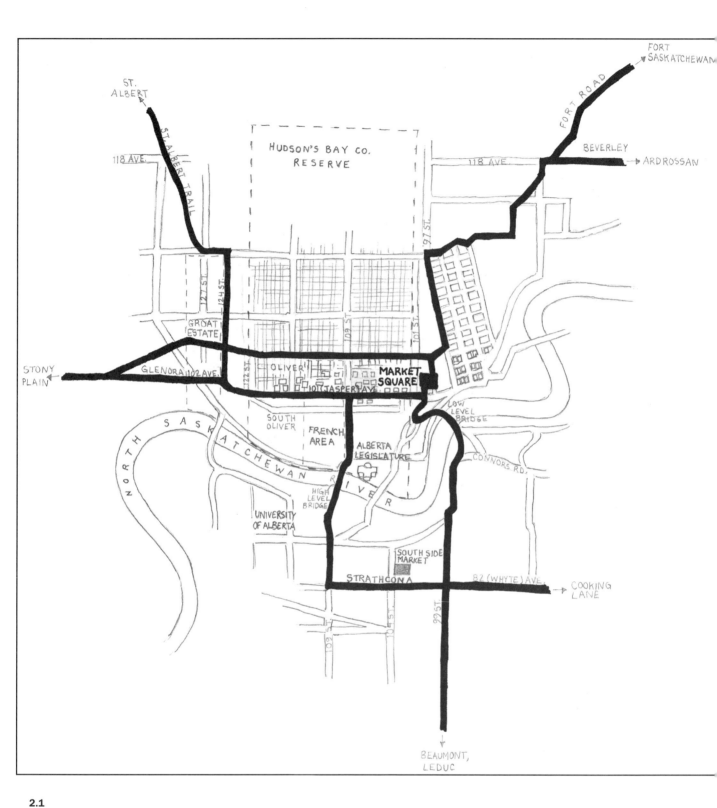

2.1

1900-1964: Routes from the east, west, north, and south brought vendors and customers to Market Square. Drawing by Barbara Budenz

2.2

On 17 July 1893, an article in the *Edmonton Bulletin* included a detailed description of the construction and plan of the town's new Fire Hall no. 1. On the upper floor, in addition to a reading room and a bedroom for firemen, was a council hall (35' x 35') and a small office for the town clerk. By 1908, when this photograph was taken, the town had become a city and had expanded to a freestanding annex built next to the firehall (visible on the right side of the photograph). CEA, EA-500-304

> Raspberries are ripe.
> Heavy Rain on Sunday last.
> New potatoes are in general use.
> Hogs are scarce. Butter plentiful.[4]

On 27 November 1888, an editorial published in the *Bulletin* claimed that "farmers as a class are doing well," most of them engaged in mixed farming and all benefitting from a "phenomenally deep, rich soil, good water, plenty of timber for fuel and building purposes, nutritious grasses, and a climate second to none."

In 1892, in recognition of Edmonton's new corporate status, the *Toronto Mail* published a feature article on Edmonton and its citizens which proclaimed the "remarkable fertility" of the region and provided details intended to impress prospective settlers:

2.3

Taken around 1907, this photograph illustrates the impressive results obtained in the gardens of Edmontonians in the early years. CEA, EB-23-48

> The potatoes ... grown in the Edmonton district are large in size and of superior quality. Turnips, cabbages, radishes, and other vegetables attain remarkably large dimensions, and preserve all the merits which are found in the root crops of ordinary growth. The exhibit of native grasses made by Edmonton at the Winnipeg Industrial Exhibition of 1891 won for it first prize.... Wild fruits are abundant in the district but as yet there has not been much effort made with the cultivated varieties.[5]

Had a public market existed in 1892, it might have provided an urban venue for the exhibition and sale of local-area produce — a link between agricultural production and urban identity. Instead, the enterprise and accomplishments of individuals, not institutions, highlighted to Edmontonians and the outside world the benefits of such a liaison.

Donald Ross, whose renown as a vegetable grower is endearingly captured in photographs showing his bulky frame standing stolidly amongst great squashes and giant cabbages, probably did more than any of Edmonton's pioneer settlers

2.4

Donald Ross, standing to the right of an impressive display of vegetables, was an Edmonton pioneer remembered not only for his garden and his interest in horticulture, but also for opening Edmonton's first hotel. PAA, Ernest Brown Collection 9071

to promote the district's agricultural potential. Employed in the early 1870s to run the Hudson's Bay Company garden, Ross went on to grow his own large vegetable garden, the produce from which he peddled in town. Ross was known to have "corresponded with other agriculturalists and received plants from Ottawa's Central Experimental Farm for trial at Edmonton. He also attracted the attention of the celebrated American botanist, Luther Burbank, who visited him in 1894 and sent plants for experiment."[6]

Ross built what were probably Edmonton's first greenhouses (one in 1895 and the second in 1900), rotating crops so as to extend the season for lettuces, cucumbers and tomatoes. An article in the *Bulletin* in 1903 claimed that "Mr. Ross knows nothing of gardening or greenhouses except what he has learned by experience during his long residence in Edmonton. But what is learned by experience is learned well, and Mr. Ross has made his garden and his greenhouses a success for himself and a credit to the district."[7] A director of the Edmonton Agricultural Society when it was formed in 1879, Ross was also a keen exhibitor of his produce, winning prizes not only in his home town but at exhibitions in Calgary, Winnipeg, and Toronto. An article describing his performance at the Western Horticultural Society's exhibition in Winnipeg in 1902 provides one account of his accomplishments as a gardener: "Mr. Ross took first prize for conical cabbage, he showed the largest turnip at the exhibition, weight 11½ lbs., and considered that he had the best rhubarb."[8]

By 1900, when Edmonton's public market opened, Donald Ross was an old timer, a veteran producer, exhibitor, promoter, and a peddler with a roster of customers. He probably never took his produce to Market Square. On 19 July 1904, Ross wrote to the city requesting that he and other peddlers be licensed in order to prevent misrepresentation by rival peddlers from "across the River." The city refused the request, explaining by return letter that no licence fees would be set until a "permanent" market — by which was probably implied a building — had been established.[9] Local-area producers who followed in Ross's footsteps, men like Frederik Frederiksen, for example, who moved a greenhouse and gardening business to Edmonton from Dawson in 1907, became regular vendors at the city market, maintaining at the same time a delivery service to bulk buyers such as hotels and boarding houses.[10] But, even in 1907, the market offered little more than a legal place to park and sell — hardly the surroundings in which to display for sale the prize vegetables, grains, and cheeses described in both local and national press of the period.

By 1892, a broad range of agricultural products was in regular production in the Edmonton region but, without a railway link, markets for these products were not as easy to come by as were newspaper articles praising the productivity of the soil. A public market, especially one located next to or near a city hall, might have consolidated rural and urban aspirations within the new corporate project in addition to providing producers with increased opportunities for direct sales.

Before Edmonton's public market opened, urban dwellers had three means of obtaining honey, eggs, poultry, locally grown vegetables, or any other product they did not produce themselves. Firstly, many would have bought from peddlers, like Donald Ross, who travelled door to door. The Chinese, who were not a presence on the city market, despite their reputation as river-bank market gardeners, became well known in Edmonton as peddlers, though certainly not until after 1900.

Secondly, items bought in bulk, like coal, wood, and hay, were probably purchased directly from rigs which were driven to town and parked in vacant lots. On 17 December 1900, just two days before the market was opened on

Rice Street, the *Bulletin* reported that "all lines of farm produce are offering freely and to-day, not with standing that it is Monday, which is usually a slow day, the streets are busy with farmers rigs." When the pre-1900 debate over the need for a public market appeared in the *Bulletin*, at least one editorialist defended these informal venues as adequate in themselves, arguing that "if the establishment of a market means the imposition of vexatious restrictions and tolls ... what the town chiefly wants of a market place it has at present without the expense of purchasing one; that is a place where loaded teams can stand awaiting business without impeding street traffic."[11]

Thirdly, local produce was also sold in retail outlets, although the relatively small volumes bought and sold limited the benefits to all parties. In 1889, for instance, R. McKernan, proprietor of the Edmonton Meat Market, "first Building East of Bulletin Office," advertised in the *Bulletin* that he had fresh butter, eggs, and potatoes for sale and that he would take farm produce in exchange.[12] Mr. McKernan was probably one of many who expanded the range of his retail business in order to broker the goods of the small local producer to the discriminating consumer.

It is not clear why, in 1895, council decided to renew the search for a market site. Maybe it was just a response to the actual and anticipated growth of the town, a perceived need to facilitate and regulate the production and sale of local foodstuffs. Perhaps council was attracted by an overture from real-estate agent Philip Heiminck who, as agent for David McDougall, was a powerful player in the development of River Lot 8. Whatever the cause, the ensuing five-year process, which increased in momentum as the years passed, was as confusing as it was anticlimactic.

Early in 1895, the Town Hall and Market Committee solicited offers of sites suitable for a public market. Although six offers were received, none was chosen, and the committee recommended instead a site referred to in the council minutes as "Block X" and not for sale at the time.[13] This was the property in River Lot 8 controlled by Heiminck and promoted by him as the best possible site for a market. Unfortunately, however, bargaining on the property was rendered impossible in 1896 when Heiminck and the town entered into an acrimonious set of dealings on another land sale issue — probably that of access to the ferry crossing from River Lot 8.

Throughout 1897, with J. H. Gariepy as chairman of the Town Hall and Market Committee, the feud between the town and Philip Heiminck escalated into litigation with the result that no progress was made on the market project. Throughout the year Heiminck wrote many letters to council regarding the market site, most of which were answered with formal refusals to bargain.[14] On 3 July 1897, the clerk wrote wearily that "a Special meeting of the Council was held on the above date to finally consider the question of a market site." The word "finally" was crossed out in this minute, giving some idea of the general level of exasperation that must have prevailed as the town tried to obtain the alluring but elusive "Block X."[15] Although some council members favoured cutting off all negotiations with Heiminck until the litigation was settled, Gariepy, who obviously wanted to hasten the acquisition process, moved that "an offer be made to P. Heiminck in his individual capacity and as Agent for David MacDougall." The town was prepared to pay $5,100 for Block X (land and buildings) including free right of way "to the ferry & proposed bridge site across the portion of River Lot 8 below the high bank." A condition of the offer was that Heiminck not appeal his suit against the town.[16] Although council voted to make this offer, Heiminck must have refused it, and the opening of a public market was again delayed.

Having failed to arrange a sale to the town on behalf of his client, Heiminck began, in November 1897, to buy the land himself, putting it in the name of his wife, Isabella. In November 1897, she bought lots 30-34 inclusive: in May 1899, she bought four lots, and in November 1900, Mrs. Heiminck bought a final lot.[17]

Throughout 1898 and 1899, the Town Hall and Market Committee attempted to deal with Heiminck for the nine lots belonging to his wife, with Henri Morel for lot 43, and with Luc Authier, carpenter and builder, for lot 44. Finally, in April 1900, council went to the ratepayers "to provide for the borrowing of $3,900.00 to acquire land for Market site."[18] Even the defeat of the by-law could not stand in council's way this time. The Finance Committee was called in to help finalize a legal agreement with the Heimincks. In August 1900, a much debated and often revised lease agrreement with Isabella Heiminck was approved by council and duly signed, effectively concluding an eight-year process to acquire a site for a public market. Less than a year later, the option to purchase the property which the city had taken care to include in the agreement was exercised when, in June 1901, the ratepayers finally approved the required money by-law.[19]

If the creation of a market had really been a civic priority between 1893 and 1900, it is difficult to imagine that a suitable site could not have been found sooner. What was a priority, it seems, was Block X, ultimately destined for redevelopment as Edmonton's civic centre. But, in 1900, any designs council might already have had on Market Square were not discussed openly.

Philip Heiminck's role in founding the city market can neither be satisfactorily explained nor overestimated. How much of his enthusiasm for the project derived from self-interest — as agent for and then owner of the land — and how much of it was based on his professed belief that a market was needed in

Edmonton, will never be known for sure. In true booster tradition, self-interest and civic interest were fused in Heiminck's imagination and rhetoric. However suspect the motives behind his letter on the subject of the market, published in the *Bulletin* on 6 April 1900, a few months before his agreement with the town was finalized, his joint claims that a market would stimulate economic growth and promote the lively and proper interaction between country and city were the first formulations of what became a refrain for decades to come:

2.5

Philip Heiminck, shown here in a photograph taken around 1880 and therefore before his arrival in Edmonton, must have been rarely photographed for this is the only image of him to be found. CEA, EA-10-689.64

> We challenge anybody in this community to give a single valid reason why we should not have a market, and we further challenge anybody to give a valid reason why the selected site is not the best, the most central, and comparatively cheapest site for our town.... We claim that there is no greater impetus to the growth of any town than a well established market.... The market represents the fixed centre for trade not only for the city housekeeper, but for ranchers, farmers and traders who live a hundred miles away; it represents a fixed hour at which we are able to find a selection of the choicest products of our fair country, at which we meet the people of Strathcona, Leduc, Beaver Lake, Ft. Saskatchewan, etc., etc., when they come to us to trade; it means the development of our export trade and the abolishment of ranky butter.

Some time around 1870, Philip Heiminck had moved from Ontario to Winnipeg where he met and married Miss Isabella Green. They had three children, two girls and a boy. In 1881, the Heimincks moved to Edmonton, where Mr. Heiminck went into the real-estate business. In 1883, the family moved to Fort Saskatchewan, returning to Edmonton about eight years later.[20] On 8 August 1891, the *Bulletin* reported that "P. Heiminck has opened his real estate office on Jasper avenue between Larue & Picard's and P. Daly's stores." In 1892, Edmonton's incorporation year, Heiminck was one of several individuals profiled in the *Toronto Mail*, where he is described as having been born and raised in Norfolk County Ontario, "another one of the numerous young men of Ontario who have made a name and a reputation for themselves by their tact and business ability in the far west."[21]

According to the article in the *Mail*, Heiminck was the "largest and best known of real estate operators west of Winnipeg," representing clients from across the west. An aggressive and apparently successful businessman, who included the HBC among his clients, Heiminck must have been as well known in Edmonton around the turn of the twentieth century as other founding citizens about whom much more is known today. He sat on council between 1902 and 1904, chairing the License and Police Committee both years. A street (107th Avenue) was named after him and it is possible that Isabella (104th Avenue) was named after his wife. Like many of his fellow citizens, he took a strong interest in issues such as the need for a railway link and, in 1897, was one of a group of men who were organized by Mayor John A. McDougall to put up $25,000 towards the building of the Low Level Bridge (completed 1902).[22] During the building boom before World War I, Heiminck, as did so many of Edmonton's wealthy citizens, built a building which he named after himself at 10153 Jasper Avenue between the ACME and Cristall blocks.[23]

Heiminck seems to have been a prickly, disagreeable person who, outside work, moved in few social circles. His exchanges with the town on real-estate matters show him to be opportunistic, quick to take offence, disposed to resort to legal process when thwarted, self-important and humourless. He routinely disputed tax assessments, refusing to pay until forced. On 28 December 1900, the *Bulletin* reported that "P. Heiminck forwarded $346.43 taxes paid under protest." On 10 February 1896, he wrote to the mayor and councillors asking to be put on a delegation to be sent to Ottawa to discuss the issue of a railway link:

> I take the liberty in offering myself for the office as a deligate [*sic*], knowing that you gentlemen fully agree with me that I am the most suitable person for the position, being thoroughly versed in the matter to be transacted, besides I might say, my business ability regarding R.R. affairs *of this kind* should make it highly desirable in bestowing upon me ample funds and full power of attorney for this delicate mission, being sure you Gentlemen will clearly see the advantages in my offer.[24]

Unfortunately for Heiminck, his confidence in his own disinterestedness was not shared; it is unlikely he received the appointment.

Philip Heiminck's death in 1922 was recorded in the *Bulletin*, 13 September 1922, but the obituary is sparse in detail, lacking in anecdote, and somewhat detached in tone. The *Bulletin*'s restraint, combined with the fact that the service was conducted at his home and not in any of the well-patronized churches, before burial in the Edmonton Cemetery, suggests that despite his long residence in Edmonton and the influence he had brought to bear on its development, Heiminck was an outsider.

It is tempting to wonder whether Philip and Isabella Heiminck patronized the market when it opened or what they thought in 1914 when the city

2.6

Even in 1910, when this photograph of Market Square was taken, it is evident that the social aspects of the Saturday markets were one of its major attractions. GA, NA-1328-64813

attempted to move it from land they had sold for the purpose. In years to come, beginning as early as 1911 when council initiated plans to move the market, a strong conviction took hold among vendors that the city was not legally free to use the Rice Street site for an alternative purpose, a conviction no doubt fuelled by the wording of the agreement between the then town and Mrs. Heiminck which specified that the land was to be used for a market. At least twice, in 1910 and again in 1939, the city's solicitor was called upon to provide legal advice on the matter, and both times he advised council that it had the legal right to change the use of the property.[25] Nevertheless, as late as the 1980s and 1990s, many of the older vendors, still unhappy about the Edmonton City Market's move to 97th Street in 1965, recounted the story of a rich woman who they mistakenly believed had donated land for a market to the city on the understanding that it would forever be dedicated to that use.

By-law No. 202 Respecting a Public Market was passed by council on 5 December 1900, just two weeks before the market opened. Hours of operation were set from 7.00 a.m. to noon and 1.00 to 6.00 p.m. every day except Sunday, and a market clerk was hired to supervise operations. From the beginning the market seems to have been a success — eagerly patronized by citizens in search of everything from coal to turnips, hay for their horses to a nice fresh chicken for the Sunday dinner.

2.7

Photographs of the weigh scales are difficult to find. This one shows a load of coal being weighed at the market scale in 1914, two years before the erection of a market building. The city charged for each load weighed. Occasionally, farmers were suspected of lying about the tare weights of their wagons so they could overcharge customers, but this never became a public issue. GA, NC-6-1242

The first so-called "Market Square" was probably more rectangular than square for it was not until 1909 that the city finally assembled the entire block, today's site of the Stanley A. Milner Library. Fenced, because in September of 1900 the town paid Philip Heiminck fifty dollars for having provided this amenity, the main feature of the market in 1900 was undoubtedly the platform weigh scale in the southeast corner for which council had obtained quotes in August of that year.[26] A one-storey wood frame office for the market clerk costing the city one hundred dollars was built nearby.[27] A minor feature would have been the often-remembered horse trough which marked the northwest corner of the site for many years — probably moved there after the entire site had been assembled. And doubtless there were a few miscellaneous buildings on the site because, in his annual report of 1908, Market Clerk Ernest Grierson noted that "the removal of the buildings added considerable [*sic*] to the size of the market grounds."[28]

All traffic to and from the site in 1900 was horsedrawn, and horses not stabled in one of many nearby livery stables would either have been tied to the fence or tethered to the wagons (rigs) from which their owners sold. Much of the trade was in bulky items such as coal, wood, hay, straw and greenfeed. Market Square must have been awhirl with dust and bits of straw and hay during windy, warm weather and a sea of mud during a rain. On 21 October 1910, a reporter for the *Bulletin* noted that "on a windy day the farmers who sell the dainty dairy butter or the dressed meats or poultry, have to keep it covered to keep off the dirty dust from the pavement or the manure from the square which a passing gust of wind might deposit upon the good-looking butter."

Throughout the market's first decade, the square became increasingly congested and unmanageable, partly due to increased selling but also because it was a gathering place. In his annual report to the city in 1909, Grierson pointed out that "the square is at present used by a large number of persons as a convenient place to feed their teams," going on to suggest that a fee should be charged for this use, whether or not weighing was done.[29] While farm produce, such as vegetables, poultry, butter, and eggs, would have been sold throughout the week, it is likely that Saturdays were the busiest of the market days, drawing families out to shop for their Sunday dinner. Beginning in 1908, and continuing until he left his position sometime at the end of 1910 or beginning of 1911, Grierson noted that "the space allotted to market purposes is greatly congested and in the near future will be entirely inadequate to accommodate the same."[30]

In early December 1900, council chose W. E. (Ernest) Grierson from among six applicants to be the market clerk. His opening salary was twenty-five dollars per month, although he negotiated this sum up rapidly in the first years of his tenure so that by September 1903 it had tripled to seventy-five dollars.[31] During his last year as clerk, 1910, the city obtained ratepayer approval to move the market to a location on 101st Street and 107th Avenue. Grierson's job, to enforce all twenty-one articles of the market by-law, endowed him with the authority of a special constable for the site, ensuring that the market clerk, later known as the market superintendent, was always a controversial figure among vendors.

Two tasks would have occupied the majority of Grierson's time: weighing loads on the platform weigh scales, and regulating activities on the square. Weigh fees were prescribed in the by-law (ten cents for every load of hay, straw,

2.8

Ernest Grierson, Market Clerk between 1900 and 1910, was the first in a long line of market overseers — subsequently referred to as "superintendents" or "managers." This portrait of Grierson appeared in the "Municipality of the City of Edmonton, Alberta Financial and Departmental Reports for the Year ended October 31st, 1910." Courtesy of the CEA

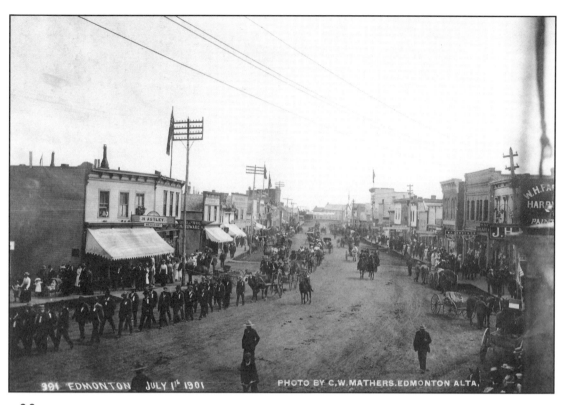

2.9

This photograph of Jasper Avenue, taken during a Dominion Day Parade on 1 July 1901, gives an impression of Edmonton's downtown just a few months after the public market opened in December, 1900. CEA, EA-10-180

or greenfeed, five cents for every load of coal and five cents for any live animal on foot, for example) and constituted the main source of revenue until 1911 when, in a move that almost caused riots on the square, the city instituted small vendor fees. In 1901, Grierson recorded an income of $336.40 in weigh fees, a figure which had risen to $1,033.40 by 1903. Even so, during Grierson's tenure, the market's annual expenditures always exceeded revenues, so that in his report of 1909 he hinted that vendors should pay to sell rather than to weigh: "the total number of loads weighed was 23,399, but the amount of weighing done was small in comparison to the amount of produce, etc., offered for sale on the market square." Although the weigh scale remained on the square until 1957, its role slowly diminished after 1911 when council, following Grierson's recommendation, introduced vendor fees as well as weigh fees.[32]

Regulating activities on the square must have become more demanding as the decade wore on, for Grierson would have devised and enforced the rules by which vendors were assigned parking and stall locations, ensured that horses and wagons moved safely about the site, supervised and assisted with the maintenance of the site, and initiated any repairs or improvements to it. It is clear from Grierson's annual reports that, in addition to managing traffic and keeping the grounds in acceptable shape, he was given "much trouble and annoyance," as were his successors, by the job of maintaining public "closets" on the site.[33]

Few vendors sold at the market without spending some of their earnings in the city, and few customers made the trip to the market without stopping elsewhere. Ranged around the market, even in 1900, were shops and businesses catering to the many needs of these two groups. Jasper Avenue, only one block south of the market, included hotels, banks, restaurants, tobacconists, drug stores, and grocery stores in the few blocks between 96th Street (Kinistino) and 101st Street (McDougall). Johnstone Walker Dry Goods store was on Jasper immediately south of the market, as were J. T. Blowey (which sold furniture, carpets, and musical instruments), the CPR Land Office, and the Imperial Bank, whose manager, G. R. F. Kirkpatrick, was one of those who contributed, as did Philip Heiminck, his own money to the building of the Low Level Bridge. Abe Cristall, who delivered at least one speech on Market Square during a prohibition rally in 1915, operated a liquor store on the corner of McDougall and Jasper, just a block south of the market.[34]

By 1900, several of Edmonton's residential districts were well enough established to supply customers to the Rice Street Market. Immediately to the west (101st Street westward to 121st Street) the Hudson's Bay reserve had begun to open up, much of it developed as residential lots. Ernest Grierson lived on 101st Street in the HBC reserve. Joseph Gariepy, who had chaired the Town Hall and Market Committee in 1897, built a grand house in 1902 at 9947 - 104th Street. About the same time, Philip Heiminck, who had lived on the southwest corner of Market Square before selling it, built a large new house for his family north of Jasper on 103rd Street, just a few blocks from the market. Walter Ramsay, who came to Edmonton in 1899 as a school teacher and went on to become the city's best known greenhouse operator and florist, was living downtown in 1900. Kathrine Granstrom of Virginia Park Greenhouses, who began attending the city market in 1929, remembered seeing Ramsay and his wife there every Saturday — he carrying a wicker basket which she filled with purchases.[35]

In addition to the residences west of 101st Street, customers in 1900 would have come from the residential areas east and north of the market, especially 95th, 96th, and 97th streets, and from areas west of the Hudson's Bay reserve. Present-day Oliver, for example, was already established as a French community around St. Joachim Church, which opened in 1899 on 110th Street. Shortly after 1900, the Highlands area, slightly to the east and quite a bit to the north of the city market began to open up as a wealthy residential area with an agricultural hinterland. Highlands supplied vendors as well as customers to the Rice Street Market.

Although no records exist to name those who travelled to Market Square in 1900 to sell loads of coal, wood, hay, cattle, poultry, butchered meat, butter, vegetables, flowers, and plants, it is likely that they came from as far away as St. Albert, Spruce Grove, Leduc, and Clover Bar and from smaller farms and market gardens close to or within the town boundaries. In 1910, a *Bulletin* reporter noticed clumps of vendors standing around the market and recognized them to be groups of neighbours from outlying towns: "they come from all around: North, south, east and west, for from twenty to fifty miles."[36] Interviews with vendors selected from these milling groups convinced the reporter that, despite the lack of a market shelter, vendors found Edmonton to be a good market town — a place where they could sell all of their produce and, best of all, realize cash for it.

One man who might have begun selling at the market before 1910, was Frederik Frederiksen. By 1907, Frederiksen was the coproprietor of Klondyke Gardens at 12340 Fort Road, having moved to Edmonton from Dawson where he and a friend abandoned the gold rush in 1899 to grow and sell vegetables. Frederiksen, who soon after his arrival in Edmonton became sole owner of the business, grew potatoes, carrots, onions, leeks, lettuce, cabbage, kohlrabi and celery as well as bedding plants to sell to home gardeners. Klondyke Gardens was well known in the city by 1909,[37] a renown which might have come partly through contacts made at the market. Certainly, from the time the first patchy vendor lists were compiled by the superintendent in the 1920s, Klondyke Gardens appeared on them.

In 1909, council made two land acquisitions around which its market planning revolved in subsequent years. In June of that year, it submitted two money by-laws to the ratepayers, both of which were approved. *By-law no. 214*, for $45,000, enabled the city to buy from druggist Donald Walter Macdonald, the last two privately owned lots on the Rice Street site, lots 39 and 40. *By-law No. 213*, for $40,000, raised enough money for the city to buy, piece by piece, a hay market site on the northeast corner of 101st Street and 107th Avenue. The hay market was expected to relieve two problems on the Rice Street site, crowding and dirt, for straw, hay, greenfeed, and coal were notorious generators of dust and flying debris. On 20 December 1910, council passed a motion stipulating that only the 101st Street site could be used for the sale of "hay, straw, green-feed and all that particular class of material, and coal." A new market by-law was passed on 17 January and, for the short term anyway, Edmonton had two markets, each of which was supposed to be offering different goods.

Between January 1911, when council's *By-law No. 307 Respecting Public Markets* was passed, to November 1914, when a new and costly market building was opened on the 101st Street site, conflicting ideas about the long-term future of the two market sites sometimes coexisted, sometimes collided, creating a confusing picture of the issues at stake. Council's moves during this period, as Alderman Lundy made clear in an interview with the *Bulletin*, were calculated to keep the Rice Street site open for future redevelopment as a civic centre, and, at the same time, to convert the market from a money-losing proposition to one that broke even or was marginally profitable. "It is the intention of the city some day to build a city hall on the centre of the present city market square," he pronounced: "Consequently, it would be foolish to erect an expensive market building there."[38] Lundy went on to suggest that the 101st Street site would be a good location for a permanent building.

Supporting council were those who deplored the chaos and disorder of the Rice Street Market and wished it out of the centre. The outcome of a February 1910 plebiscite on the best location for a market building, which favoured the 101st Street site (698 votes against 345 for Rice Street), constituted the high point of public support for council's aims.[39] Although some supporters of the 101st Street site must have changed sides in the years to come, one group remained steadfast in its quest to relocate the market. At least two chapters of the IODE, the Beaver Hill and the Westward Ho chapters, wrote in 1911 to "the Mayor and City Council" to request that "no other building but the city hall" be constructed on the market grounds. The Beaver Hill Chapter went so far as to resolve:

> that this Municipal Chapter, realizing the great natural advantages of Edmonton, as a beautiful residential as well as industrial city, and having in view the fact that its dignity as the capital city of this great Province, involves the obligation of worthily sustaining that position, would urge upon the Municipal bodies interested and the citizens at large, the imperative need of a comprehensive and scientifically studied plan for future development — and improvement as such a plan as shall place Edmonton in line with practically all the progressive cities of the world.[40]

The IODE's arguments were rooted in the City Beautiful movement which, with its promotion of gardens and parks as fitting contexts for formal government functions, became a planning orthodoxy about this time. In Alberta, it was reflected both in the Thomas H. Mawson plan for Calgary (1914) and in the Morell and Nichols plan created for Edmonton's civic centre in 1912.

Those who favoured keeping the Edmonton City Market on Rice Street argued that the 101st Street site was too far from the city centre and its businesses. These people, mainly vendors, customers, owners of adjacent businesses, and even market clerk Ernest Grierson promoted the continuation of the *status quo* on Rice Street with one improvement — the building of a market structure to shelter trading. In his final annual report in 1910, Grierson wrote that "if it were possible to erect a comfortable and commodious building and pave and lay out the grounds with convenient walks, where loads could be placed in proper position, it would add much to the appearance of the square, and be a great convenience to buyers and sellers, as well as a great advantage to all concerned."[41] In April 1910, Kenny McLeod, who was soon to build the McLeod Building just to the east of the market, was one of a delegation of three who addressed council to protest the market's removal from Rice Street.[42] And in March 1910, a month after the plebiscite, a reporter for the *Bulletin* grumped that while it had been clear for many years that the people wanted a market building on Rice Street, the city had simply been procrastinating for ten years. "The market building is to remain a castle in the air," he claimed.[43] Although little resistance to the 101st Street site was expressed between 1911 and 1914, as the city concentrated on its civic centre planning, the attractions of the Rice Street site resurfaced as soon as the long-anticipated move was attempted.

By-law No. 307 Respecting Public Markets, passed by the Edmonton City Council on 17 January 1911, was written with change in mind. Council, determined to create "a first class Market By-Law for this City," had taken some time to draft it, beginning in May 1910 when it decided to review market regulations in other cities.[44] In addition to naming the two market sites (a south-side market was added after Edmonton's amalgamation with Strathcona in 1912), *By-law No. 307* created a new reporting structure, with the clerk reporting directly to the city commissioners, not to council. It also gave the commissioners the power to hire a private company to manage public markets and to introduce vendor fees in addition to weigh fees. It restricted the sale of hay and coal to the 101st Street site after 1 February 1911. Within months of being passed *By-law No. 307* required amending, first when the private management scheme collapsed, and then when citizen delegations, persuaded council to reallow the sale of hay and coal on the Rice Street Market.

D. C. Robertson, who replaced Grierson as market clerk in 1911, remained in the position throughout the next volatile decade without leaving any imprint on the location debate. In early 1911, he remained in the background while the professional management group, Kelly and Ennes, faced the vigorous opposition to vendor fees. In his annual report of 1912, Robertson fed council and the administration the bureaucratic line that they needed to embark on the 1913 exercise to design a new market building for 101st Street:

> I avail myself of this opportunity to strongly recommend the speedy erection
> of a proper market building, where sellers and buyers and their merchandise

will be protected against weather influences, such a building becoming more and more urgent in the city of the size and growth of Edmonton. Cold storage facilities, moreover, will make it possible for a wider contributory district to avail itself of Edmonton's market conditions and this will add to the levelling of the high cost of living and better the health conditions in the city.[45]

Throughout 1913, Robertson was a member of the committee which planned and designed the new market on 101st Street and, in 1914 and 1915, with no evidence of regret, he supervised the vacating and the reinhabiting of the Rice Street site.

A week before *By-law No. 307* was passed, council decided to contract the day-to-day management of its two markets to a private firm. The firm of Kelly and Ennes was hired for a yearly contract amount of $2,020, "for which they agree to keep the two markets (Rice Street and First Street), scales and buildings in repair, weigh all goods brought to the scales and keep a record of the weighing of such goods." According to the *Bulletin*'s report, "besides the prices for weighing, a fee of 10 cents per day is charged each farmer occupying a stand on the market."[46]

Kelly and Ennes were not equipped to face the vendors' resistance to the imposition of selling fees. On 4 February 1911, the *Bulletin* reported that the attempt to enforce this fee-paying regulation had:

> caused a miniature riot at the First Street Market.... Three farmers flatly refused to pay their fees for standing on the grounds, while all the others did so, only under compulsion. One man objected to paying his market fee on entering but agreed to do so before leaving. On departure he saw the gate open and made an attempt to rush it.

By the time council met on 28 February, at which meeting they were petitioned by a group from the United Farmers of Alberta to take back the management of the markets, "Mr. Kelly expressed his willingness to hand back the lease to the City."[47] Thus ended the city's only experiment in delegating the management of its public markets until October 1998, but the hated vendor fees lived on.

The Kelly and Ennes experiment raised questions about how well the city was delivering market services to the public and, to a lesser extent, about the role played by the market in the life of the city. A reporter for the *Bulletin* wondered why "instead of making one good market and making it pay expenses, we have created two markets which can only be made to pay expenses by collecting excessive charges on the business done." This reporter, pronouncing on the benefits of "one good market," returned to a formulation reminiscent of Heiminck's made more than a decade earlier:

A good market, with moderate fees charged and reasonable conveniences afforded is the best means the city has of holding trade against the competition of other towns where such favorable conditions exist. It is the strongest inducement the city can offer for getting the farmers of the district to produce the dairy, poultry and other products needed by the townsman and for making the farmer a frequent visitor to the city and a more liberal patron of the city stores.[48]

But by 1912, as the city embarked on its first major attempt to plan and build a civic centre, its vision was shaped more by the ideals of the City Beautiful movement and the new orthodoxies of planning than it was by the almost anachronistic idea that Edmonton's urban identity was linked to its agricultural hinterland.

Edmonton's first civic centre plan was prepared by an American landscape architecture firm, Morell and Nichols, with well-known architect C. L. (Lionel) Gibbs acting as liaison between the city, the parks commission, and the consultant.[49] Gibbs, a vocal advocate of city planning, took a special interest in this project. In March 1911, Gibbs defined a civic centre as "the hub of any civic plan, the culminating point laid out with a special view to impressing the stranger with an idea of the city's importance and taste." Gibbs's list of the kinds of facilities that would go to make up such a centre included a city hall, public library, museums, "Central Education establishments," and smaller components "of a quasi public sort, such as leading establishments devoted to public recreation, dramatic, musical and otherwise, with a clientele covering the whole city."[50] A market of any sort does not appear on the list prepared by Gibbs. In their report, Morell and Nichols handed back to the city in spades what they had been dealt as terms of reference.[51]

Dated 1 November 1912 and discussed later that month by council, the Morell and Nichols' plan was infused with the ideology that informed it. The opening section laid out the history and benefits of town planning. Gibbs and his colleagues were addressed and flattered for their "large progressive ideas," and their "great faith in the City's future." It was no surprise that Morell and Nichols' account of the "advantages to be gained from the adoption of an intelligent City Plan" complemented Gibbs's ideas on the subject. In their view, a city plan:

> will give due importance to each field of municipal improvements. It will furnish a nucleus around which people's sentiment can crystalize [*sic*]. It will help to culminate the unity of city life by bringing together the different parts of the city, but more than anything else, it will tend to create city orderliness and beauty where otherwise there will continue to exist a lack of unity in practical arrangement and an absence of dignity and harmony.

2.10

When Morell and Nichols prepared their proposal for Edmonton's civic centre (1912), they assumed the market would be moved well away from the centre to 107th Avenue and 101st Street. This particular view looks north from the site then occupied by Market Square. CEA, EA-362-68

Orderliness and beauty, dignity and harmony, were not terms that sprang to mind as descriptors of the Rice Street Market, and Morell and Nichols simply assumed, for the purposes of their plan, that the market would move to the 101st Street site as the city had arranged. Had the first civic centre plan been officially accepted and partially or wholly implemented, the Rice Street site would not have been available to be reclaimed as it was in 1915. However, when council was unable, in March 1913, to get the consent of ratepayers to borrow $2,712,193.34 to buy the remainder of the land needed to accommodate the Morell and Nichols plan, it simply faded into the background, leaving scope for the market to spring into the public view as a project in its own right.[52]

The market component of the Morell and Nichols plan, peripheral though it was, offered the city its only scope for action after the defeat of the money by-law in March 1913. Both market sites were owned by the city and ratepayers had already approved the erection of a building on the 101st Street site. So, although the collapse of the main plan removed the pressure to close the Rice Street Market, the city decided to move ahead with the design and construction of a new market on 101st Street. The Rice Street site, had the project worked out as anticipated, was to have been converted to a public park until it was needed for redevelopment.

Practical considerations must also have figured in the city's decision to close the Rice Street Market. Throughout 1911 and 1912, council had spent as little as possible on improvements to the market sites — not wanting to anticipate the outcome of the planning process. Also, amalgamation with Strathcona brought a third market (South Side Market) into the city's fold, and its role in the overall delivery of market services had to be considered. In mid-August 1912, Mayor Armstrong wrote to council suggesting that the market committee meet with the commissioners to "go thoroughly into matters pertaining to better market facilities in the City on both sides of the river."[53] As it turned out, the major task of this new committee was to initiate and follow through with the design of the 101st Street market building.

Under the leadership of Mayor Armstrong who, when he had been an alderman in 1909, had spoken about the "urgent necessity of the early construction of a suitable Market Building,"[54] the market committee was restructured in mid-1912. Two aldermen (East and May), Mayor Armstrong, two commissioners (Chalmers and Harrison), Market Superintendent Robertson and City Architect A. M. Jeffers began meeting on a regular basis to plan and design the new facility.[55] By the time council was finally ready to call for tenders, 30 September 1913, Mayor Armstrong had been replaced by Mayor Short, the design had gone through several permutations, each one responding to a different set of design requirements, and the office of the city architect was about

2.11

When this photograph of Market Square was taken in 1913, the Civic Block had just opened and a new market building was being built on 107th Avenue and 101st Street. GA, NC-6-581

to be abolished, taking with it the distinguished architect who had laboured to provide a design acceptable to the committee.

Allan Merrick Jeffers came to Edmonton in April 1907 from the United States. Born in Pawtucket, Rhode Island, in 1875, he had studied and practised architecture there before coming to Alberta, where he was hired by the Alberta Department of Public Works as chief draughtsman in May 1907. A couple of months later, he was promoted to the position of provincial architect. Probably best known as the designer of the Alberta Legislature Building, Jeffers designed a number of other buildings for the province, including the official residence of the Governor General.[56]

Before the legislature building had been completed and occupied, Jeffers was wooed away from the provincial government to become, in February 1912, head of the newly created City Architecture Department. There he designed, among other things, the Civic Block, built in 1912 to accommodate council and the expanding civic administration on a site kitty-corner to the Rice Street Market. The design phase of the new market building followed immediately after the opening of the Civic Block.

Jeffers's attempt to design the 101st Street market building must have been one of his more frustrating projects. The inability of Mayor Armstrong's working committee to agree on important matters of function made design almost impossible. Questions raised but never answered included: who would occupy the administrative portion of the project; how many horses would be stabled;

whether the direct producer/consumer sales model would be scaled up to allow middlemen to sell under specified conditions; whether the city would provide an auctioneering service in the building. Jeffers produced a number of very different designs before, sometime in August or September of 1913, the project was turned over to A. W. Wheeler, also of the architect's office, to prepare specifications and plans.[57]

Jeffers left the employ of the city in November 1913, when the architect's office was abolished, though he was rehired when the office was reconstituted in February, 1914. By June of 1915, he had entered private practice in Edmonton. In 1922, he left Edmonton for Prince Rupert and then Los Angeles, where he died in 1926. Of all Jeffers's public projects, the design of the 101st Street market building may be the least known. It was certainly the least successful, a fact which had less to do with the talents of the designer than with the confusion and indecision which plagued the design process.

Jeffers's first design proposal to the market committee, which was reviewed at its meeting of 6 November 1912 and described a few days later in the *Bulletin*, met with little expressed enthusiasm and provoked some public anxiety, despite its conformity to the ideals and design principles of the Morell and Nichols report.

> The plans indicate that the market building when complete will be a fine sample of this class of building. Speaking broadly, the building will be somewhat the shape of a horseshoe. It will be three stories high, with frontage on First street and other sides of the block. Provision will be made for offices in the wings facing on first street and Queens avenue. Arcade-like entrances will lead through to the market proper. Inside there will be long rows of stalls wherein the market gardeners and other vendors of produce will be able to deal directly with the consumer.[58]

The Retail Merchants' Association of Edmonton was vocal in its criticism of the 101st Street market design. It would provide farmers with better facilities, according to the retail merchants, than many of their own shops and would be sure to attract middlemen — either farmers selling for neighbours or enterprisers selling for farmers.[59] Nevertheless, the city proceeded with the project. On 4 March 1913, council passed a by-law for $110,960, "for the purpose of erecting and equipping market buildings on the First Street Market Site."

Jeffers's second design, submitted to the market committee in mid-May 1913, followed a marathon meeting held five days earlier to review the building's requirements. The committee had visited the site, talked about the number of teams needing on-site stabling and even reviewed plans for the market building in Cleveland, Ohio. Jeffers's "sketch plan," which showed a building 50 feet wide, 120 feet long and two storeys high, was immediately rejected as not grand enough and the committee decided to start again from scratch after looking at plans from a host of other cities. Despite Jeffers's protests, Toronto and Winnipeg were telegrammed for copies of their plans and Alderman Livingstone, who was about to embark on a long trip, was asked to get plans from every city he visited.

In July 1913, the market committee finally approved a design, but not before (at its June meeting) it considered moving the entire project back to Rice Street.[60] Poor Jeffers, in the throes of designing for 101st Street, was asked in June to prepare sketch plans for a new market on Rice Street, and only the city solicitor's opinion that money approved for 101st Street could not simply be applied to another site refocussed the project. The approved design, which consisted of a $36,000 administration building, a $32,000 market building and a $15,000 stable went forward to council in July with many details still unresolved. It was not until 30 September of that year that tenders were finally called — a year during which the subject of the market building came up at council meetings at least twelve times between February 4 and September 30.

Market Superintendent Robertson, in his annual report for the market department at the end of 1913, provided a detailed description of the design, including the size, disposition and layout of the buildings which were to be built in the fiscal year 1914.

> The Market Building is arranged with front and rear, as well as, twelve side entrance doors. Produce, meats, etc., will be exposed for sale inside the building on marble top counters which go to make up the eighteen stalls and outside from wagons under sheds twenty-four feet wide, which extend on both sides for the entire length of the building. A walk ten feet wide extends around the entire structure under the wagon sheds, thus intending purchasers from wagons are always sure of protection from inclement weather while inspecting produce before purchasing. The basement contains heating and ventilating apparatus and storage rooms for produce.[61]

Opened 7 November 1914, the 101st Street market building was a spectacular failure, rejected so decidedly by customers and then vendors that within weeks of its opening, it was empty, and within months had been reallocated to other uses. Somehow, despite the results of the 1910 plebiscite and the objectives spelled out in the Morell and Nichols report, the city's attempt to move and upgrade the Rice Street Market sparked a popular and effective resistance to the move.

New City Market

Removed from Rice St. to 101st St. Cor. Nelson Ave.

The new building is greatly to the advantage of the merchants. Everything sanitary and full up-to-date in every respect. It is nicely divided into stalls, every stall fitted in the best and most sanitary methods available and inspected by the health officers.

Street Railway Gives Free Return From Market

Take advantage of this and visit the New City Market. Ask the conductor when leaving the street car at the market, for a transfer which you can use after your shopping is finished.

THE FOLLOWING MAY BE OBTAINED AT THE RIGHT PRICE

MEATS, POULTRY, VEGETABLES, GAME, FRUIT, HAY, GRAIN, COAL AND WOOD

The public is cordially invited to visit the new Market. Courteous treatment is gladly given.

Open Saturday 'till 10 o'clock

2.12

The city went to great lengths to induce Edmontonians to patronize its new market. This advertisement appeared in the *Edmonton Journal*, 13 November 1914. Courtesy of the *Edmonton Journal*

In the months immediately preceding the opening of the 101st Street market, there were signs of resistance to it. The most indirect and mysterious of these was the emergence of a private market in the Empire Auditorium on 102nd Street. Its manager, E. J. Strata, described to a *Journal* reporter the renovations which would create eighty-three well-equipped and sanitary stalls: "38 stalls in what is now known as the Auditorium, will be used for meats and green goods, the 30 stalls situated to the south, for poultry and the 15 stalls on the corner, will be used for the sale of meat by wholesale." Housewives were invited to bring extra baked goods to the manager "who will sell them and charge a small commission." Prominent Edmonton women, including members of the Consumers' League, were said to be interested in the project.[62] It seems unlikely that the Empire Auditorium market lasted long, but the timing of its appearance suggests that consumers were worried about the proposed disappearance of the Rice Street Market and that they did not expect the new building on 101st Street to replace it.

Despite vigorous promotion of the 101st Street market by the city and a measure of support from some quarters, including the *Journal*, resistance to it grew. On 8 October 1914, a delegate of the stallholders association presented council with a petition asking that the Rice Street Market not be closed. Five days later, on the advice of the Parks and Market Committee, the city approved a three-point policy aimed at protecting its considerable investment in "a new central market." The Rice Street Market was to "be closed on the 5th of November and the new first Street market be opened on Saturday the 7th November." Then the Rice Street site was to "be seeded and put into grass, to be used as a Public Square, Playground or Park, until such time as it may be required for any other purpose." Finally, twenty dollars were to be put aside for cash prizes "for the best exhibitions of Alberta produce shewen [*sic*]at the official opening of the new market."[63]

The *Journal* supported the city's decision to close the Rice Street Market. An article published in the 5 November 1914 edition, just two days before the 101st Street market was to open, reminded Edmontonians that the city was merely acting on the advice of its citizens in the 1910 referendum, "and it is certainly a trifle late to revive the subject now." As for arguments that the new market was out of the way, the *Journal* found this claim "absurd": "with a double-tracked street car line passing right in front of the market building, buyers should find it convenient, and it could not be better situated for those bringing in produce from the country."

Resistance to the new market was quiet but persistent. On 10 November, a representative of the stallholders group from the Rice Street Market complained to council that vendors "were unable to get accommodation in the new market

2.13

When this photograph of the market building on 101st Street was taken in 1919, it had long ceased to be used for its intended purpose. Between 1923 and 1943, the building became well known as Edmonton's technical school. GA, NC-6-4964

building." On 8 December, council received a petition from property owners adjacent to the Rice Street market site asking that the Rice Street Market be reopened. On 14 December, the United Farmers of Alberta wrote to the Parks and Market Committee warning it to advertise for customers because "owing to lack of patronage the stall-holders were unable to sell any produce."[64] On Christmas Eve of that year, Commissioner Harrison was authorized "to advertise the market and to adopt measures to boost it."[65] But, somehow, over the Christmas season, the project failed entirely so that, by 17 January 1915, the *Bulletin* ran an article under the headline: "City Market Will be Re-established Upon the Rice Street Site." Alderman Williamson was reported as declaring, "the Fact that money has been spent on the First street site is no reason why it should be retained."

The three-point market plan adopted by council on 26 January 1915 represented a one hundred and eighty degree turn from the one adopted two and a half months earlier. Firstly, the Rice Street site was to be cleared of "all material and temporary buildings and farmers permitted to tie teams there for a fee of 10c." Secondly, a portion of the 101st Street Market was to be "leased to the Police Department." And thirdly, the commissioners were asked to "prepare plans and estimates for a temporary market building on the Rice Street site."

Despite a reluctance to abandon the 101st Street site, this plan was finally implemented. In January 1916, Alderman Williamson, who headed the market committee, reversed his opinion of a year earlier and attempted to sabotage the new plan, advising against a market building and recommending a park instead.[66] More persuasive were the actions of the United Farmers of Alberta who declined to hold their convention in Edmonton that year to protest the city's stance on markets. The farmers met in Lethbridge instead.[67] Finally though, it was at the urging of women lobbying under the banner of the Consumers' League, that council again went to the electorate on 20 June 1916 to ask for money to build "an inexpensive market building on Dominion Square, Rice Street."[68] According to one report, council "showed some diffidence" when deciding whether to respond to this request, "but being impressed with the fact that only temporary buildings were asked for," it finally decided to go to the people.[69] When the voters approved the construction of a "temporary building" on Rice Street, Edmonton's sixteen-year-old Market Square had been effectively reclaimed for the next half century, despite the reservations of many of the civic governments which followed.

Between June and December of 1916, council approved a miscellaneous expenditure for a market building on "Dominion Square" — $3,781.88. Also in 1916, a general debt debenture in the amount of $110,960 is recorded in the city's financial statements for the "First Street Market Buildings."[70] The difference between these two figures is a measure of the gulf that existed between corporate and popular attitudes towards the Edmonton City Market.

The story of the Edmonton City Market's precarious existence, especially until the 1916 building secured the Rice Street site for the purpose, uncovers the conflicting ideas and values that lay at the heart of Edmonton's corporate culture. In retrospect, the outcome of this first phase of the market's history was more ironic than triumphant. The decision in 1900 to put the market on the Rice Street site, a decision which may have been regretted almost immediately by civic officials, stacked the deck against a monumental solution to conceiving and constructing a civic centre. In the years between 1893 and 1916, the market's site cards were shuffled, dealt, and played. Trapped by its own moves, the city lost in its bid of 1914 to relocate the market away from the centre, locking itself into another half century during which the clutter and chaos of the Edmonton City Market set the tone for its corporate image.

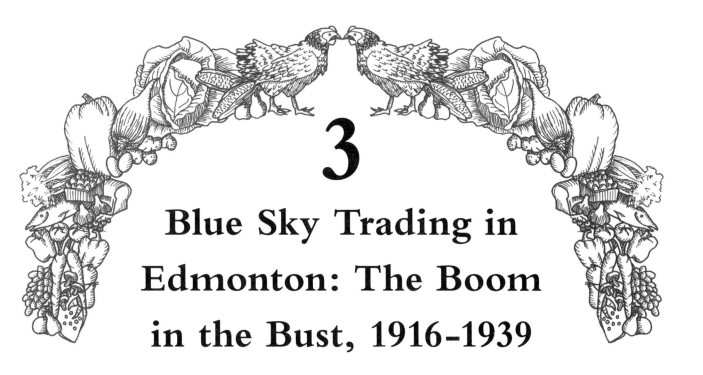

3

Blue Sky Trading in Edmonton: The Boom in the Bust, 1916-1939

The two decades between World Wars I and II were not stellar years for the city of Edmonton, but throughout them the Edmonton City Market's fortunes shone. The collapse in land values which deflated Edmonton's economy in 1913-14, bankrupting many and dragging down tax revenues, removed development pressure from the Rice Street site, rendering acceptable the decision to build an instantly scruffy market building on prime property. As the local real estate slump blended into a decade of world depression, the market attracted increasing numbers of vendors and customers, drawing from a widening range of constituencies to support mainline and peripheral activities on the square. Between 1916 and 1939, horse and wagon were almost supplanted by truck and car, a change reflected in the geography of the square and in how it was perceived and used. In 1933, the market's popularity gave rise to a scheme to enlarge it as a make-work project. Individuals and firms were engaged on the project to work off unpaid taxes and, once the addition was complete, vendor capacity (both permanent and Saturday) had been increased. By 1939, the market had become the "fixed centre for trade" and predictable source of the countryside's "choicest products" that, in 1900, Philip Heiminck had argued was a city's best asset.

Council's reluctant decision in 1916 to build a "temporary building" on Market Square initiated the market's renaissance. The Consumers' League had pressed for it, arguing that any building which would provide shelter for buyers and sellers would be acceptable.[1] The day before the required money by-law went to the electorate, the *Edmonton Bulletin* reported that, "with the case of the 101st street building before them, council showed some diffidence in dealing with the subject, but being impressed with the fact that only temporary buildings were asked for, they finally decided to submit the ... question.... Are you in favor of a temporary market being established on the Rice street site?"[2]

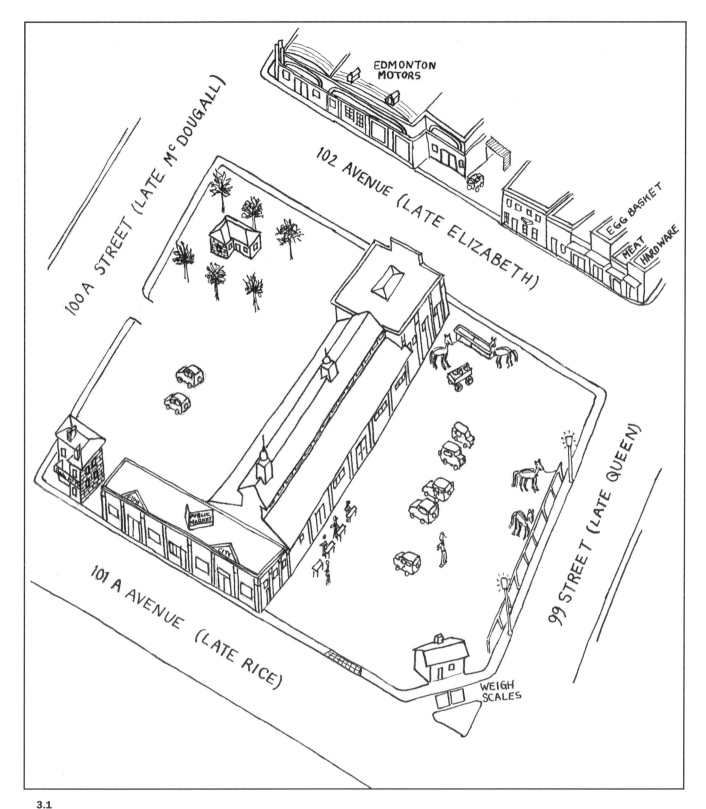

Labels within the drawing:

EDMONTON MOTORS

100 A STREET (LATE McDOUGALL)

102 AVENUE (LATE ELIZABETH)

EGG BASKET

MEAT

HARDWARE

PUBLIC MARKET

FISH

CITY

101 A AVENUE (LATE RICE)

99 STREET (LATE QUEEN)

WEIGH SCALES

3.1

1916-1939: Market Square flourished at the heart of the city. Drawing by Barbara Budenz

3.2

Under pressure from Edmonton's citizens, council finally agreed to build this "temporary" market building in 1916. Its main entrance, shown here as it must have looked just after it opened, faced onto Rice Street (101A Avenue), a major shopping street in the young city. Within a few years, the open walls (visible at the back) were filled in to create a farmers' hall. A fish market and public washrooms were added to the Rice Street facade. See fig. 3.12. GA, NC-6-2643

Council's ambivalence towards a scheme which could interfere with a future civic centre development explains the market building's meagre budget and perfunctory design, if not the disappearance of the drawings from public record. In October 1916, the Parks and Market Committee recommended to council a $9,000 ceiling to the building budget but aldermen balked at the expense. A week later, council agreed to the construction of "a brick building 46 x 48 ft. with an extended open shed 96 ft. north" and authorized the commissioners to call for tenders.[3]

Probably built to a simple set of plans and specifications prepared in the office of the city architect, the contract was given to Zenith Construction Company whose bid for the project was the lowest at $3,596. Although council agreed to increase the appropriation to $4,000 to cover "watermains, advertising and sundries," it appears the specifications were compromised. Alderman Pheasey raised several questions at council wondering why, for example, fir flooring had been substituted for the specified maple. A "miscellaneous expenditure" entry in the city's financial statements for 1916 — $3,781.88 for a "Market Building in Dominion Square" — is probably the most accurate public record of the cost of a building which was to 'grace' the city's main downtown square until 1964. In June 1917, council accepted the market building as complete and satisfactory despite "the several changes from the original specifications."[4]

Opened in mid-1917, and expanded two years later by the addition of an attached fish market, the Edmonton City (or Rice Street) Market settled into an

3.3

When the federal government opened a new Post Office in Edmonton in 1910, it was the most impressive building downtown. Its clock tower quickly became a landmark. The Post Office was demolished in 1972 to build a hotel, but the workings of the clock were saved and incorporated into a modern clock tower on the same site. CEA, EA-371-10

urban context which had been enriched in the preceding years by three major buildings, the dominion government's main Post Office (opened 1910), the Civic Block (opened 1913), and the McLeod Building (opened January, 1915). Far from dragging down the value of this prime real estate, the revitalized city market brought people, activities, and economic life to the centre, building an identity which matched its location at 'the heart of the city.'

In October 1910, when the federal government opened a new three-storey, copper-roofed Post Office, complete with a 130-foot high clock tower, on the corner of Rice and McDougall, just south of Market Square, a *Bulletin* reporter commented that "with its wide corridors, modern oak fittings, mosaic floor and lofty ceiling, supported by great pillars [the Post Office] seems to belong to another city."[5] By 1917, the Post Office had become an Edmonton landmark, its clock tower a reference point for all those coming to shop or sell in the new

3.4

From the time the Civic Block opened in 1913 until a new city hall was built in 1957, Market Square and the various activities which took place there could be viewed by those occupying civic offices. This photograph was taken in 1932, the year a hunger march originating in the square turned into an ugly confrontation between police and workers. CEA, EA-0-2

market building. What the market gained from the Post Office — a degree of dignity by association and the practical benefits of being situated across the street from a landmark building — it probably returned. Drawing customers and vendors from the city and its surrounding countryside, the market benefitted all public and commercial services located at the centre.

The six-storey, $250,000 Civic Block, designed by A. M. Jeffers and opened in 1913 just east and north of Market Square, was reluctantly abandoned by vendors and customers in the 1914 move to 101st Street and reclaimed in the 1915 return to Rice, a reclamation which had the effect, if not the intention, of cementing the relationship between city hall and market. Intended as a substitute for the hall the city was not prepared to build in 1912, the architect's department made no secret of the limited vision which attended the Civic Block's construction. In his annual report, Jeffers admitted that no attempt had been made to "elaborate the architectural lines [of the Civic Block], as it is a general belief that some day this site will demand a more pretentious structure."[6] Thus it was that between 1917, when the "temporary" market building opened, and 1957, when the Civic Block was finally replaced by a structure deemed

3.5

This drawing of the McLeod Building, dated 1914, was done by John R. Dow, the architect engaged by businessman K. A. McLeod to design his business block. McLeod, impressed by a building he had seen in Spokane, Washington, sought out the same designer, but he had his project built to such high specifications that he ran out of money half-way through construction. The project lay dormant for several months while McLeod raised the necessary money to finish it. For decades, the McLeod Building was a prestigious address for many businesses. In 1995, it was designated a Provincial Historic Resource. GA, NC-6-148

worthy of the term "City Hall," the town hall and market, up to then separated as a matter of unarticulated policy, found themselves practically colocated. It was a colocation that served the market symbolically by strengthening its civic associations, and practically by placing it in the day-to-day orbit of the mayor and aldermen. But the association also served the city, because the market, with its small staff and minuscule budget was, by definition, diverse and eclectic in the scope of its operations.[7] Through the market, the city's connections with its many constituencies (voters as well as groups and organizations made up of voters) were expanded and enriched.

In January 1915, when K. A. (Kenny) McLeod proudly opened the nine-storey, 210-room, luxuriously finished and appointed McLeod Building, just west of Market Square across McDougall Street, the 101st Street market was in the process of being abandoned as vendors and customers trickled back to Rice Street. McLeod must have been delighted. An advocate of the market's return to Rice Street, McLeod doubtless believed that his new office building would be more desirable to tenants with the market as a next-door neighbour. He would certainly have voted for the erection of a building — even a temporary one — on Market Square and, from the verandah of his house on 103rd Street, could have watched it being built. For McLeod, an alderman in 1900 when the market opened, the Post Office, Civic Block, and McLeod Building grouped around Market Square probably constituted a popular and practical conception of an ideal civic centre, one which, though never given civic sanction, became the *de facto* reality of the 1920s and 1930s.

Between 1917 and 1939, the market's hold on a key situation in the city's geography was not challenged. Its rhythms, which changed with the days of the week and with the seasons, complemented those of the city, and its patrons

3.6

This photograph, probably taken in the mid-1920s on a summer day when the outside stalls on Market Square were filled with fresh vegetables, attracted the attention of Jack McMann when he saw it about seventy years later. His parents, Allan and Ella McMann, are the smiling couple looking directly into the camera. CEA, EA-122-66

were also patrons of the streetcar system, the livery stables, car dealerships, seed companies, hardware stores, furniture emporiums and other retail stores located downtown. Saturdays, when business receded from the centre, housewives and families took over the market and its surrounding shops, many of them arriving by streetcar. Vendors came from all quarters and in all sorts of vehicles.

Jack McMann's first trips to the city market must have begun shortly after 1917, but he did not remember them until a few years later. Born in Edmonton in 1916, Jack made weekly visits to the market with his parents from their house at 11648 – 95th Street. He particularly looked forward to his weekly treat, a jam–filled oatmeal cookie referred to by its maker as a "pauvre gâteau d'une fermière":

> We would shop first at the market and then across the street and up a bit to James Ramsey to do our grocery shopping. Then we would take the streetcar home. We took the streetcar until my father got a car — which was in 1926.[8]

3.7

For many years, cars and horses co-existed on Market Square, as this photograph, taken around 1937, shows.
Courtesy of Betty Bre-Win

On weekdays, Market Square was quieter, although smaller numbers of vendors inside the building carried on trade as usual. Drivers frequently stopped at the horse trough to allow their horses to drink, and although feeding hay on the square had been forbidden for years to cut down on litter, it was an accommodating spot to tie up for a nosebag of oats. In May 1926, Mrs. Mabel Dean objected to this rule, arguing that it was cruel to horses whose owners had no grain to feed. She suggested horse-owners be asked to pay a little extra to cover the cleaning, but Market Superintendent Edgar Kendall rejected her argument:

> She says [horse-owners] would be willing to pay a little extra, to pay the expense of cleaning. They do lots of grumbling now at having to pay .15 for tying up. I do not think we should allow them to feed hay again as the Council stopped them before around 1913, owing to the complaints they got from the stores and merchants along the streets, as the wind storms blow all the hay and dirt across the market into the stores, so if we allow them again, I am sure we shall have the same trouble.[9]

In August 1928, Kendall wrote Mayor Bury to report a complaint from a Mr. Carswell whose horse had been injured on the jagged fence while resting on Market Square, explaining that "the rail around the market fence what the

3.8

On week-days Market Square was often used for activities that drew casual spectators. Here, captured in a photograph taken around 1926, the Fire Department is conducting an inspection. CEA, EA-10-998

farmers tie there [*sic*] Horses to, is in very bad shape."[10] This led to a repair of the 432-foot rail on the north, east, and west sides of the square "with eight foot strips [of iron] turned down 2 inches on the front side and 1 inch on the back."[11] Ten years later, J. Munro of Munro Hardware on 102nd Avenue just north of Market Square wanted the city to remove this fence and create a new entrance to the market but the city refused. The fence was still needed for tying horses according to the superintendent, and adding an entrance to the square from the north, the police believed, would merely have aggravated an existing congestion problem.[12]

Keeping the square in reasonable condition for pedestrians was an ongoing challenge for Superintendent Kendall. In March 1928, he wrote Mayor Bury, asking for "a few loads of cinders to spread on the Market Square from the North End of the building, through to the Street, along where people walk, and where the wagons stand, as it is just one mud hole."[13] In the fall of that year, the commissioners asked the city's engineer to investigate a complaint about "excessive dust blowing off the market square." The engineer's first solution, laying down gravel and oil, was rejected for its price tag of $2,425, leaving Kendall to implement the second solution — keeping in touch with the street cleaners and

3.9

This aerial view of Market Square taken in 1929 shows the diagonal path line linking the Post Office and the Civic Block. CEA, EA-64-4

having "the Street Flusher go over it when conditions are bad."[14] The following year, Kendall asked for "40 or 50 yds of gravel, for to fill in some bad holes on the Market Square, and along where the farmers and Market Gardener's, stand with there wagons, on Saturdays, they have to stand pretty near over there boot tops, in mud and water, to sell there produce, after a rain [*sic*]."[15]

Market Square's central location was convenient for pedestrians, who wore a diagonal path across it to the Civic Block — reportedly to pay their utility bills. In 1930, the path was compromised when the city decided to increase motor vehicle parking on the east side of the square. There was an immediate outcry. In October 1930, the *Journal* reported that the city had received a "flood of complaints ... that parking of cars in the market square is blocking the diagonal walk across the square."[16] Despite Kendall's lack of sympathy for the complainants, it appears the path was not obliterated that year. In February 1934, the issue was returned to the civic agenda by Alderman Ogilvie who wanted the diagonal pathway from the Post Office to the Civic Block retained. The police, in their capacity as traffic regulators, recommended against it, arguing that to keep it would reduce available parking and "as this is the only vacant space in the centre of the city it would work a hardship on the motorists."[17] The commissioners, apparently to pacify Ogilvie, came up with an elaborate plan to "demark a footpath diagonally across the market square for the convenience of pedestrians by inserting planks in the ground."[18] In April 1934, Mayor Knott sent the city's engineer a sketch showing how the path could be retained by restricting parking on some stalls, an idea the engineer rejected, saying it would reduce the capacity of the lot from 210 to 180 stalls.[19] Eventually, of course, the diagonal path disappeared, but the 1930–34 debate over whether to retain or eliminate it still resonates.

The market building, upon which so little attention was lavished in the months before its 1917 opening, became a landmark in its own right. Few who sold or shopped there have been able to embellish their memories of its character and atmosphere with descriptive

3.10

Natural lighting inside the market building came either from clerestory windows located above the wooden beams or from low windows located around the periphery. This photograph, taken of the R. Hinse Poultry stall around 1958, conveys the quality of light inside the old market building. Courtesy of Grace Kipling

detail, a testament to its unremarkable appearance. Situated on the western half of Market Square, the building ran north and south with a main entrance on Rice Street (101A Avenue). Six large partitioned stalls in the south end of the building were rented to retail vendors — mainly butchers and greengrocers — who paid weekly rates. The larger portion of the building, often called the farmers' hall, stretched north from the stores, with doors placed along the sides through which vendors unloaded their produce. In December 1927, the farmers' hall was flooded "owing to the doors on the west side of the building being six or seven inches lower than the ground outside."[20] According to Kendall, water running from the roof during a thaw drained into the market building, requiring some alterations to the level of grade outside the doors. Long, low wooden tables (stalls), some equipped with storage shelves behind, were rented out in three- or seven-foot modules with the larger ones reserved for market gardeners. Clerestory windows and a few side windows, some of which were blocked by vendors' displays, let in minimal light until a skylight was added in the mid-1930s. Although the south end of the building was apparently heated by a hot-air furnace in the basement while the farmers' hall was warmed by two coal stoves in the centre and small gas heaters on the narrow side aisles, greengrocers had produce freeze next to the walls and vendors in the farmers' hall took turns in winter warming themselves at the pot-bellied stoves. There was no insulation in the walls and in winter most vendors dressed for the outdoors. In summer, flies were a problem but the alternative, window screens, filtered out light — a dilemma which led to several altercations between the market superintendent and the MOH in the 1930s.[21]

The plan to include six retail outlets in the market building may have originated in a request put forth by the Consumers' League to council on 14 November 1916. Although the idea was rejected by the Parks and Market Committee, which recommended instead that the "Dominion Square Market should be used purely as a farmers' market," the retail stalls were clearly featured in the 1916 design.[22] Quickly they became a defining feature of the city market, expanding the range of products sold and offering customers a set of stable vendors operating on fixed retail hours. The model proved durable and was elaborated twice: once in 1919 when a fishmarket was added just west of (but attached to) the market, and again in 1933 when six balancing retail stalls were added to the north end of the building.

If the retail stores provided continuity and stability to the city market, the so-called farmers' hall was the setting for the weekly scrums known as the Saturday markets. It seems likely that space inside the building was rapidly taken on Saturdays, especially between 1 May and 31 October, despite the increase in the Saturday rental fee from ten cents per stall in 1916 to twenty-five cents per stall in 1917. Early in May 1928, for example, Superintendent Kendall reported proudly to the mayor: "I have rented every Stall in the Market Building to the Market Gardeners and Florists, it was quite a job to satisfy them all, there was only one application, that I could not give a permanent Stall but I think I can place him Temporary until someone gives up on July 1/28."[23]

Most stallholders agreed to rent an assigned stall for the six-month summer season (May to October) and many retained the same stall for the winter season (October to May). They paid a specified weekly rate, which was collected one week in advance. Stalls not paid for on this basis were rented out on demand for a daily rate. In 1928, when Kendall was preparing a new set of market rules, he considered increasing the 1926 rates, which had varied from four dollars per week for the most desirable stalls to two dollars and fifty cents per week for those which received less exposure to traffic.[24] In addition to stall rental fees, market gardeners who lived within city limits paid business taxes which were based on a percentage of the rental fee. In August 1929, Norman P. Finnemore wrote to Mayor Bury to challenge the assessment of his business tax, suggesting it should be reduced from $7.70 to $4.45, but he was not successful. In January 1935, Mayor Clarke wrote Kendall asking for a report on the possibility

3.11

On 24 May 1925, this crowd assembled on Market Square for Victoria Day celebrations. GA, NC-6-11698

of imposing a business tax on out-of-town vendors, but Kendall advised against it: "I do not think myself that any of them should have to pay a business tax, as they are paying there [*sic*] Market fees, for to sell their produce, and I know some of them only take a few dollars on Saturdays, during these hard times."[25]

After he had allocated all the inside stalls for a six-month season, Kendall was free to allocate outside space to the east of the market building on a first-come first-served basis. In 1933, well before the beginning of the summer season, Kendall estimated that thirty-five to forty vendors were selling outside each week.[26]

In 1924, when Peter and Mary Oppelt first travelled to the market from their farm in the Fort Saskatchewan area, competition for the outside stalls was fierce.

They travelled by horse and wagon over mud roads, carrying a whole load of rhubarb and arriving about 3 o'clock in the morning. They tied the horses at the Market Square and waited till morning.[27]

By 1932, as stallholder Norman Finnemore complained in a letter urging the city to allow farmers to reserve an outside space, "vendors actually had to take up their stands on Friday afternoon [and] sleep there all Friday night in order to do business on Saturday."[28]

In 1932, Peter and Mary Oppelt no longer lined up for an outside selling space. By then, the couple had a dedicated stall inside the building and were on their way, with the assistance of their nine children, to operating first one and then two of the retail stores. From 1924 to 1978, members of the Oppelt family were a continuous presence at the city market.

> A Saturday was never missed to go to the market. Rain or snow or forty degrees below zero, we got there somehow. Sometimes, when it was very cold, we would take the load to Edmonton on a Friday night, leave it overnight at the market, and take the train back the next morning to sell it. There were times too, that when Dad took sick or the old truck broke down, my mother, with two big suitcases filled with fifty pounds of homemade butter in each, would walk from our place at the Fort to the railway station to take the train to Edmonton CN station and then walk from there with the heavy load to the market.[29]

The market's vitality in the years that followed the building's 1917 opening are partly known through the stories of rural and urban vendors who, like the Oppelts, were inspired by it to create lasting businesses. Flore Bilodeau, for example, first came to the market from Beaumont in 1923, when she was thirteen years old. Her father's sudden death from pleurisy in 1923 left a wife with twelve young children to raise. On Saturday mornings, Flore and her mother would hitch the horse to the democrat, already loaded with 150 pounds of butter and other dairy produce, and drive to the market, stopping at Arctic Ice in Rossdale on the way. When they arrived, there would "usually be a line up," Flore said, "waiting for the butter and cream." She liked handling the horse, which she would stable for the day at one of the livery barns off Market Square, and she enjoyed learning to speak English and meeting her mother's customers. So naturally, as a young married woman in the early 1930s, Flore Hinse immediately thought of the market when she and her husband were having trouble making ends meet. The egg and poultry business she started quickly grew to become their sole means of income and eventually grew into a legacy she passed on to children and grandchildren.[30]

Charles and Peter Juchli, brothers who came to Edmonton from Switzerland in 1913, relied on the city market to convert their interest in horticulture into a living. In 1916, they started a business together in the Bonnie Doon area, where Peter remained. A few years later, Charles bought Highland Park Greenhouses at 8849 - 87 Street and began his own business. In 1920, Charles married

3.12

The facade the old market building presented to Rice Street (101A Avenue) remained much the same from 1919, when the washrooms and fish market were added, to 1964, when the market was demolished. CEA, ET-17-17

Augustine Accarias, a young woman of French–Algerian descent who reportedly loved selling at the city market. From the early 1920s through the early 1950s, Charles Juchli raised everything from prize Swiss pansies and carnations to hothouse tomatoes and long English cucumbers, all sold at the market by Augustine. It was Charles Juchli who donated to the market the one decorative feature remembered by patrons and vendors. In the early 1930s, he shot a moose in the Fawcett area, just north of Westlock. A much larger moose than he could mount as a trophy at home, it presided over the farmers' hall — first from over the south door and then from a spot over the higher ceilinged north door — long after Juchli himself had retired from his market stall.[31]

The instant success of the first market building created pressures for expansion, and, less than two years after it opened, the Parks and Markets Committee recommended that council erect "a sectional fish market adjoining the present building."[32] The addition, which must have included converting the open shed to an enclosed shelter, was linked to the main building by a public lavatory and cost more than the original building.[33] The fish shops yielded consistently higher rents than any of the other retail spaces — twenty dollars a week per tenant until the mid-1930s — and there was no turnover of tenants. Prince Rupert Fish Market and Mr. and Mrs. James Jones each took two of the four stalls in 1919 and, when Mrs. James Jones retired, probably some time in 1956, her stalls were taken over by Prince Rupert. In April 1927, Harry Mandlis,

We Handle Only the Best

All Varieties in Season.

If unable to call, telephone your order to

MRS. JAMES JONES

Opp. Post Office, Phone 22531   WE DELIVER

3.13

Mrs. James Jones regularly advertised her fish store in local programs and in the city newspapers. These two advertisements, taken from a prize list put out by the Edmonton Horticultural and Vacant Lots Garden Association in 1933 and from an undated Pantages Theatre program, are typical. Courtesy of the Edmonton Horticultural Society and the CEA

DURING LENT EAT FISH

Red Spring Salmon, lb........25c
Chicken Halibut, lb. 25c
Fresh Ling Cod, lb. 25c
Fresh Silver Smelts, lb. 30c
Fresh Lemon Soles, 2 lbs. ..35c
Fillet of Soles, 2 lbs. 35c
Fresh Herrings, 2 lbs. 35c
Fresh Shrimp, per lb. 35c
Fresh Crabs, each 25c and 30c
Fresh Caught Cold Lake
    Trout, 2 lbs. 35c
Fresh Caught Whitefish, lb. 15c
Fresh Caught Pickerel,
    per lb. 12½c
Fresh Caught Jackfish, lb. ..10c
Fresh Sealshipt Oysters, pt. 75c
Fresh Shell Oysters, dozen 55c

Fresh and Smoked Fish

MRS. J. JONES

3—STALLS—4
CITY FISH MARKET
2531—Phone—2531

All Orders Promptly
Attended To.

WE DELIVER

founder and owner of Prince Rupert Fish Market, notified the commissioners of his intention to vacate, but was persuaded to stay when the city offered to share costs on improvements to the building.[34] John Martland, the city's building inspector and architect, designed new display windows facing Rice Street for a total cost of $299.25.[35] This cost-sharing arrangement worked so well that in 1928 the fish stores and the city again split the cost of a project to provide wire fencing outside the stores to prevent boxes of fish stored there from being pilfered.[36] And, in April 1937, the two shops installed new refrigeration in return for the city's agreement to spend $322 on lath and plaster.[37]

In 1923, Mandlis hired sixteen-year-old Roy Heeks as a delivery boy for Prince Rupert Fish Market. Roy, born in 1907 in Toulon, Manitoba, came to Edmonton with his parents in 1914. On Saturday mornings, the family shopped at the city market. It was Roy's mother, a customer of Prince Rupert Fish, who got her son the job — eager, he said, to reap some of the benefits of his six-dollar-a-week pay. A keen worker, Roy delivered fish all over the city, relying on his bicycle for transportation. One of Prince Rupert's best customers was the

Eat Fish for Health

Choice Fresh Fish Daily From Ocean and Lakes.

REMEMBER. Fish is our Business, not a sideline.

MRS. JAMES JONES

Wholesale and Retail

PHONE 22531   WE DELIVER

Johnson Café, run by well-known Greek restaurateur Con Johnson. In 1938, when Mandlis retired, Roy bought the business on very good terms, continuing to run it from the market even after its 1965 move to 97th Street.[38]

The Joneses, according to butcher Joe Bre-Win, were Cockney Londoners whose entry into the fish business in Edmonton was deliberate and planned. The death of Mr. Jones, not long after their arrival in Canada, occasioned the renaming of the business after Mrs. James Jones. Mrs. Jones advertised her store widely in newspapers and theatre programs until her retirement. Roy Heeks remembered that it was she who gave him his first lessons in filleting fish and that, when he married Hazel in September 1930, Mrs. Jones surprised the young couple with a set of silverware for a wedding gift.

Far from being viewed as a wartime extravagance, the opening of the new market building in 1917, especially a building which had cost the city so little to build, was consistent with prevailing views about the need for thrift and economy in daily life. "Since war has broken out," an article in the *Edmonton Daily Capital* in 1914 ran, "public markets have sprung up all over the Dominion of Canada and are being largely patronized by the housewives who are now anxious to economize in the price of their foodstuffs." Going to markets to buy "direct from the producers" was promoted as an economical practice.[39] In June 1916, when council asked the electorate's approval to build on Rice Street, the *Bulletin* particularly urged women to vote for it — "to facilitate the condition of living!"[40]

The practice of thrift and economy was one of three goals of the Vacant Lots Garden Club, formed in March 1916, supported by both the IODE and the Civic Improvement League, and partially responsible for allowing a number of urban farmers to create market businesses. Also dedicated to stimulating "an interest in the love of plants and the cultivation of the soil through the utilization of the vacant land lying within the city limits" and to developing civic pride by encouraging the "beautification of the city," the Vacant Lots Garden Club, which amalgamated with the Edmonton Horticultural Society shortly after it was formed, played an important role in the life of the city in the 1920s and 1930s.[41] By 1918, enthusiast J. E. Pember proclaimed that the scheme had transformed the city's appearance since "nearly 8000 lots have been allocated and are today under intensive cultivation."[42]

One urban farmer who created a business on rented land was Mr. Wallish, who may have begun selling at the market as early as 1919. Wallish rented an acre on 73rd Street just north of 121st Avenue. According to Robert Wallish, one of three children, his father came to Canada in 1913 and worked in Edmonton as a teamster before starting a gardening business and, in 1925, marrying a young Alsatian-born woman who had been working as a cook and housekeeper for Miss Maddock, head of Llanarthney School for Girls on 121st Street. "We operated that land like a farm," Robert remembered. "We had horses for work and for taking the vegetables to market on Saturdays in summer by buggy. In the winter, my dad used a sleigh with lots of heavy blankets to keep the produce from freezing." Years later, before they acquired their own truck, the Wallishes employed the service of city trucker Reg Dockstader to drive them to the market on Saturday mornings. According to Reg, who drove other vendors, "the market gardeners those days were all within the city boundaries and many people rented land from the city to grow vegetables."[43]

In 1928, the Wallishes found themselves in a heated dispute with Edgar Kendall, the market superintendent, over stall allocation. In September of that year, Mayor Bury received a letter from Miss Maddock criticizing Kendall for refusing the Wallishes the stall they had rented during the summer months.[44] The stall in question, sometimes referred to as the "charity stall," was occupied during the winter season by a succession of ladies' groups selling coffee and home baking to raise money for charitable causes. Kendall insisted that the Wallishes had taken the stall on the understanding they would give it up at the beginning of October. The Wallishes, who were supported in their claim to keep it by their own legal counsel and by Norman Finnemore, then secretary-treasurer of the Edmonton and District Market Gardeners and Florists Association, were nevertheless forced to give up the charity stall. Mayor Bury, annoyed that the superintendent's authority had been challenged, informed Finnemore "that there must be no departure from nor any weakening of the long established principle that stallholders have no right or interest in any particular stall."[45]

Edgar Kendall, the superintendent who stamped his style and personality on the city market during the interwar period, rarely lost battles with stallholders. Remembered by Joe Bre-Win to have been a "short little man" who slung a leather purse to collect his rents on "an army belt with a strap over his shoulder," Kendall prided himself on running the market by the rules and at a profit.[46] A city employee since 1907, he was promoted to the job of superintendent in 1924 but, by his own claim in October 1924, he had already "worked on the Market a good number of years."[47] When he retired on 30 June 1941, the city presented him with a travelling case, an appropriate gift in view of the inventive justifications he provided every year for extending his summer holiday.[48] In 1932, for example, he asked for three weeks leave of absence juxtaposed to his holidays, "as my Health is very poor, and I intend going to California. I have been under the Doctors care for some time, with stomach trouble very bad."[49] And, in 1933, he needed two extra weeks so that he could both visit his sick sister in Hamilton and attend the Chicago World's Fair.[50]

As Superintendent of Markets, Kendall's jurisdiction extended beyond Rice Street (arbitrarily named the "Central Market" in the 1917 by-law) to include the North Side and the South Side Markets. Practically speaking, the North Side Market, once referred to as the haymarket, withered away after the closure of the market building on 101st Street although hay and probably coal were sold there for some time. The South Side Market and weigh scale, located on 104 Street and 83 Avenue and taken over by Edmonton as part of the 1912 amalgamation agreement with Strathcona, was practically moribund until it was closed some time in the 1950s. The Rice Street, (or Edmonton City) Market occupied almost all Kendall's time and generated more than ninety percent of his department's revenues. Kendall supervised market staff, collected rents from vendors, allocated stalls, enforced the market by-law, kept records, and reported to the mayor and commissioners on both a regular and an as-required basis.

In addition to the superintendent, a weighmaster and two fulltime janitors were required to keep the Rice Street Market in operation six days a week. The weighmaster spent most of his time supervising the weighing of large loads and keeping records but, as Kendall explained when an internal audit in 1935 required him to justify his staffing model, "the balance of his time is occupied, collecting on the market, relieving men on half day Holidays as they take separate days off owing to the market and scales being open 6 days a week."[51] Ernest Tookey occupied the position of weighmaster for much of the 1920s and 1930s, retiring in 1933. In 1927, he took six months off to undergo an operation "caused by handling [a] heavy coal scuttle during the winter I worked in the old scales building which has since been torn down."[52] In 1929, Tookey's monthly salary was increased by Mayor Bury to $110 per month, a figure which exceeded the maximum salary for his category of worker but was intended as a recognition of his "long and faithful service."[53]

The day janitor began work at 6.30 a.m. and was relieved at 3.30 p.m. by the night janitor. A. Jackson, day janitor for many years, took over from Tookey as weighmaster in 1933. Described by Kendall in 1935 as "a most reliable and trustworthy man," Jackson retired at the end of 1939 — not long before Kendall also retired. Janitors, many of them hired on a temporary basis to fill in for vacation absences, often remained at the market for many years. An exception was a night janitor whose occasional "spells of drunkenness" were the ultimate cause of his dismissal. One such spell, which caused the employee to fall into a drunken stupor in the men's comfort station while trying to clean it, exhausted the patience of his employer, and he was fired.[54]

Throughout the 1920s, the mayor often intervened in the process of hiring at the market. In 1928, for example, Kendall was looking for someone to act as a relief worker throughout the summer holiday season. Mayor Bury advised him to accept an application from a Mr. A. E. Smith: "I want to get him the position unless there is some other person who has a decidedly prior claim. Mr. Smith has worked for the City for some time in several departments."[55]

As the depression deepened in the 1930s, all hirings and contracts were measured against city employment and wage policies and were sometimes challenged by unions. In April 1934, for instance, the secretary of a union local, Brotherhood of Painters, Decorators & Paperhangers of America, complained that the city's policy of letting general contracts on projects at the city market favoured contractors who hired non-union workers. The commissioners' reply presented the case that general contractors spread the work more widely while workers were protected by the city's "Fair Wage" conditions.[56]

The small-scale, highly individualized and dispersed nature of the market's operations created ongoing opportunities for the city to connect with its citizens on many levels — some of them informal and personal and others more formal and bureaucratic. Although Kendall was in the forefront of all matters connected with the market, the mayor, aldermen, commissioners, MOH, police chief, and other senior administrators could be drawn into day-to-day affairs on the square. Accounts of these dealings cast light in two directions. While they help to fill in the colours and textures of a thriving period in the market's history, often rendering it in comic tones, they also offer perspectives on the city's corporate history, highlighting the concerns of key elected and non-elected officials and the values they brought to civic life.

In *By-law No. 13 to Regulate Public Markets*, passed 30 November 1917, the city laid out the framework within which Edmonton's markets were to operate until 1964, the year the market building was demolished. More comprehensive than its predecessors, *By-law No. 13* delineated the responsibilities of the market superintendent, placing him "under the supervision and direction of the Commissioners." There was scope within the by-law for the commissioners "to make rules and regulations" and, although vendors' fees were set, the commissioners were free to make changes to fees and leases "as [they] shall from time to time determine." While most conflicts and disputes arising at the market during the 1920s and 1930s revolved around the superintendent's interpretation of the by-law, two incidents in the early 1920s raised questions about the market as an instrument of policy.

In 1923, the Retail Butchers and Merchants of Edmonton claimed that meat vendors (retail butchers and producer farmers) at the market obtained unfair advantages in the form of low capital costs and rents. In December 1923, when butchers occupied three of the six stalls at the south end of the market, paying rents of twenty dollars per week, and thirteen farmers were selling meat from the farmers' hall, and paying rents of six dollars per week, council received a petition from the retail butchers and merchants arguing that they were "not averse to the actual retailing of meat in the City Market providing that the farmer so retailing meat pay to the City a fee commensurate with the extent of the privilege enjoyed so that the *bona fide* Retail Butcher will not be labouring under a hardship which constitutes a serious menace to his ability to continue in business." Start-up costs for a retail butcher were estimated by the petitioners at $2,520, while monthly operating costs were said to average $583.50. According to the butchers,

> when such regulations involving so much expense, are considered necessary for a Retail store, there is no justification for allowing parties to rent a stall by the day, cut up meat in any sort of way, throw it on a dilapidated piece of oilcloth, have it coughed over, handled by anyone who comes along, and finally sold, contaminated as it is bound to have become, sacrificing the health of the community on the alter [*sic*] of a mistaken idea of economical marketing.[57]

Complaints from the retail butchers were sympathetically received but not acted upon, raising questions about the role played by the city market in the overall system of food marketing in Edmonton. Through the market, the city took a direct role in stimulating agricultural production — both within city limits and in surrounding communities — and in creating opportunities for economic activity downtown. As long as it remained committed to this policy, the city was best served by blurring the lines between market vendors and their retail counterparts. For example, the regulation stipulating that market vendors sell only their own produce was not always strictly enforced despite the retail sector's hostility to so-called hucksters on the city market. Flore Hinse, for instance, before becoming a producer of her own poultry, collected eggs from farm women in the Beaumont area and sold them at the market, returning "pin-money" to the wives who sometimes kept the income a secret from their husbands.[58] Vendors frequently sold items for neighbours either to make up a lack in their own offerings or to do a small service. The scale of these infractions was hardly punishable, leading Kendall, in April 1933, to recommend to Mayor Knott a measure of laxity in enforcing the rule.[59]

The role played by market vendors in the wholesale marketing of food was also raised in the early 1920s, but desultory debate and lack of action favoured an ambiguous outcome. *By-law No. 13* allowed farmers to sell wholesale in a specified location and at a specified early-morning time. Minimum quantities for most goods were established (e.g., three dozen bunches of onions, quarters of beef, whole sheep, twenty-five pounds of butter), and the superintendent was authorized to set minimum quantities for nonlisted items. In March 1924, the by-law committee of council, motivated partly by council's desire to reduce the numbers of peddlers on Edmonton's streets, introduced the possibility of enhancing these provisions by establishing a "Growers Marketing Association" at the city market through which farmers could sell their produce in bulk. In the end, the city solicitor's advice to council that it could not restrict peddling removed the incentive to expand the market's role in bulk sales and the project was dropped, leaving the conditions under which vendors could sell wholesale vague and undefined.[60]

Competition for stall space at the market throughout the 1920s and 1930s, a sign of the value to vendors of having a stall there, created a need for criteria which could be consulted when choosing one applicant vendor over another or to help settle disputes among existing vendors. By 1927, it was apparent from the phrasing of letters of inquiry and complaint that, though not broadcast, the criteria for stall allocation were public knowledge. Preference was given to those who had sold longest on the market and to those who were prepared to sell year-round. Applicants with no other means of livelihood were given favourable consideration. City taxpayers were preferred over rural vendors and, if necessary, the length of time the applicant had been a taxpayer was taken into account.

The city's policy of favouring taxpayers in the allocation of market stalls was a tacit acknowledgement that the market played a role in the local economy. Those on the outside of the policy could be critical of it. Jean Henri, a rural farmer from Strathcona, wrote the commissioners and objected to the city's policy of favouring its own taxpayers: "Those city gardners [*sic*] should even pay more than they do now because they are not the ones who bring the public on the Mkt it is the farmers who do and if they pay city taxes they have the convenience of the city."[61] Taxpayers, of course, appealed to this criterion whenever it stood to advance their claim. In April 1929, F. E. Moroney wrote the mayor asking that his taxpaying friend Antonio Tonsi, who did not like the stall he had been assigned, be given the stalls of a nontaxpayer on the market, arguing that "Tonsi is on the market every week steady, and in addition to vegetables he has a large flower display." Moroney concluded his letter by itemizing the taxes paid by Tonsi.[62] In January 1932, when Max Baader asked the mayor to intercede with Kendall on his behalf for a stall, he too presented his case as a taxpayer: "I know that many of them have their Greenhouses out of the City limit to avoid Taxes, my Propertys [*sic*]and Greenhouses are in the City and I have to pay Taxes. I think it would be only fair to me to have a chance to sell my Products."[63]

A taxpayer who was refused a stall on the market by Kendall raised the spectre of discrimination that was not convincingly dispelled by the city's handling of the formal complaint. In October 1927, the legal firm of Robertson, Winkler & Hawe wrote the commissioners on behalf of an unnamed Chinese client who had applied for a stall only to be told that "it was a rule of the market that no Chinamen would be rented space on the market for the sale of produce." Chinese market gardeners, the legal firm pointed out, paid taxes and business taxes to the city. Only a policy of discrimination could have accounted for his client's not getting a stall.[64] The lawyer was quickly assured by Mayor Bury that Kendall "had no authority to exclude anyone the market on the ground of race and that any tax-payer of the City of good character and carrying on his business in proper way was entitled to use the market." However, Bury went on to imply another explanation for Kendall's refusal — the city's prior commitment to vendors "who have established themselves and their business on the faith and assurance that they will be continued to be given all necessary facilities [at the market]."[65] Although Mayor Bury was required to send a similar letter to the Chinese consul general in Ottawa after Chow Kwo-Hsien wrote asking him to "take immediate steps to adjust this trouble in the interest of British justice and fair-play," there is no indication that the Chinese applicant persevered in his application for a market stall or that other Chinese market gardeners became vendors there.[66]

In November 1927, when Peter Juchli sold Bonnie Doon French Gardens to Marcel Aldry and Henry Valentin, all the stall allocation criteria were invoked to deal with the resulting dilemma. Juchli's stalls, A and B, were well placed in the farmers' hall and the new owners, anxious to retain them, wrote to Kendall: "We are prepared to pay the going rental for these stalls; we are prepared to occupy them the year round and will sell in these stalls only the produce of our own gardens."[67] But other vendors, eager to improve their location, argued that Aldry and Valentin, as newcomers, had to move to the bottom of the line. Several requests for the stalls were received, and Kendall, intimidated by the challenge, asked the mayor to decide "and get this trouble settled."[68] In the end, H. A. Bannard was awarded stalls A and B after writing a second letter of application emphasizing his credentials:

> Perhaps I should have stated that I have been on the Market for the last ten years. And I stand on the Mkt. all the year round. I have never held two stalls on the Mkt. At the present time I hold stall "G" permanent and half of Stall "E" temporary since July of this year. I have been a resident and taxpayer since April 1907. I own the property on which I live. And I depend entirely on Gardening for a living.[69]

This case became a precedent for Kendall, who referred to it in January 1933 in a letter to Mayor Knott when the buyers of S. Magee Greenhouses wanted to be assured of their stall: "I remember when P. Juchli sold out, H. Bannard put in a claim for his stalls and the man that bought him out had to go where we could put him."[70]

The value of a market stall was well appreciated by Kathrine and Marius Granstrom when, as newlyweds, they bought a greenhouse business in Edmonton, in November 1928, in partnership with Marius's brother Pete. Kathrine and Marius, both immigrants from Denmark, met and married in Saskatchewan, where Marius, a returned soldier from World War I, was trying his hand at homesteading. Through Pete they heard about a greenhouse in the Highlands area which had been empty for three years. Once owned by market vendors, the Blochlingers, it was sold to the Granstroms by Con Johnson, owner of the Johnson Café. By February 1929, the Granstroms were preparing to take bedding plants to the market, having obtained tulip, daffodil, narcissus, crocus, and iris stock from a Dutch supplier, and in the spring of 1929, they secured their first stall — a small one on a centre aisle which they later exchanged for a double stall on the west side with its own loading entrance. Pete returned to Denmark in 1935, selling his share of the business to his brother, but Virginia Park Greenhouses, run by Kathrine and Marius with their children Rita, Greta, Ellen, and especially Ray, maintained their stall at the city market until, in 1993, they withdrew to concentrate on greenhouse sales.[71]

In addition to the greenhouse business, which was gradually turned towards a speciality in cut flowers and bedding plants, the Granstroms rented land west towards Concordia College. On this they grew potatoes, carrots, lettuce, celery, cucumbers, cabbages, and other vegetable crops which they sold at the market and also direct to large purchase customers such as the "Mounties" (RCMP). In 1938, they built an additional roothouse, one in which the cabbages could be stored on racks while the celery roots were packed tightly together in rows standing upwards because, as Kathrine said, long storage in root cellars was more important in the years when few fresh vegetables were shipped to Edmonton from the United States. Conceived around the market, which was to become its major retail outlet and primary means of building a customer base, Virginia Park Greenhouses became a family-owned-and-operated business which drew its customers from all corners of the city.

The Granstroms, who remember seeing fights break out at the market, caused Kendall no problems during the turbulent 1920s and 1930s, because their names never appeared on lists of troublemakers, such as the one naming vendors who would not pay Saturday rates for their stalls when Dominion Day dictated changing the main market day from Saturday to Friday.[72] Nor were the Granstroms ever involved in the fights which figured from time to time in Kendall's reports to the Mayor. In August 1928, for example, the couple renting stalls 28 and 29 became embroiled in a fist fight with the couple renting stall 30. Although Kendall had not witnessed the fight himself, his report represented one of the couples as "agitators," who should be "put off" the market for their cursing and swearing alone, and the other couple as "two of the quietest persons on the market."[73] In the end, after Kendall's clear-cut interpretation of events had been challenged by vendors, the dispute was solved simply by separating the stalls of the two combatants.

In 1933, the Bergers were backed up by Ronald C. Neal, secretary treasurer of the Edmonton and District Market Gardeners and Florists' Association, in a dispute with the Whittons over a stall, an intervention the Bergers must have appreciated as they were not assertive in putting forward their own case. When Louise Marletaz married François Berger in 1926, shortly after she arrived in Canada from Switzerland, she joined him in running Belvedere Gardens at 137 Avenue and 58 Street. François, who already had a market stall, liked selling there and so did his wife as soon as she lost her shyness about speaking English. One of her first memories of the market was her failure to sell turnips after conveying the impression to a prospective buyer that they were hollow.[74] Neal supported the Bergers partly because they "[stood] on the market all the year round, every Saturday & every week-day in the summer months" and also because of some alleged duplicity on the part of Whitton. "Last year Mr. Whitton ran a bluff, or tried to, a sales lady was on the stand with vegetables, supposedly grown by Mr. Whitton, but we have a written statement from the weed inspector that it was practically an impossibility for Mr. Whitton to have grown them."[75]

3.14

When Louise Marletaz and François Berger married in 1926, they became market-gardeners and regular vendors at the city market. They and their children enjoyed buying snapshots taken of them by roving photographers on Jasper Avenue on Saturdays. Louise could only remember that this photo was taken soon after her arrival in Canada from Switzerland. Courtesy of Louise Berger and family

In rare cases, the mayor was moved by the intemperance of a market vendor to act swiftly and in his own voice. In May 1935, Mayor Clarke wrote to John Chapman, butcher, notifying him that the lease "held by you for some time" had been cancelled. Two reasons were given:

> First, your reported blasphemy and insults hurld [*sic*] at the Market Superintendent in the presence of citizens who could not possibly be interested in your troubles; and Second, your action in calling the mayor up at his house over the phone, and swearing and using other language so loudly that guests in the Mayor's house could hear the words coming over this phone.[76]

Kendall, doubtless pleased that Chapman, had been expelled, was not always pleased at mayoral intervention. In 1928, as part of an exercise in reviewing and revising the market rules, Kendall had written to Mayor Bury: "I do not want you to think I am interfering with your affairs, none watever [*sic*], but I think the renting of the stalls, should be left to the Superintendent in charge, as he should know best. [*sic*] and it will save you quite a lot of trouble from different applicants coming over to see you all the time."[77] And in July 1933, he complained to Mayor Knott and the commissioners that his authority in dealings with five "troublemakers" had been challenged: "these men boast around that I cannot put them out, if I do they will go to the mayor and they will get back again, I have got all this kind of stuff to put up with."[78]

If vendors tended to quarrel among themselves and with the superintendent over the issue of stall allocation, those who sold eggs at the market encountered a different set of frustrations. By federal (then dominion) law, all eggs sold at the market had to be examined and graded immediately prior to being sold by a process known as 'egg-candling.' The candler, who was paid per dozen eggs candled, inspected each egg in front of a light, rolling as many as four at a time in her hands before passing them through a template to determine their size.[79] During the 1920s and 1930s, this process was overseen by the dominion government's senior egg inspector for Alberta, R. H. Ennismore, whose office on Jasper Avenue and 99 Street guaranteed easy access to Market Square. Delays in the candling process resulted in arguments and complaints from vendors, while the two collaborating levels of government often had to struggle to present a united front.

In May 1926, Ennismore and the commissioners disagreed over which level of government should act on the following case. A female vendor was reported to the city by Ennismore for "bringing in eggs after the candlers and inspectors have left the market and also [for] selling low grade eggs for the high grade or mixing them." But, he continued, "the repeated offences made by this woman are very petty and not sufficient to enable us to take into court [*sic*]." He recommended a solution described as "the custom in markets in the east" which would have seen Superintendent Kendall confiscate the eggs and suspend the vendor for a specified period of time. The commissioners, however, preferred "dramatic legal action" by the higher level of government and even had the MOH, Dr. T. H. Whitelaw, write Ennismore asking him to take action on "unsound or inferior eggs."[80]

A more successful collaboration between the city and the dominion government resulted when, in 1927, Strathcona vendor Jean Henri mistakenly complained to Ennismore through his lawyer, Mr. Poirier of Milner, Carr, Dafoe & Poirier, that he was losing business to the slow candling service. Ennismore wrote Poirier to explain that his own responsibility was limited to enforcing the egg act, although he sometimes "[gave] a hand in relieving the congestion at the candling booth." Mr. Henri's attitude, Ennismore continued, was antagonistic: "unless your client is prepared to co-operate with us or at least meet us half way, there will always be friction." Working with Mayor Bury, who in turn contacted the food inspector Mr. Lord, who involved the MOH Dr. Whitelaw, Ennismore generated an account of the events which had so excited Mr. Henri. On a Saturday morning when 600 dozen eggs were presented for candling, the candler's assistant was absent due to illness. Vendors had been asked to present their eggs in shifts, an aggravation to Henri who managed to get twelve dozen candled first thing but had to wait for the remaining forty-eight dozen. The issue died down when Mayor Bury wrote a soothing explanatory letter to Mr. Henri's lawyer explaining the unusual circumstances.[81]

Eggs left unattended, either in the candling booth or at nearby stalls, were sometimes stolen. When "thirty dozen firsts" belonging to a blind vendor and said to be worth twelve dollars disappeared from the candling booth, Ennismore suggested to the mayor that the city — not himself or the candling staff — reimburse the owner:

> As you know, the candler herself has given this service to us for little or nothing for the past six years and we feel it would be too much of a hardship to force her to pay for them. We as you know, have no funds at our command except our own personal money but we would be pleased even then to assist in this reimbursement of the owner of the eggs.[82]

Kendall rejected the suggestion that the city was responsible, arguing that Ennismore had opened the egg-candling booth to retailers as well as market vendors, thus undermining security: "I know it is pretty hard for the blind man, to have to stand this loss as he his [*sic*] trying to make a living, and he as [*sic*] had 2 cases stolen before out of his wagon, just the same I do not think it is up to us, to pay for these losses."[83] In the end, the city paid half the market value of the eggs "whilst the balance [was] made up by the egg-candling staff personally." To forestall similar incidents, Kendall's janitors were given the keys to the booth and the responsibility to keep it secure.

The operations, facilities, and location of the Edmonton City Market favoured its use by individuals and by social-service organizations, church parishes, agricultural and horticultural associations, and even socio-political groups. In its many dealings over access to the market or use of the building or square, the city connected with some of its important constituencies while the market gained status and customers.

The tradition, which evolved some time after 1917, whereby one stall in the market was given over each week to a different ladies' group to be operated as a refreshment stall, extended the range of the market's customers and provided the city with an opportunity to distribute delicate favours. Coffee, tea, and home baking were sold by the ladies and the proceeds applied to the charitable causes they represented. While the origins of the tradition are unclear, it may have started around 1926, when a petition submitted to the city from a group of ladies "asking if better accommodations can be provided at the city market for the supply of hot water" was redirected to Kendall.[84] Certainly it had become an established tradition by 1928 when the Wallishes resisted vacating the dedicated stall. When the United Farm Women of Alberta wrote Mayor Clarke, on 5 December 1935, offering two preferred dates on which to sell their cooking, he referred them immediately to Kendall.[85] The charity stall, which became increasingly important in the 1940s, inducing Mayor Fry to make special arrangements to obtain sugar and coffee rations for it, offered the ladies considerable access to the consuming public and ensured that the market would be patronized by the members of these often influential groups.

Because the city market drew so many of its vendors from rural communities around Edmonton, mayors were sometimes called upon to answer questions posed by farmers or respond to their expressed concerns. In 1926, for example, when a Mr. Babcock from Hattonford, Alberta, wrote asking "what potatoes are bringing on the Edmonton Market," he received the following polite and detailed reply: "In answer to your inquiry, our market Superintendent states that potatoes are bringing 70, 75 & 80 cents per bushel wholesale although about two weeks ago they did not range higher than around 60 cents. They have been retailed from 95 cents to $1.00 per bushel, but just now prices are varied considerable [*sic*] according to the demand and quality of produce."[86]

In February 1930, Fred Wagner, a farmer from Spruce Grove, wrote Mayor Douglas to express his concern on hearing that weekly vendor rates were to be increased: "If to [*sic*] much Difficulty is placed against the farmers when they come to Edmonton to sell there [*sic*] produce, they may stay at Home and Trade at the Country Stores." Mayor Douglas replied that he had read the letter "with interest" and would "do what [he could] to protect the farmers in their dealings on the Market."[87]

For Edmonton's French Catholic community west of 109th Street, attending the city market was simply an accepted feature of civic life. When François Morin arrived in Edmonton with his family in 1930 and settled near St. Joachim Church, he routinely took his mother to the market to shop on Saturdays, although he did not say whether they heard about the market from their neighbours or by reading an advertisement in the Cathedral Year Book.[88] In any case, a few years later, in January 1936, Commissioner Mitchell wrote to the Reverend Father Leo Nelligan of St. Joseph's Cathedral to apologize for having to reduce the size of the city's market advertisement in the yearbook. Father Nelligan was gracious, assuring the commissioner that, despite the smaller advertisement, the city market would be duly promoted. He would, he

---

Edmonton and District Market Gardeners and Florists' Association

Any of our members will be pleased to assist you in your gardening problems.

BEDDING, POT AND ROCK PLANTS, PERENNIALS TREES, SHRUBS, PEONIES AND DAHLIAS

Cut Flowers in Season

Visit the City Market for the finest vegetables of the well known Edmonton quality.

FROM PRODUCER TO CONSUMER

LOOK FOR THE MEMBERSHIP CARDS DISPLAYED ON THE STALLS.

3.15

For years the Edmonton and District Market Gardeners and Florists' Association represented market vendors in negotiations with the city over issues related to the market. This advertisement, which appeared in the prize list for the garden show held in 1933 by the Edmonton Horticultural and Vacant Lots Garden Association, conveys the important role the city market played as a direct-marketing outlet for Edmonton's market-gardeners. Courtesy of the Edmonton Horticultural Society

wrote Commissioner Mitchell, "take advantage of every opportunity to remind [his parishioners] that it is their duty to patronize those who have favored us with an advertisement, as we realize that there must be reciprocity in matters of this kind." The advertisement, which was constructed to resemble a personal message from Superintendent Kendall and the commissioners, promoted the benefits to customers of the 1933 expansion to the market building and emphasized the market's role as a public service.[89]

As a venue for annual agricultural shows or exhibitions, the market building brought the city occasional revenue and more goodwill, while the resulting shows helped to maintain the high profile of agriculture in the city. Joe Bre-Win, long-time butcher at the market, first entered the building in the mid-1920s when his Grade 8 class from Alex Taylor School was taken there for the annual poultry show, an event he particularly remembered for the opportunities it presented to "swipe" eggs. A few decades later, annual flower exhibits put on by the Edmonton Horticultural and Vacant Lots Garden Association in the market building nurtured in Joe an adult interest in gardening.[90]

Annual shows sponsored by the Edmonton Poultry Association were held at the end of January and beginning of February. In 1926, the manager of the poultry association wrote to announce the dates of the 1927 show and to request the usual arrangement: "use of the Market Building heated and lighted in lieu of a grant." The request was granted on condition that the building be left on the Friday evening in good shape for the Saturday morning market.[91] Only twice did the poultry association not fulfill its side of the bargain. On 4 February 1929, Kendall wrote the Mayor complaining that the building "smelled pretty strong, especially where they had the water tanks, for the Ducks and Swans to swim in." In addition, he said,

> we had some water pipes burst, through there [sic] carelessness, with some of the men leaving a door wide open, all the time they were using it, and we warned them before about this, as we knew it would freeze up, unless the door was kept closed, we had an awful mess with it, as it flooded the comfort stations out, and we had to close them down, until we got them repaired.[92]

By comparison, the complaint registered in 1940 was mild. When an alderman complained to the acting MOH of the excessive dust left after the show, the latter wrote Kendall: "I would be glad if you would arrange to have the rafters and ceiling cleaned before the opening of the market tomorrow."[93]

Annual shows sponsored by the Edmonton Horticultural and Vacant Lots Garden Association and held throughout the 1920s and 1930s in a variety of downtown venues, eventually found a home in the Edmonton City Market, despite initial opposition from the Edmonton and District Market Gardeners and Florists' Association, which often assumed the role of spokesman for market vendors and may have wanted to downplay recreational gardening in favour of urban agriculture. In 1935, Ronald Neal, secretary treasurer of the market gardeners association, wrote to the mayor complaining that the annual flower show was a major disruption to stallholders and that it constituted a loss of rent to the city and a loss of sales opportunities to market gardeners:

> If this is to be allowed the building will cease to be a market, but will be a hall for the use of every Dog or Cat Show that want a public building to show in. The market is paying a good revenue to the City & is an asset that must be protected. We would therefore ask you to *refuse* the Horticultural Society the use of this building.[94]

By the 1940s, despite these protests, the city market was hosting one or more of the horticultural association's annual shows every year.

No complaint was lodged by the market gardeners association when the Edmonton Tree Planting Association, in honour of Arbour Day, asked to distribute trees for planting on boulevards from the market building. At least once, on Saturday 5 May and Monday 7 May 1928, for example, the association was given a stall from which to distribute trees.[95]

Causes which presented agriculture as entertainment and instruction were popular in the 1930s, and the city promoted them through its market. In 1936, the horticultural association, after a request from its president, W. J. Cardy, to the commissioners, held its fourth annual fall potato show in the market building and found the location so congenial that it returned in subsequent years. The show, which represented a collaboration between the association and the University of Alberta "to rid the community of various potatoe [sic] diseases," was intended to appeal to growers and consumers.[96] The *Bulletin* sponsored the 1936 show and previewed it in an article appearing 15 October 1936. Mrs. Joseph A. Clarke, the mayor's wife, was scheduled to distribute prizes in all eleven classes. Mr. Andrews, the government potato grader, was to be present to discuss potato diseases, and J. W. Marritt of the University of Alberta was to superintend the show. The preview article further announced that "the stalls in the market will be gaily decorated for the show, which is open from two o'clock in the afternoon until nine in the evening."

Also in 1936, the Edmonton Chamber of Commerce obtained approval from Commissioner Mitchell to use the market building on 20 and 21 January 1937

3.16

Market Square was a favourite marshalling ground for parades. Here, workers' groups are setting off from the square on 1 May 1937 for their annual May Day parade. CEA, EA-160-1240

for the Provincial Seed Fair, although in this case a nominal charge of five dollars was set to cover utilities.[97] After the show, C. S. Longman, field crops commissioner, wrote to thank Commissioner Mitchell: "This space was most suitable in every way for the purpose, and we were very pleased indeed to have the privilege of holding our seed fair in that building."[98]

Market Square's central location, its civic associations, and the flexibility of its open spaces made it a favourite martialling ground for parades and an occasional site for special events and demonstrations. In the 1930s, parades and demonstrations set to begin from Market Square were linked to left-wing organizations and groups often viewed suspiciously by city and provincial governments. The majority of these parades, including those held each year on May Day, were peaceful events. The 1932 Hunger March, which resulted in a riot in Market Square, was another matter altogether.

Although Market Square was merely a backdrop for the riot which broke out on Tuesday, 20 December 1932, after a hunger march set to begin there had been thwarted, its civic setting reinforced the impression that excessive force had been used against the marchers. In December 1932, organizations including the

Canadian Labour Defence League and the Communist Party planned a march from Market Square to the legislature to advertise the plight of workers and farmers. Feelings ran high when the city refused organizers a parade licence and it was clear that marchers would not be satisfied with the one permission they had been granted — the use of Market Square for a meeting. Both levels of government prepared for trouble. Police Chief Shute apparently ordered hardware stores around Market Square to close and their owners to remove any hardware or equipment which could be used as clubs or weapons.[99] When, after speeches, the assembled workers decided to proceed with their march, they were met "in front of the market building" by a reported 115 mounted RCMP with batons, as well as an unspecified number on foot. "Once back in the square marchers commenced booing the policemen and hurled several stones as the officers reformed their ranks opposite the market building." The *Journal* reported in picaresque terms the eight minutes of "fierce fighting" followed by a longer period of general disorder. "Hundreds of spectators," according to the *Journal*, had taken refuge in the fish market while hundreds more had repaired to the roof of the market building for a better view, threatening its collapse.

> A woman, coming out of a fish shop in the market building was caught in the maelstrom as the mounted men first started to break up the parade.
>
> She screamed, and throwing her parcel of fish high in the air, ran across the street in the thick of things and apparently, and amazingly, made her way to safety without trouble.[100]

Events rendered by the *Journal* as comic raise questions about the city market's potential to serve interests perceived by council as subversive. Winnipeg's public market, thought to have been a breeding ground for radical elements earlier in the century, was closed down as a direct result of the 1919 Winnipeg General Strike there. Fifteen years later, Edmonton's square was the meeting site of potentially radical groups such as the Unemployed Association, which met at 7:15 in the evening of 14 May 1934. A set of notes taken at the meeting reported that "there were about 1,000 present at one time on this meeting but many persons just come to see what will happen. There was no appeal to go around City block ... same as some unemployed leaders proposed to do before."[101]

But in the 1930s, Edmonton's civic governments, especially that of Mayor Daniel Knott (1931-34), who was himself active in labour movements, were not likely to emphasize the market as a breeding ground for radicals. Quite the opposite. In 1933, Mayor Knott seized on the market as an opportunity to ease the financial strains of the depression for the ordinary citizen by expanding the market building in a highly successful make-work project.

3.17

This photograph was one of several published in the *Edmonton Journal* on 5 July 1929 of unemployed men on Market Square. The accompanying article describes 150 men marching from Market Square to the legislature to "demand relief." They were met there by the Minister of Labour, who asked for their names and for particulars of their situation. Here, they have returned to the square to prepare the material requested by the minister. GA, NC-6-12553(d)

Had the depression not created social and economic conditions favourable to the city market, Alderman C. L. Gibbs, an influence on the civic centre plan of 1912 which had nearly resulted in the market's displacement in 1914, might have been successful in reviving a similar displacement project. Elected alderman in 1925, a position he held until his death in 1934, Alderman Gibbs acted swiftly to return civic centre planning to council's agenda. In December 1925, he argued that the approaching construction of a new CNR station warranted a "general policy of developing an attractive entrance from the Canadian National Railway to Jasper Avenue." His plan was to give the commissioners scope to "obtain exchange options, or make exchanges of land, subject to an agreement that the City will make an effective commencement with a Civic Centre scheme by June 1st, 1927."[102] Twenty-six lots were identified as needing to be acquired, but in November 1926 two money by-laws which would have funded the acquisitions, one for $175,000 and the other for $206,000, were turned down. Although a few of the properties were acquired as forfeitures in the depression to come, the opportunity to revive full-scale civic centre planning did not present itself again for almost twenty years — until after the end of World War II.[103]

Other initiatives taken by Alderman Gibbs in the 1920s could have undermined the market's hold on its prime location, had there been pressure to build there. In September 1926, for example, council endorsed Gibbs's recommendation that architectural guidelines be developed for the civic centre so that the city could "prescribe the architectural design, facing material, cornice and building line on structures on all lots facing and abutting on the area proposed."[104] Any proposed changes to the market would have come under scrutiny. Then, in the summer of 1927, council set up a committee to deal with town planning issues chaired by Alderman Gibbs — a step leading to the formation of a town planning commission two years later. Although the Edmonton Horticultural and Vacant Lots Garden Association was one of the many organizations asked to participate, the Edmonton and District Market Gardeners and Florists' Association was not.[105] Alderman Gibbs died suddenly on 5 September 1934 while on business in Sault Ste. Marie, Ontario, thus removing from the civic scene a determined advocate for city planning. Even before he died, the depression had raised practical rather than aesthetic concerns to the top of the city's agenda, paving the way to a building project Gibbs would have probably deplored — the expansion of the city market.

The plan to expand the market was, among other things, a practical response to that institution's apparent vitality — a tacit acknowledgement of the market's success in stimulating and sustaining the near-barter economy. Although vendors selling at the market were far from immune to the economic hardships which prevailed during the depression, low overheads and a large customer base favoured their survival. From 1929 on through the 1930s, the market continued to generate an atmosphere of bustle and prosperity even as vendors' profits diminished and customers had to search harder for bargains. In June 1932, when a *Journal* reporter wrote in glowing terms about the market's enticing atmosphere, he also touched on its economics: "while the smaller and more occasional operators may take in only a few dollars per day, which quite likely they expend on groceries and supplies before they go home, several of the largest stands, with heaped up stocks of plants and vegetables, have been doing business this season, on Saturdays, to the tune of about $100.00 each."[106] Even a few dollars a day would have helped Mrs. A. Morris, who, in August 1933, wrote Mayor Knott in desperation: "I have my husband. also two sons. out of employment. we are. almost on our last dollar. Please. advise. if it would be in order to make washing soap and sell same on. market. every saturday to help keep things going. we. are. British. subjects [*sic*]."[107] And when Mayor Knott had checked to make sure Mrs. Morris would not require a licence to sell soap, he was able to write her with an invitation to contact Mr. Kendall for a stall. Mayor Knott, who had already initiated the market expansion project, was especially tuned to the social and economic benefits it offered during hard times.

It was likely under Mayor Knott that relief vouchers were made redeemable at the city market, a policy which put city money directly into vendors pockets, enabling them to pay their stall rents back to the city. In March 1932, Norman Finnemore, writing on behalf of the market gardeners association, suggested the idea to the commissioners.[108] He believed it would protect farmers who would otherwise have to sell their produce to large stores "at prices below the cost of production." The very short distance travelled by relief voucher money was emphasized in a story told by Joe Bre-Win, whose father accepted vouchers from customers only to find himself short of cash when Kendall came to collect the rent. When Kendall threatened to evict the Bre-Wins, Joe's father asked the superintendent to try redeeming the vouchers himself. At the time, according to Joe, redemption of the vouchers was impossible because the city had exhausted its credit with the Imperial Bank. Needless to say, Bre-Win's Meat Market was given a couple of weeks free rent.[109]

Even before Mayor Knott took office in November 1931, the city adjusted its stall and store rents downwards to help keep vendors in business. Mayor Bury, in 1929, and Mayor Douglas, in 1931, both responded to requests to reduce rates. In 1932, Mayor Knott too was approached. A petition from stallholders asked that the farmers' stalls be reduced from thirty-five to twenty-five cents per day, while the six shop owners proposed substantial reductions — the three butchers from $20 to $16 and the others from $15 to $12 and from $12 to $9.50. In December of the same year, further reductions were requested from all the store owners, including Harry Mandlis and Mrs. James Jones, whose rents were reduced from $20 per week to $17.50.[110]

Vendors' financial problems intensified when the addition to the market opened in 1933. In September 1933, Kendall wrote to Mayor Knott recommending that weekly rentals at the north end be reduced drastically "on the understanding that it is for the purpose of giving these people a chance to establish themselves as part of the Market."[111] Howard Bre-Win, who had been lucky enough to obtain one of the six stores at a rent of $17 per week, had it reduced to $13, a figure which moved down again in 1934 to $9.00 and, a year later, to $8.50.

Howard Bre-Win, who moved to Edmonton from Litchfield, Staffordshire, in 1912, with his wife and twin sons, and who worked for many years as a

3.18

In May 1938, when this photograph of Bre-Win's Meat Market was taken, Howard Bre-Win was owner and butcher. His sons, Harold and Joe, worked for him part-time. Not long afterward, Joe joined his father in the business and continued to run it until 1972. Courtesy of Betty Bre-Win

butcher for Burns and Company, had taken a position in 1930 with Patrick and Brown at the south end of the market building. When the 1933 addition was under construction, Bre-Win applied for one of the new stores and was pleasantly surprised, not only to be awarded a stall but to be given first choice. He chose the stall by the window which he kept, in spite of the depression, until his death in 1956 when Bre-Win's was taken over full time by his son, Joe.

Joe recalled the difficulties starting up a business during the depression: "Sometimes we'd get farmers coming in asking us if we'd be interested in buying a few sheep or a veal calf." Joe and his brother would take the streetcar after work to its western terminus where they would meet a farmer in a horse-drawn sleigh. Together they would travel to the farm, slaughter the one or more animals on offer and return to the market in the farmer's sleigh or wagon. The next morning, the city meat inspector would be called to do the inspection so butchering could proceed. Eliminating the middleman was one strategy the Bre-Wins used to stay solvent during hard times, but the low capital costs and the frequent rent adjustments at the market were important. According to Joe, "there were a lot of butchers who would set up for the winter months, when they didn't have to worry about buying ice or refrigeration." Referred to as "snowflake butchers," they went promptly out of business in the summer.[112]

Janitors hired to spell off full-time market staff for summer holidays were chosen carefully during the depression. In June 1930, Mayor Douglas wrote Kendall asking him to "give the work to someone in real need as we are confronted every day with men of this type who find it impossible to secure work."[113] In 1932, Mayor Knott wrote Kendall acquiescing in his choice of a relief janitor but warning that "there may be some criticisms due to employing a single man who is not a taxpayer."[114] In 1933, Kendall hired a Mr. Lang who was not only behind in his taxes, married and with one child but "as [sic] not had a steady job for years."[115]

The city acted quickly during the 1930s on complaints about vendors whose income was not completely dependent on market sales. One such complainant was Mr. B Caswell, a market gardener who wrote Commissioner Mitchell about an employee of the Royal Alexandra Hospital who was also maintaining "three stands in the Edmonton Market Place, thus taking away the needed opportunities of many who depend on that occupation for a livelihood."[116] The following spring, the Edmonton and District Market Gardeners and Florists' Association registered a similar complaint: "This market gardening is our living, not very good these days either, not just extra pocket money as in the case of a man who already has a good position."[117]

The origins of the idea to expand the market in 1933 as a make-work project are not clear, but it might have occurred to Mayor Knott as early as 1932 when he began to instruct the city engineer, A. W. Haddow, to consider hiring unemployed men on market renovation projects.[118] In December 1932, the city's architect, John Martland, sent Commissioner Mitchell estimates for an extension — sixty feet by one hundred and fifteen feet — to the market building, and, in January 1933, he was instructed to prepare plans.[119] The commissioners further instructed Martland to set up the project as a tax-relief program: "The idea would be primarily to provide work for those unemployed home-owners who are unable at present to discharge their tax arrears."[120]

The economics of the 1933 market expansion were carefully worked out before it was approved by council. Superintendent Kendall calculated at $5,808 the annual revenue the addition should return to the city, based on the assumption that weekly rentals for the six new stores would average fourteen dollars per week.[121] In presenting the project to council on 27 February 1933, the commissioners rounded revenue estimates down to $5,000. The capital cost was estimated at $5,500. They argued that "by utilizing the services of tradesmen who are at present unemployed and owing taxes to the City probably 80 or 90% of the cost of the labor could be credited towards payment of these taxes." A request from A. Farmilo, secretary of the Edmonton Trades and Labor Council, that the project be expanded by building a public comfort station estimated at an additional $4,500, was rejected by council.[122] The MOH promoted improved veal inspection facilities and a covered structure to house live fowl, while Minnie Bowen of the Alberta Humane Society wrote to the Mayor asking that "provision be made to protect the vendors of livestock from the weather."[123] Somehow the city limited its project to the original concept.

Well before 29 May 1933, when the *Journal* announced the city's intention both to extend the market building at a cost of $6,000 and to give the work to "unemployed tax payers in arrears," small contractors had proclaimed their interest. Hancock-Jones Lumber Co., for example, wanted to furnish supplies of lumber and "to have the same credited against taxes." But Martland was cautioned "that other Lumber Merchants in town have indicated a similar wish to be considered and when the work is due to be proceeded with it would be well to consider as to making a distribution of the City's requirements in this regard."[124] In the end, seven tenders were received for lumber and mill work. Of eight electrical bids received, only two were able to include the required deposit slips.[125] On 27 July 1933, the commissioners sent to J. Hodgson, city comptroller, a list of tenders accepted for the extension, all of which were to be paid in the form of credits to property tax arrears.[126]

Individuals also worked on the market expansion project. In March 1933, A. E. Sibun, secretary of the Amalgamated Carpenters of Canada, sent the commissioners a list of "our unemployed married men, ... who are City taxpayers."[127] Men hoping to secure work on the project sent applications even before it was officially advertised, and their letters were usually forwarded to John Martland for consideration.[128] When, on 7 July 1933, the *Journal* announced that the project was underway, more than two hundred names were said to be on the list from which Martland would draw his workers.

The expansion project was managed directly by the architect's department. The commissioners stipulated to Martland that workers were all to be "selected from the list of tradesmen in your hands who are unemployed and not in receipt of relief and who are in *arrear* as to their taxes due the City, it being stipulated of course that the men selected are competent to fulfill the respective requirements." Each worker signed a contract which had been set up for the project agreeing that wages would be credited on the arrears of taxes and Martland was asked to distribute the work "as widely as possibly consistent with carrying on the construction efficiently and economically."[129]

Early in July, the city prepared a press release claiming that "the popularity of the City Market has rendered necessary a new extension to the market

Building" and that "applications are already being received to rent the stalls." Howard Bre-Win was sent an acknowledgement of his "application for a butcher's stall in the new market Addition."[130] Another applicant, Joe Gaudio, wanted to sell "imported products such as cheese, Olive oil, Italian fruits and other high grade merchandise carried by grocery stores."[131] Late in August, the names of the successful applicants were announced, although butcher W. Tudge was replaced by Joe Milne in September when the former's application was protested by the legal firm of Tigh & Wilson. Mr. Tudge, it appeared, had operated a meat market on 100th Avenue just south of the market and was legally obliged to refrain from going into business within six blocks of his former premises.[132]

The completion of the market addition and its somewhat triumphant opening in September 1933 represented what, in retrospect, was the high point in the relationship between the city and its public market. The article in the *Journal* headlined, "Enlarged Market Houses 231 Stalls," claimed that one hundred and fifty-eight farmers' stalls, sixty-one larger stalls for market gardeners and twelve retail stores were in use but that, even so, "there was an overflow of stalls in the open air on the east side of the building" where fruit and vegetables were being sold.[133] By embracing the market as an instrument of public policy, and extending the benefits of the near-barter economy it represented through a make-work construction project, the city had used the market both to alleviate economic hardship and to enhance the image of the city centre.

Between 1933 and the outbreak of World War II in 1939, only the on-going struggles of vendors to pay stall rents could have undermined successive councils' confidence in the vitality of the Edmonton City Market. Customers still attended in droves and vendors continued to value their stalls as their living. In 1938, Arthur Close, a Morinville farmer and market vendor since 1930, married Geneva Hardy and brought her into the gardening business which, through market sales, remained their only source of income for the next twenty years.[134] In 1939, Robert Simonet, a market vendor who carried on experiments in plant breeding from his south-side greenhouses, broke the code of the double flowering petunia — a discovery which eventually led to personal wealth as a supplier of seed and fame in the agricultural community.[135] On the surface, the market in 1939 was as much a credit to the city as it had been at the time of the 1933 expansion.

Beneath the surface, however, undercurrents signalled change. A request in January 1937 from Lang Jae Ly to build a small grocery on the southwest corner of Market Square was turned down on the grounds "that it is not the City's policy to place any further buildings on the Market Square, pending some permanent improvements being made."[136] By 1939, when the federal government first began to cast its eyes on Market Square as a site for a new federal building, the notion that the market site was a target for alternative development became common currency.[137] Uneasy vendors apparently framed their concerns by invoking the agreement that had been made in 1901 between Isabella Heiminck and the city, because, in early September, City Solicitor Thomas Garside prepared a detailed letter addressing "certain statements which have been made to the effect that the City cannot legally use this land for any purpose other than as a market site."[138]

Garside's letter, which detailed the painstaking land assembly process begun in 1901 when the city exercised its option to buy lots formerly leased from Mrs. Heiminck for public market. In it he made a distinction between buying land "for the specific purpose of using the same as a market site" and buying it on the understanding that it would always and only be used for the purpose of a market. The city, argued Garside, had legislative powers to establish a market on any site, "and therefore the discretion of the Council as to how the property should be used if no longer required for a market site could not successfully be challenged." He concluded with the judgment that,

> it would appear that Mrs. Heiminck was paid a reasonable amount by the City for the lots and the transaction could not in any sense be deemed to be a dedication to the City imposing a trust. Therefore in my opinion the statement as to the lots being sold "for the purposes of a public market" does not operate as a restriction against any other use, and neither Mrs. Heiminck nor her successors nor any other person could merely on the strength of that statement prevent the Council of the City using the lots for other purposes should Council see fit to do so.

While threats to the longevity of the market on the Rice Street site were beginning to surface, Superintendent Kendall, whose opinions on the issue are not recorded, was also under attack. In June 1938, Alderman Grout had complained to the commissioners that Kendall was lax in enforcing the rules. "I would like to state," wrote Grout, "that the market should have a younger Manager, a man full of pep and energy, with up to date ideas about running a market."[139] Alderman Grout pursued this theme a few months later in another letter to the commissioners, advising that Kendall be replaced by a "competent business manager."[140] A curious note, handwritten on Alderman Grout's letter and dated 19 January 1939, suggests that the alderman's zeal in reviving the market was not absolutely consistent with evolving plans for the market site: "Matter discussed by Cmr. Hodgson with Ald. Grout. Mr. Kendall not ready to retire. No real scope in market for live business man."

Between 1916 and 1939, Edmonton's modest investment in a "temporary" market building had yielded impressive returns. Throughout hard times, the market grew in numbers of vendors and customers, but it also grew in cultural significance. Small businesses, urban and rural, had been nurtured to adulthood there. Customers had grown up with the market as a key cultural reference. The market building brought agricultural and horticultural products and sometimes issues to urbanites. Market Square brought entertainment and occasionally drama to the heart of the city. Although the market had out-performed the city's expectations as these had been framed for the short term in 1916, the return of civic centre planning in 1939 was a threat. The outbreak of World War II in 1939 put the lid back on the pot in which the civic centre plans had begun to simmer and opened the way to five or six more years during which the market reigned unchallenged at the centre. Nevertheless, it was increasingly evident that the future of the Edmonton City Market was uncertain.

4

The Market and
the Civic Centre,
1940–1964

On Valentines Day, 1942, the *Edmonton Journal* ran a short article headlined, "Butter and Egg Men Purvey Philosophy, Too, at Market." Its author, affecting astonishment at the contrast between supermarket shopping and shopping at the Edmonton City Market, described stallholders as "farmer philosophers, many of whom double-talked in quaint European accents." Intended to be complimentary, the condescension in the author's tone situated the market outside the cultural mainstream, foreshadowing the future. On the surface, the market continued to flourish during World War II, drawing crowds on Saturdays, attracting new vendors, and undergoing something of a facelift under the direction of a newly appointed market superintendent. Beneath the surface, however, currents of change were in play. A 1942 scheme to replace the building was entertained by the city administration — then deferred out of patriotism. The discovery of oil in Leduc in 1946, which boosted the economy and stimulated the city's population to grow from 90,000 in 1939 to 370,000 in 1965, eroded agriculture's profile in the community at large.[1] The market, the only public service offered by the city which expressed agriculture as a civic value, began to lose status. Between 1947 and 1963, as successive councils stumbled from one civic centre concept to the next, juggling the elements that were to define the city's image for the future, the market was slowly but surely moved to the edge of the planning board. Well before 1963, the city market was eliminated as a core component of Edmonton's civic centre plan, clearing the way for its relocation to a site commensurate with its loss of status.

Edgar Kendall's last two years as market superintendent were spared the turmoil of relocation planning when, in September 1939, Britain declared war on Germany. As late as 29 August 1939, the *Journal* reported that the federal government favoured Market Square as the site for its new office building, but the arrival of an international war a couple of days later put government building on hold and stifled the rumours that had sparked stallholders to question the legality of changing Market Square's use.

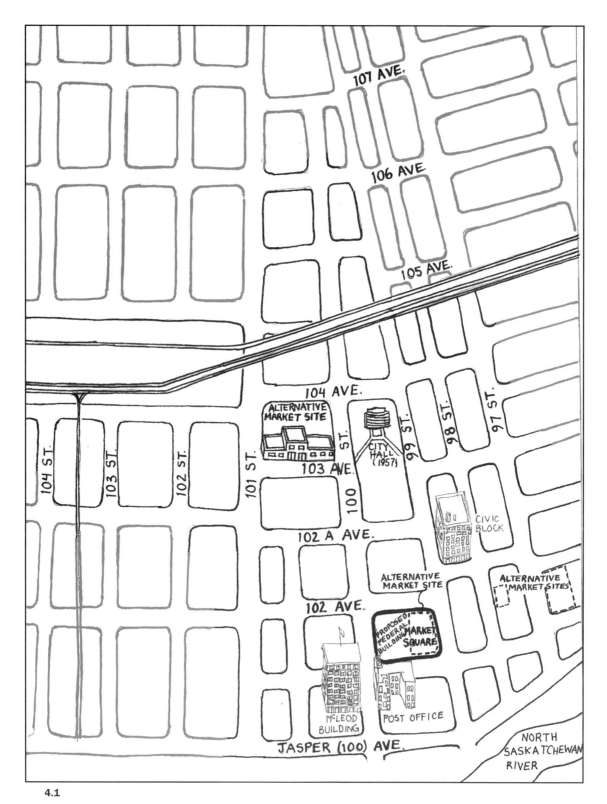

4.1

1945-1963: If not Market Square, where to put a new city market? Drawing by Barbara Budenz

War brought peace to Kendall's last months at the market. In May 1940, he oversaw the installation of new weigh scales.[2] Early in 1941, he facilitated a request sent to Commissioner Gibb by the Canadian Corps Association Boys Band to use Market Square two nights a week for band drill.[3] In March 1941, while the market was still under Kendall's supervision, the city entered into a collaborative radio-advertising venture with the stallholders whereby CFRN radio station was contracted to air one hundred fifteen-minute programs promoting particular vendors and their products. The city was to pay $280 or half the total amount, while stallholders contributed their share according to a formula which recognized the coverage they received.[4] And in May 1941, just a month before his departure, Kendall sent the commissioners a list of roof repairs needed.[5]

It was during Kendall's last years as superintendent and just before the federal government began to bargain with the city for Market Square that Arthur and Geneva Close decided to make their living as vendors at the market. Art was a year old in 1911 when he moved from Ohio to Morinville, Alberta, with his parents. Intent on farming, the family had brought with them all their possessions, including a cow and a team of oxen. In August 1930, Art made his first trip to the market to sell vegetables grown on his father's farm and, late in the 1930s, must have felt secure enough about the future of the enterprise to propose vegetable farming to Geneva as a living. Art and Geneva married in 1938, rented a room on 95 Street and 107A Avenue, and set to work growing vegetables and taking them to the market to sell. When his father died, soon after his marriage, Art sold the Morinville farm, relocated his mother to Edmonton and rented ten acres on 95th Street and 123 Avenue from the city. Some years later, when the city subdivided this acreage, Art and Geneva bought ten acres just north of the then city boundary to farm.

For almost twenty years, from 1938 to 1957, when Art decided to go into the television repair business, Art and Geneva made their living growing vegetables and selling them at the market. They worked the land with a single horse. They did not use fertilizers or pesticides. In fact, they did not even water their vegetables, although Geneva said they never had any crop failures. Potatoes, cabbages, onions, beets, carrots and other vegetables were stored in long roothouses — up to 70 feet long according to Geneva — which they built themselves. Art was the chief gardener while Geneva spent her time selling at the market, except when she gave over her place there to Art's mother. Her son Arthur used to love taking the bus to the market after school to help his grandmother sell. On those days, Geneva weeded, sometimes helped by neighbour women who liked to earn a little "pin money" in the afternoons. Art's help in the summer was another neighbour, Bud White. First hired when he was a schoolboy, Bud stayed on to become a permanent employee and a close friend.

4.2

Joe Bre-Win's pride in his car dates this photograph as having been taken in the late 1950s.
He is standing ouside Bre-Win's Meat Market at the north end of the market building. In
the background are the modern lines of the Edmonton Motors building which stood on the
northeast corner of 102nd Avenue and 100th Street in what, today, is Sir Winston Churchill
Square. Courtesy of Betty Bre-Win

Art and Geneva did not become wealthy on the income they earned at the
city market, but they lived a comfortable life. They built their own house on
95th Street just north of 122 Avenue, very near their first rented acreage. They
got to know many fellow-vendors, including the Oppelts, the Templemans, the
Arends, and Peter Lupul, and they had regular customers, like Percy Page, coach
of the Edmonton Grads and lieutenant-governor of Alberta, 1959 to 1965. He
became a friendly acquaintance.[6]

Geneva Close also knew Howard Bre-Win and his twin sons, Harold and
Joe. In 1939, Joe, who had been working in a pipe and tobacco store on Jasper
Avenue, began to work full-time in his father's butcher store. Energetic and
hard-working but also observant and fun-loving, Joe made his career at the city
market, moving Bre-Win's Meat Market to the new market building on 97th
Street when the old building was finally closed in 1964. Joe remembered playing
a trick on Edgar Kendall late in the 1930s when an empty store came available
at the north end of the building. When Howard Bre-Win and his greengrocer
neighbour, Mr. Teare, asked Kendall if they could divide the space intended for
three into two, thus expanding their businesses, Kendall refused. One night Joe

and his brother Harold dismantled the walls between the three stores and reconfigured them as two. To their delight, Kendall failed to notice the reorganization, even when he came to collect the rents. It was not until he began to look for the space to rent it that Kendall realized a trick had been played on him.[7]

Kendall's inefficacy during the last years of his tenure as superintendent is poignantly evident in his failure to influence the choice of his successor. Two weeks before his departure, he recommended to the commissioners that Harry Miller, long-time caretaker at the market, be made superintendent.[8] Miller, who had applied for the job on 7 April 1941 and on whose behalf two other letters of recommendation had been sent to the city, stressed his twelve years of service to the market department and the experience he had already gained during Kendall's vacations and absences. Miller was overlooked for the job, however, as were other applicants, in favour of C. J. (Clarence) Ingram, already head of the Civic Employment Bureau. Ingram's appointment to the job of market superintendent, made on the understanding that he would remain head of both units, was the first in a series of administrative restructurings which reflected the market's diminishing civic status.[9]

A more seasoned bureaucrat than Kendall, Ingram set about immediately after his July 1941 appointment to enhance his managerial reputation by taming the unruly market. His first action as superintendent, a request to the commissioners to place a "No Parking" sign in the loading lane west of the market, set the tone for his seven-and-a-half-year tenure there.[10] Two weeks after his appointment, Ingram had completed a written assessment of his new job and laid out the approach he intended to take. There was, he suggested, "a defeatist attitude among the staff and among the stall-holders, which apparently shows previous lack of control." He proposed to take a more disciplinarian approach, setting up rules "suitable to present day requirements" and then enforcing them "even to the extent of evacuating non-co-operating renters or group ring-leaders in order to obtain harmony and to conduct a clean establishment with standardized displays to attract the public."[11]

Although Ingram's proposals to upgrade the building, improve accounting and financial reporting systems, and create a new set of rules were all implemented, and although he was generally accepted by vendors who found him helpful and friendly, he failed to ingratiate himself with the senior administration. His quiet departure in the fall of 1948 was preceded by a virtual demotion when, after requesting a thirty dollar per month increase in his salary in November 1947 to make it "comparable to what was paid in other 'junior departments'," Ingram received the following reply: "The Commissioners have considered your letter of November 27th but do not feel justified in considering any increase in salary."[12]

While no record explains why the commissioners chose to bring the market together with the Civic Employment Bureau under one manager and under the same roof, the co-location caused no friction on either side. Set up in the spring of 1937 (although an earlier incarnation of it promoted by the Edmonton Trades and Labour Council in 1912 had operated briefly in 1914-15), the employment bureau was a registry and job-matching service for poor and unemployed residents of Edmonton, particularly those on relief. When the bureau's first superintendent resigned in the fall of 1937, Ingram was appointed to head it. Believing that those needing the bureau would prefer to access it in the market building, Ingram had suggested creating office space for it in the northwest corner of the market as early as 1938.[13] Until 1951, when the Civic Employment Bureau was absorbed into the Personnel Department, it operated from an office in the market building.

Apparently determined to set his stamp on the market, Ingram initiated repairs and renovations to the building within weeks of becoming superintendent. In 1941, in addition to the roofing repairs which Kendall had requested before his departure, Ingram carried out a program of "standardizing stalls and removing vendors' modifications, opening up the farmers hall by removing the wall between the 1933 addition and the original building, [and] installing an office on the north west corner of the farmers' hall next to a new egg-candling room."[14] He also had some new heating units installed. The *Edmonton Journal* followed the repairs, reporting on 16 December 1941 that they were almost complete.

In March 1942, Ingram continued the upgrading program, sending the commissioners a long list of repairs accompanied by cost estimates. This list included improving ventilation where "strong odors arising from fish markets and comfort stations [were] not conducive to enter to purchase foodstuffs" and fixing the drainage in the south-end retail stores "as the sewerage backs up in the fish markets and numbers one, two and three meat stalls."[15] Ingram's 1941 and 1942 renovations, which included renewing brickwork in the walls and chimneys, served to increase the superintendent's stature among vendors and probably among shoppers.[16] Except for routine and emergency maintenance projects, the 1941-42 renovations were the last carried out on the 1916 structure.[17]

Despite his expressed intention to move gradually with the program of change because "many new regulations applied at one time might be somewhat too much of a disturbing factor in dealing with stall-holders,"[18] by the beginning of August Ingram, had drafted a new set of rules for which he sought approval. He planned to print them in pamphlet-form for distribution to stallholders so "they would become acquainted with existing rules and would be more tractable when obeyance [*sic*] was requested." An advocate of written (not verbal) agreements with vendors, Ingram also decided to create a "blue print" of the floor plan "showing the location, the stall number and the cost of each stall."[19]

Ingram's approach to administration did not impress the commissioners who likely saw little scope in the position of market superintendent. In August 1941, Ingram sought approval to change the radio-advertising contract Kendall had organized with CFRN:

> Inasmuch as there has been some disagreement among the tenants as to who should pay and whether each were receiving the same publicity as the other and that the majority have the same goods to sell, we feel that the individual tenant should be responsible for his own particular type of advertising and that we continue under our control the fifteen minute semi-weekly broadcast for six months ... and advertise the market as a unit.[20]

But Commissioner Gibb ignored the issue, recommending that Ingram attend to the alterations project instead. Early in 1942, Ingram suggested increasing the weigh rates for coal to fifteen cents, but the commissioners turned the proposal down because "the coal companies are having a particularly hard time just now to make ends meet under the severe competition from gas."[21] A couple of months later, Ingram attempted, without success, to have the market by-law amended to prevent frozen chicken being sold on the market. The commissioners solicited the opinion of the MOH, who wrote that "freezing is recognized as an effective method of preserving many types of foodstuffs" and that "from the standpoint of health, we would not raise any objections to the sale of chicken in the frozen state."[22]

Ingram's conception of a public market lacked appreciation for the direct relationship between agricultural producer and urban consumer that lay at the heart of the institution. Striving always for efficiency, he found himself at odds with both stallholders and commissioners. In March 1942, he wrote to the stallholders suggesting that the prices they charged for their produce were too high and did not take into account the elimination of the middleman. "The policy of high prices reduces the volume of sales," he argued, "and, in the long run, the seller is the loser."[23] At least one stallholder, Mrs. N. P. Finnemore, disagreed in writing, listing the reasons stores were sometimes able to charge less than cost for a particular product and detailing the amount of work that went into raising a crop to be sold on the market. "Instead of complaints," she said, "there should be encouragement for the workers giving their fine service."[24]

In August 1942, Ingram asked the commissioners to bend the rules to allow three "firms" to sell on the market, but Commissioner Gibb dismissed the proposal: "We cannot see how the Commissioners can agree to such rentals ...

ALBERTA
DEPARTMENT OF AGRICULTURE

GROW A GARDEN IN 1942

Grow more foodstuffs in the garden.
Can and store more vegetables and fruit.
Live-at-home and help Canada's war effort.

The Department of Agriculture tests and propagates vegetables
and fruit varieties at the Provincial Horticultural Station, Brooks.

Write for information.

HON. D. B. MacMILLAN,   J. R. SWEENEY,
Minister of Agriculture.   Deputy Minister.

4.3

Local production of food was promoted during World War II for patriotic reasons. This advertisement comes from the prize list for the garden show held in 1942 by the Edmonton Horticultural and Vacant Lots Garden Association. Courtesy of the Edmonton Horticultural Society

this is hardly the function of a public market."[25]

In May 1944, Ingram was presented with a petition from six stallholders to remove Western Produce Company as a stallholder. They argued that it was a contravention of the rules to give a stall to a nonproducer. Although Ingram attempted to defend his action with the commissioners by arguing that many producers supplemented their own produce with purchased items, he was instructed by Commissioner Gibb to have the stall vacated.[26]

Only a few disagreements between Ingram and individual vendors found their way to the desks of mayor or commissioners, suggesting either that Ingram had been successful in obtaining compliance from vendors or that elected officials and senior administrators were increasingly remote from market affairs. In February 1944, unable to make fruit-stall operator L. L. Misener comply with his requests that the condition of Misener's shop be improved, Ingram asked Commissioner Hodgson to deliver the ultimate threat: "In view of this non-co-operation and complaints by other stallholders, we can do no other but to advise you that should this condition not be remedied immediately and your premises kept in good condition hereafter, that we will have no option but to give you notice to vacate."[27]

The city market remained busy during, and immediately after, World War II, undisturbed by talk of displacement. The promotion of local food production as a form of patriotism played to the market's strong suit and the market staff, building, and square were all conscripted for wartime uses.

In June 1942, for instance, the city was persuaded by W. H. J. Tisdale, director of the Canadian Wool Board, to "loan" Harry Miller, the weighmaster, to weigh wool at two registered warehouses in Edmonton. Commissioner Gibb had not been receptive to the request when it was first made but was convinced by Tisdale that "[the city's] co-operation would mean material assistance in an important piece of war work."[28]

Also in 1942, an elaborate intervention by Mayor Fry with the Wartime Price and Trade Board in Ottawa on behalf of the ladies' charity stall at the market, offers a perspective on wartime restrictions and affirms the ongoing interest of ladies' groups in running their market stall. In September 1942, Fry wrote Donald Gordon, the board's administrator, to make a case for obtaining a ration card to supply the charity stall. Several of the ladies' societies involved in the venture had had their card application turned down on the grounds that they were "only casually operating a restaurant," said Fry, who explained the history of the institution and argued for its necessity on the grounds that "those using the City market stalls are unable to leave the building during market days and the operation and maintenance of the refreshment stall meets a real need." Fry's proposed solution was that a ration card be issued to the city of Edmonton which would itself "purchase the rationed commodities."[29] By the end of October, a scheme had been worked out whereby the ladies' groups organized under the name of the "Market Caterers Club" with Superintendent Ingram as secretary:

> The Market Superintendent will purchase the required quantities of tea, coffee, sugar, etc., per week and the same will be handed to the particular ladies' association carrying on the stall for the particular week concerned. The maximum weekly amount required for the purposes of the market refreshment booth are: 3 lbs of sugar, 2 lbs of coffee and 2 pounds of tea.[30]

Market Square, always available for activities needing a central outdoor location, was in demand between 1939 and 1945 by groups concerned with the war effort. In addition to its use two nights a week for drill by the Canadian Corps Association Boys Band, it was sometimes requested for fund-raising events. In February 1943, for instance, Mayor Henry approved a request from the president of the Kinsmen Club that Market Square be made available on 16 June for an auction in aid of the Milk for Britain Fund.[31] The third annual auction held on Market Square to raise money for Britain, the 1943 event raised more than $4,000 or 40,000 quarts of milk and kept an eager group of buyers on the square until past midnight.[32] Although these events drew large crowds, there is no record that vendors opposed them.

Vendors did oppose Ingram's 1943 initiative to rent some space in the north end of the farmers' hall to a group of U.S. engineers for a camouflage unit. In March 1943, a group of vendors drew up a petition against Ingram's action and

4.4

This was the crowd that gathered on Market Square in June 1943 for a Patriotic Auction Sale. According to the *Edmonton Journal*, which reported on the event in its issue of 17 June 1943, six local auctioneers donated their services. Many items were bought more than once as they were turned back for a second and even third selling. CEA, EA-160-1955

took it to council. Asked to comment, Ingram argued that many of those who signed the petition would not be affected by the new tenant at all, while the inconvenience to others would amount to a slight stall shortage in summer. The $125 monthly rent to be paid by the army, he said, was more than could be generated by stall rents, and, finally, the gesture demonstrated involvement "in helping to win the war."[33] The finance committee, to which the matter was referred in April 1943, dismissed the petitioners' claims on the main issue but upheld their request that an advisory committee be set up to prevent such a misunderstanding in the future, all of which was duly reported in the *Journal* the following day.[34]

The controversy which erupted when Ingram rented space in the market building to the American army was cast in practical — not political — terms. Vendors complained about losing stall space; they did not complain about the presence of the army. Although Ingram responded primarily on the pragmatic level, arguing that the benefits outweighed any possible disadvantages, he attributed the opposition mainly to a few individuals who he accused of exaggeration and of inciting opposition. Behind this incident lies the faint suggestion of racial/political tensions.

Ingram himself was not above slurs or insults based on the cultural stereotypes of the time. In 1942, he attempted to have two "unnaturalized aliens" charged with a contravention of the market by-law because they were selling bread on Market Square which had been baked in a local bakery. However, when the MOH failed to identify a health concern and the city solicitor stated that "the City would be on uncertain ground in attempting to prevent such delivery under the marketing by-law," the commissioners casually let the matter drop.[35] A couple of years later, when writing to the commissioners about a dispute with a long-time stallholder, Ingram denounced the vendor's complaints as "false, defamatory and typical German propaganda."[36] Although Ingram's slurs were infrequent and far from virulent or obsessive, his attitudes and manners were probably fairly typical of his time and place. German and eastern European vendors selling at the city market between 1939 and 1945 may have been subjected to occasional hostility or insult from fellow vendors or customers and to a consequent reduction of business.

Betty (Oppelt) Bre-Win, born in Alberta in 1928, was careful not to speak German during the war. Betty's father, Peter Oppelt, had been born in 1885 in Hofheim, near Wurzburg, Germany, and her mother, Mary, was German-speaking with an Austrian background. When anti-German feeling began to develop well before 1939, the senior Oppelts instructed their nine children to speak only English at the market.

In 1943, when she was fifteen years old, Betty decided to leave school and help her mother full-time at the market. In addition to their farmers' stall, the Oppelts had been operating two of the retail fruit stores, but Mrs. Oppelt sold the smaller one, named the larger one Oppelt's Fruit, and trained Betty to run it: "I would run the business for her during the week and she would help me on Saturdays. Even though I was very young, I already had a lot of experience. I had sold at the stall in the farmers' section of the market each Saturday since I was ten years old."

It was a career Betty took to. For the next twenty years, she worked in partnership with her parents, running one and helping out with another of

4.5

In 1948, five years after she began working full time at the city market, Betty Oppelt was photographed standing outside the market building. To the right, just visible at the edge of the photograph, is a sign for the egg-candling station. Courtesy of Betty Bre-Win

4.6

Mary Oppelt, shown here in a photograph taken in 1955, enjoyed selling at the city market. According to her children, in addition to selling at the city market. According to her children, in addition to selling farm and garden produce of all sorts, Mary sold a number of handicraft items, including large rag rugs which she would make to order in the winter for her customers. Courtesy of Betty Bre-Win

the market retail outlets. She formed friendships with the other store owners, particularly those at the north end of the farmers' hall. In 1964, Betty and five other of the retail vendors, including her mother and Joe Bre-Win — who she married in 1969 — decided to open stores in the new market building on 97th Street. By the time Betty sold her business in 1979, she had worked continuously at the city market for close to forty years.[37]

Between December 1941 and the end of March 1942, just a little over a year before Betty Oppelt opted for a career at the city market, a plan to replace the market building with a new and bigger one reached the drawing board of City Architect John Martland. Supported eagerly by the retail stall operators from the south end of the building, who drew up and signed a petition arguing that a "modern, convenient structure" was necessary to remedy "the dangerous, unsanitary and run-down condition of that section of the market building in which we operate," the proposed two-storey, full-basement building was to extend 186 feet along 101A Avenue and 90 feet along 100th Street at a depth of 30 feet.[38] The petitioners' argued that a new building would be a "much needed asset to the city in any beautification or city Planning effort." But, just as the war had intervened in the federal government's negotiations to acquire Market Square in 1939, so it intervened in the 1941-42 initiative to construct a new market building there. An article in the *Journal* anticipated the outcome:

Edmonton needs a new and modern market building. It could do with two or
three other civic buildings, such as an auditorium in the downtown section of
the city. But it should wait until the war is over before it undertakes extensive
public works programs of any kind. They will help then to bridge the change-
over period from war to peace; today they could not help but divert materials
and workers from the only job to which Edmonton and all Canada is committed — the winning of the war.[39]

In March 1942, council approved a little more than a thousand dollars for
improvements to the south end of the market building but agreed that "in their
opinion it would be better to delay construction of the proposed new building ...
until after the war."[40]

What is surprising about the 1942 plan for a new market building on the
Rice Street site is not that the project was nipped in the bud but that it was
allowed to bud at all. The emergence of the new-building proposal, however
badly timed, suggests that despite the city's long-nurtured but inchoate plans
to redevelop its civic centre and in spite of the interest expressed by the federal
government in acquiring Market Square for its new building, there was still a
scrap of support in 1942 for the idea of redeveloping the square as a market.
By the spring of 1943, however, signs that the city had reverted to its prewar
plan to move the market were unambiguous. In February 1943, the city solicitor
reminded Mayor Henry that "the power to establish a market is a legislative one,
and markets once established may be abandoned or changed at the pleasure of
the Council."[41] And the next month, Norman Finnemore received a letter from
the mayor emphasizing "that the city has the right to vary the use of the site at
its discretion."[42]

In February 1946, when he sent the commissioners a detailed account of the
physical decrepitude of the market building, the 1942 proposal and the decision
to lay it aside until after the war may well have been at the back of Ingram's
mind. Possibly hoping for a revival of the scheme, Ingram listed the building's
most acute problems and offered his opinion "that the old structure is in such a
state that casual repairs are useless particularly as there is no foundation to build
from." He requested that the city architect "make a careful examination of the
premises and submit a written report to you concerning the safety and condition
of same."[43] As Ingram had anticipated, City Architect and Building Inspector
M. C. (Max) Dewar, who had replaced John Martland in 1943, agreed with him
"that the buildings on the extreme south have outlived their usefulness and no
further expense should be incurred in their maintenance."[44] However, in place
of the building project put forward in 1942, Commissioner Hodgson advised
inaction. Ingram was informed that the south end of the building "is not in such

a dangerous condition as to constitute a public menace," and tenants were to be told that low rentals would compensate for bad conditions.[45] With the market's future dependent on the prescriptions of a nonexistent civic centre plan, council was understandably reluctant to approve extra expenditures.

The on-going popularity of the market among customers, and its continued desirability as a direct sales outlet for farmers and as a retail opportunity for small business, made threats of its closure seem exaggerated or unreal. In 1943, when Pat Brennan arrived in Edmonton from Regina with her husband, she already knew about the city market. A friend in Regina had told her to be sure to go there for fresh vegetables and poultry. Pregnant with her first child, she walked to the market on Saturday mornings from the Mayflower Apartment building on 118th Street which overlooked the Saskatchewan River valley, getting there as early as possible to beat the crowds and to obtain the pick of the produce. Throughout the 1940s, 1950s, and 1960s, Pat made the Saturday morning market part of the family routine, a habit she maintained long after her seven children had left home and started families of their own.[46]

Neither was the condition of the market building or the insecurity of its status an inhibition to Bill Elliott when he and his father went in on a store there in 1945. The idea for the venture came from his father and, in retrospect, Bill realized it was a ploy to settle him in a respectable business. The business they bought for $500 was at the north end of the building next to Morphread's candy store (operated at the time by the Jaegers) and right across from the fruit store operated by Betty Oppelt. Soon after he moved in, Bill worked out a deal with Vivien Jaeger to split between them the space occupied by an empty store. A few years later, when Mary Malcolm and her husband bought the candy business and converted it into a health food store, Bill and the Malcolms retained the same arrangement. Bill made a few tenant improvements to his space, adding a layer of flooring and installing a big "Marchand heater," and he liked the work well enough to buy out his father's share and stay on until 1964 when the old building was finally closed. Although he moved to the new building on 97th Street, asking for the smallest space available, Bill had barely moved in before he decided to close his fruit and vegetable business.[47]

The return of civic centre planning to the city's agenda in 1947 raised a guillotine over the city market and its retail businesses, including Bill Elliott's new fruit store. Postwar prosperity stimulated new expectations for growth and wealth. Edmonton, still lacking a city hall, had not decided upon the major elements that would go to make up its civic centre, a state of affairs which made responding to the federal government's revived interest in Market Square difficult, especially since any decision to put the federal building there would raise the immediate question of what to do with the old market.[48] Two plans prepared

4.7

Bill Elliott was persuaded by a freelance painter to have this sign painted on the window of his
fruit and vegetable store sometime around 1950. He liked the result and took a photograph
of it. Courtesy of Bill Elliott

in 1947, one by the Edmonton Town Planning Commission and its chairman,
Cecil Burgess (Burgess Plan), and the other by the city architect, Max Dewar
(Dewar Plan), attempted to convert Edmonton's civic aspirations into concep-
tual and architectural terms. Both plans recommended moving the market from
Market Square, a move which vendors and customers were quick to perceive as
a loss of status. Had location criteria for a new market site been made explicit,
the gap in values between the city and its market would have been highlighted
rather than obscured. While vendors and patrons articulated their demands
for centrality and accessibility, council and its administration quietly sought an
inexpensive and inconspicuous site. The formal and monumental features of
both the Burgess and Dewar plans excluded, conceptually and practically, a centrally located market.

The Burgess Plan, dated 15 April 1947, recommended creating a central open
area between 99th and 100th streets and between 102nd and 103rd avenues
(today's Sir Winston Churchill Square). The new federal building was to be
located north of this open area. A new city hall would be built on the east of the
new square while the market site, on the south, was to accommodate an auditorium and arts centre. A replacement market was to be built west of 100th Street
between the lanes at the back of 102A and 104th avenues — assuming the lots

not owned by either the federal government or the city could be acquired at the assessed value of $42,220. Burgess, who believed that "the operations of a market are not altogether consistent with the scenic requirements of a civic centre," chose this site because "it would have no undue prominence in the general scene."[49]

> The scheme showed public buildings dominating each side of 100th Street from the post office to the C.N.R. Station. These were to act as a barrier to business development. Properties on the east side of 99th Street and the south side of 101A Avenue were to face large open spaces in the Civic Centre. These open spaces were to be used primarily for off-street parking. The main buildings envisaged by the Plan were a civic auditorium with museum and art centre, a new City Hall, a federal building, and a communications building. The market was to be removed, its site taken by the City Hall, and a new market found elsewhere in the retail section of the city.[50]

The failure of both Burgess and Dewar to accommodate the federal government's interest in Market Square was enough to permanently block acceptance and implementation of their plans, because there was no ready sponsor for an auditorium and arts centre on Market Square as per the Burgess plan, and no immediate plan to build a new city hall as per the Dewar plan. Instead of acting on either plan, the city continued to negotiate with the federal government over Market Square and even entertained a proposal from a private group to construct a fifteen-storey hotel in the block Burgess had advised be converted to a formal open space. Dewar, who did not want the federal building to go on Market Square, was furious when he heard about the hotel negotiations:

> On what grounds the city commissioners would recommend to the city council the acceptance of this proposal and its adoption by council is beyond my comprehension.... It seems that an outside influence is only required to dangle a luscious proposal before the eyes of the city and our civic administrators rush madly about and practically offer the proposer the keys of the city.[51]

Dewar submitted a new plan to council at its meeting of 16 June 1948, suggesting that the hotel be built on Market Square with the federal building taking the site on 103rd Avenue west of 100th Street that had been proposed for a market. Although Council rejected Dewar's revised plan by a vote of eight to three and remained committed to the plan to build a hotel on the block north of Market Square, the proposed hotel was never built and the federal government remained interested in Market Square as a site for its new building.[52]

Through the last half of 1948 and all of 1949, in an effort to satisfy the interests of the federal government and to accomplish its own goal of closing the market or moving it to a less prominent site, the city embarked on a dizzying merry-go-round of decisions and counterdecisions which, by early 1950, saw the participants back where they had started two years earlier. While the federal government tried to push forward with its plans to build on Market Square, first obtaining an agreement with the city to develop the site in return for $100,000 to assist in relocating the market (February 1949) and then obtaining rezoning approval from the planning commission (March 1949), the city was having trouble relocating the market. In August 1949, the 103 Avenue site was selected for the new market but, when the design prepared by the city architect suggested a price tag of $300,000, aldermen and commissioners began to balk. "Ald. Parsons disagreed with proposed site," reported the *Journal*, "saying it was too expensive for bldg. to be used 1 day a week. His objection was supported by Ald. Bowcott."[53] When the commissioners reported to council on 3 October 1949 that, in addition to the exorbitant building costs, "the land on which it is proposed to erect the new structure is too valuable for market purposes," council decided to initiate a new site search.[54]

A lumberyard site on 97th Street between 101A and 102 avenues was proposed, considered, and then rejected when the property's owner wanted to charge more than twice the city's evaluation of $44,000, but, by December 1940, John Martland, former city architect and designer of the short-lived 1942 proposal, had been hired to design a market and creche on a small site at 98th Street and 101A Avenue — just a block and a half to the east of Market Square. Martland's task was to design a two-storey structure with a full basement and a roof playground. The basement and ground floor levels were to be occupied by the city market while a creche would take over the second storey and roof.[55] Before the design was complete, however, it too was cancelled. Early in January, the city briefly considered moving the market back into the building on 101st Street and 107th Avenue that had been vacated in 1915, but, before this desperate idea could be examined and found wanting, the federal government was reluctantly persuaded to move its building to a site on 107th Street.[56] Thus, quite unexpectedly and for a reason peripheral to any civic centre plan, the market retained its hold on Market Square.

Three years of insecurity over the future of the city market politicized the normally apolitical vendors, aroused some concern among customers, and highlighted the issues in the debate over the market's role (or nonrole) in the civic centre. Norman Finnemore, who had formerly represented vendors' interests as secretary treasurer of the Edmonton Market Gardeners and Florists' Association, began to write the city as chairman of the now active and vigilant Edmonton

City Market Committee. Thomas Templeman, Mrs. Mary Oppelt, Norman Peck (Leduc) and N. J. Jensen (Riverdale Greenhouses) were also members of the committee, and they kept a close watch on any city initiative affecting the market, asking questions, reviewing and criticizing plans, and lobbying council over issues of concern.[57]

Perhaps the stallholders' committee was made suspicious of the city's motives by assurances given as late as March 1948 that there was "no immediate prospect of the market being moved from its present location," especially when, in October 1948, the commissioners refused to upgrade the home-cooking booth because "there is some prospect that the building will be demolished in a very short time."[58] By February 1949, when plans to move the market were in full swing, Finnemore argued that, although the city was not legally bound to perpetuate the market on Market Square, it was morally bound to provide an alternative site that was both central and accessible.[59]

The design developed by chief architect Dewar's office for the 103rd Avenue market building satisfied the farmers, but the omission of a retail section raised two issues. At a personal level, eliminating the stores would have had serious economic consequences for retail vendors who believed they had contributed to the market's success since 1917. Committee member and retail vendor, Mrs. Mary Oppelt, appeared at council on 12 September 1949 to plead this case and was supported by Norman Finnemore, stallholder, who claimed that "there has never been any friction between the stall operators and the retail stores in the market." At a theoretical level, the question of a retail component was problematic. The maximum fourteen retail stores (six in the north end, six in the south end, and two fish stores) had played an important stabilizing role at the city market, attracting customers throughout the week and generating a significant percentage of the market's overall revenue.[60] But their existence required occasional defending against claims by rival retailers who believed market store owners were being subsidized by low rents. Commissioner Hodgson was against including retail stores in a new market, wondering whether it is "the responsibility or a desirable feature of municipal administration to provide retail outlets for ordinary store business."[61] Howard Bre-Win attended the 26 September 1949 council meeting to plead the practical side of the case, arguing that retail vendors paid business taxes and utilities as did other stores, that the city was free to set fair rental rates, and that the result would be a benefit to the market. This argument, neither lost nor won in relation to the 103rd Avenue site, was carried on in relation to the 98th Street design.

When the 103rd Avenue site was abandoned by the city for a much smaller and less accessible site on 98th Street, the stallholders committee engaged the legal firm of Duncan, Johnson, Miskew, Dechene, Bishop & Blackstock to

4.8

When Dorothy and Jim Hurlbut bought this house at 78th Street and 128th Avenue in 1948, intending to grow vegetables for the city market, their first job was to clear the stinkweed from the site. To render the ground suitable for gardening, they grew a large crop of potatoes there. Courtesy of Dorothy Hurlbut

represent their interests. In early January 1950, H. J. Bishop represented the stallholders' objections to the 98th Street design, noting a reduction in loading space from 227 feet to 119 feet, the provision of only three entrances for 49 stalls on the ground floor and 142 stalls in the basement, the smallness of the site, and the fact that "no provision has been made for the present store operators in the City Market." Bishop argued that the stores "have provided a useful feature of the market" but that the 98th Street site was simply too small to include them, necessitating a search for a more suitable location.[62]

Coverage in the newspapers of the plan to build a federal building on Market Square and to relocate the city market provoked some letters from readers, and at least one, Winifred M. Scott, secretary of the CCF Women's Club, wrote directly to Mayor Parsons arguing that the market "is a distinct asset to our city," supplying "numbers of our citizens with a means of livelihood." "While we realize that there is no direct intention of doing away with it," Mrs. Scott wrote presciently, "we feel that to place the market on a site that is not easily accessible would destroy the market just as effectively, only it would take a little longer."[63]

Dorothy and Jim Hurlbut were well aware of the market's uncertain future when they decided, in 1948, to begin a market-gardening business and to

4.9

By 1970, when this photograph was taken, the Hurlbuts had bought and developed Ardrossan Greenhouses, turning it into a large and profitable business. Courtesy of Dorothy Hurlbut

orchestrate their sales through the city market. Dorothy, older sister of Betty Oppelt and daughter of Mary and Peter Oppelt, had sold at the market since she was a youngster. In 1940, three years before Betty left school to run a retail fruit and vegetable store at the market, Dorothy married Jim Hurlbut, but it was not until he was demobilized in 1942 that they began to consider how they would make their living. Jim got a job with J. B. Starkey driving a coal truck, and Dorothy decided to use a cold frame to grow a few things to take to the market. She did so well that in 1948 they made a big decision: they bought about five acres of land on 78th Street and 122nd Avenue, built a greenhouse, grew a garden, obtained an inside stall at the market, and launched what went on to become a large and prosperous market-gardening business. It was on the basis of their excellent sales that, in 1953, the Hurlbuts bought a quarter section in Ardrossan on which to expand.

Between 1954 and 1986, Dorothy and Jim built their business to become a multigreenhouse operation, selling directly to their customers at the market and wholesale to IGA, Nick's Landscaping, and Apache Seeds. For the first ten years in Ardrossan, in addition to market gardening, they operated the majority of their quarter section as a mixed farm, growing grain, raising cattle and pigs, and keeping about one thousand chickens. At the same time, they gradually

4.10

Dorothy Hurlbut worked in the greenhouses herself and supervised the staff hired to work there. Here, the centre of the greenhouse is taken up by flats of bedding plants. Bedding plant season was always the busiest time at the market. Courtesy of Dorothy Hurlbut

expanded their greenhouse business, adding one or two greenhouses per year as they could afford them, constantly devising new and more efficient means of getting water to the plants and of regulating the temperature and humidity inside the greenhouses, painstakingly monitoring the growth cycle of the plants, and carrying out the myriad tasks of seeding, transplanting, reorganizing the plants in the greenhouses, watering, and preparing to take them to market. Dorothy took bedding plants, vegetables, and eggs to the market each Saturday. Around 1964, the Hurlbuts sold most of the quarter section, keeping only about twenty acres for the market-gardening business. By the time they sold Ardrossan Greenhouses in 1986, the business had grown into a modern complex with its own shopping centre, no longer dependent on the market for its sales but still drawing many of the customers the Hurlbuts had come to know there.[64]

Neither did uncertainty over the market's future dissuade Peter Lupul from buying a business there in 1950. Peter, who was raised in Warwick, a few miles north of Vegreville, came to Edmonton in 1939 in search of work and began driving for Capitol Packers. It was then that he acquired an interest in cutting meat, so he worked as a butcher's assistant in a shop on Rice Street before

4.11

By 1955, when this photograph of Peter Lupul was taken, he had owned a butcher shop at the south end of the market building for five years and was so satisfied with the business he expanded it at every opportunity. Courtesy of Peter Lupul

signing up in the Royal Canadian Army Service Corps in 1942. When he returned from Europe and was discharged in 1946, he moved about from one job to another before deciding to take a job in 1949 with Garth Bennett, owner of Daily Meats at the market. Garth, who wanted to retire, made it easy for Peter to buy him out. With a $690 army gratuity, Lupul bought his first supply of meat, and the forty-five dollars in the till at the end of his first day in business marked the beginning of a thirty-year career at the city market. Before the old building was closed in 1964, Peter had bought out the butcher shops on either side of him, including one that sold horsemeat. Horsemeat brought in a lot of customers, according to Peter, but it was not his preferred line. Instead, he sought out good suppliers of mainline meats including pure Angus beef, which he purchased from Canadian Meats in Lethbridge and sold to the young lawyers and business people who patronized his store.[65]

4.12

Saturdays were the busiest days for all the retail vendors, including butcher Peter Lupul. Peter enjoyed meeting and getting to know his customers, many of whom were politicians, lawyers and businessmen. According to Peter, many of the men who worked downtown stopped to buy meat on their way home after work. Courtesy of Peter Lupul

Peter Lupul had barely launched his business when, between January and October 1950, the short-lived Detwiler scheme for the development of a privately run civic centre in Edmonton briefly dazzled the Edmonton City Council. L. E. Detwiler, managing consultant, First New Amsterdam Corporation, New York City, wooed council with an elaborate multimillion dollar proposal to develop a large and tempting array of facilities on land south of 104th Avenue to Jasper Avenue between 99th and 100th streets in return for a ninety-nine year lease on the property, property tax exemption, and twenty-five percent of the antici-pated profits. In addition to a 2,500-seat auditorium, a public museum and art gallery, and a variety of commercial buildings, restaurants, and clubs, the archi-tects of the Detwiler plan, alert to local issues, allowed for a market, although there was understandable confusion as to "whether this is to be along the lines of Edmonton's present farmers' market, or rather a super-market." Commissioner

4.13

This photograph of Mary and Laurie Malcolm was probably taken around 1955. The Malcolms bought a store in the north end of the city market which had long been known for its chocolates and candy. Mary converted it to the Natural Health Centre and soon developed her own strong following. Courtesy of Mazelle Nohr

Hodgson was quoted as claiming that "the farmers' market in its present form would be wiped out entirely by the Detwiler project."[66] In the end, although council went so far as to vote five to four in favour of the plan and had the Edmonton Charter amended by the province in order to allow the city to lease its downtown to a corporation, the public voted against the scheme in a referendum held during the November civic election.[67] Impossible as it would have been to devise a civic centre scheme more philosophically opposed than Detwiler's to the idea of a locally based farmers' market, its claim on the attentions of the council throughout 1950 finally loosened the federal government's hold on Market Square.[68] In this way, the collapse of the Detwiler scheme gave the market its last fourteen years in the city centre. Except for a brief period in 1954, when Market Square was examined as a possible site for the province's Jubilee Auditorium, even the city's parsimonious approach to repairs did not seem to undermine the market's sustained popularity among vendors and citizens.[69]

Around 1950, oblivious to the possible implications of the Detwiler or other civic centre schemes, Mary Malcolm and her husband, Laurie, bought the Vita

Bar, a small health-food shop next to the Edmonton Journal building on 101st Street, and decided to move it to the market as soon as the opportunity arose. The chance came about two years later when the Jaegers decided to sell the candy business they had acquired from its founders, the Morphreads. Mary, whose interest in natural foods had grown up around her own health problems, did not really want the candy business, though according to her daughter, Mazelle, she kept it going for a short time. She did, however, believe that the liaison with the market would be a good one for her business. From about 1952 until the building closed in 1964, Mary shared the north end of the market with Bill Elliott, Joe Bre-Win, and Betty Oppelt. Born near Belfast, Ireland, in 1917, Mary came to Canada with her parents in 1926 and settled with them in a farming community near Wainright, Alberta. It was there that, at the age of nineteen, she married the local teacher, Wilfrid Laurier Malcolm. They moved around a bit during the first years of their marriage, settling in Edmonton when Laurie left teaching and took a job with the federal government. When she developed rheumatoid arthritis at twenty-two, just after her second child was born, Mary read an advertisement in the paper for the Ball Clinic in Excelsior Springs, Missouri, decided to attend it, and returned to Canada convinced that diet was the only way to treat her ailment. Buying the Vita Bar (renamed Natural Health Centre) was an extension of her interest in the relationship between diet and health. Mary loved meeting and talking to customers, and she found the atmosphere in the old market congenial. She described it as a place where "old friends came to meet." She bought honey from the Regameys and, to obtain the best quality carrots and cabbage for juicing, contracted with a market farmer to grow them without using pesticides or fertilizers.[70]

Mary Malcolm remembered Market Square as a busy place when she first moved her business there, a place filled on Saturdays with cars, trucks, and even some horses and wagons. On Saturday mornings in the early 1940s, traffic on the square was so bad that the new superintendent, C. J. Ingram, was persuaded to hire Mr. Lawrence, the humane officer, who proposed his services as a traffic regulator for the modest compensation of two dollars per Saturday.[71] Six years later, Lawrence asked for, and received, an increase of four dollars per day, a raise he justified by claiming exemplary past service, "which is very hard and trying at times due to the fact that the parking situation seems to be getting more difficult all the time."[72]

On days other than Saturdays, Market Square was an ideal place to start a parade, test new fire-fighting equipment, or erect a new home or a model garden display. Events on the square were known to attract onlookers to the roof of the market building and, in 1945, Ingram wrote the commissioners about this problem. Access, he wrote, was gained from the building on the southeast

4.14

When a small crowd gathered on Market Square on 15 March 1948 to watch the fire department test a new ladder, Betty Oppelt was ready with her camera. Courtesy of Betty Bre-Win

4.15

Market Square was a central location for a variety of charitable causes, including this model home demonstration set up to raise funds for the Children's Aid home and advertised in an undated Pantages Theatre Program. Courtesy of the PAA (96.611, file 9)

corner of Market Square, which was occupied by the real-estate and insurance firm, Bagley and McManus,[73] thus enabling "any person to cross over to the roof of the market." When an event took place on the square, Ingram said, "people, particularly children, go up on the market roof to secure a grandstand view of what is happening."[74]

At least two groups made regular use of Market Square as a parade mar-shalling area. Starting in the mid-fifties, the Alberta Motor Association picked a morning in June for a School Patrol parade from Market Square followed by a picnic — a day intended to promote safe pedestrian habits among school children and to reward those who acted as patrols. And between 1958 and 1964, the year Market Square began its conversion into the Centennial (now Stanley A. Milner) Library, the Canadian Legion used Market Square on 11 November to marshall a Remembrance Day parade.[75]

Perhaps the most transformative make-over of Market Square occurred each December when the city sold outside "stalls" to vendors selling Christmas trees. In November 1950, Ingram's successor as superintendent, N. J. McIntyre, recommended to the commissioners that annual Christmas tree sales be stopped as the revenue, at ten dollars per stall for a total of one hundred dollars, did not justify the cost of clean-up afterwards. The commissioners, believing "the practice should be continued as a public service," suggested that McIntyre raise the stall rents to twenty-five dollars to offset costs.[76]

Between 1939 and 1964, a series of small changes to the buildings and layout of Market Square imperceptibly eroded the market's urban image. The decreasing importance and eventual elimination of the weigh scales marked the end of a period when public weights were indelibly associated with the public market. Parking unrelated to market activities began to take more space on the square and became an independent generator of revenue for the city, undermining the market's former dominance of the site. The addition of nonmarket functions to the square blurred the market's image in its downtown setting. The replacement, in 1957, of the Civic Block by a new city hall removed the market from the direct purview of mayor and council but, more importantly, effected a symbolic separation of the two functions. And perhaps most important, but least documented, was the gradual shrinking of the outdoor Saturday markets until, by the end of the 1950s, almost all selling took place within the shabby old building slated for demolition.

Uses not related to the market had been accommodated on Market Square since 1900 in buildings the city acquired with the land, but by the 1920s, it seems that only a brick house and a detached barn remained available for rent on the southwest corner of the site opposite the Post Office. It is possible that this house had been built by Philip Heiminck shortly before he sold the property, for in 1900, he added a brick veneer stable and outhouses to his dwelling on McDougall at the corner of Rice. In 1919, when the fish stores were built, Sam McCoppen was renting 9944 - 101A Avenue for his undertaking-and-ambulance business and using the barn for storage. Towards the end of Kendall's tenure as superintendent, Mr. Ennismore, the federal government egg inspector, persuaded the city to convert this barn to a detached egg-candling facility, although Ingram returned the function to the market building as soon as he became superintendent. Between 1929 and 1951, the real estate and insurance firm of Bagley and McManus was an unobtrusive presence at 9944 - 101A Avenue.

4.16

Bagley & McManus Insurance occupied an old house, possibly built by Philip Heiminck before 1900, at 9944 – 101A Avenue on the south west corner of Market Square. Stairs located behind Bagley and McManus, and intended for use by the upstairs tenants, were sometimes used by citizens wanting a view from the roof of the market building — a situation which Superintendent Ingram took pains to remedy. CEA, EA-10-569

The opening of the AMA building in 1944 on the northwest corner of Market Square signalled a change of city policy and reinforced the city's assertion that the market did not have the exclusive legal right to Market Square.[77] The AMA moved from the square in 1950, leaving its building to the city, but in 1953, when fire damage to Queen City Meat Market threatened the operations of that venerable business, council agreed to the erection of a temporary building on the southeast corner of Market Square.[78]

Throughout the 1940s and 1950s, as the numbers of farmers' rigs drawn by horses diminished and then disappeared altogether, the city increased its exploitation of Market Square for parking revenue.[79] Since only a little of this parking was metred for the use of market patrons, the effect was to deprive the market of space traditionally used for overflow parking and for outdoor stalls on Saturdays. In 1947, for example, Ingram added "ten new heated car stalls on the East side of the market Square" and was able to rent them immediately. "This will increase our revenue ... as all heated car stalls rent at $24.00 per year."[80] Two years later, under Ingram's successor, N. J. McIntyre, the yearly parking rate for a "heated stall" was doubled to forty-eight dollars per year.[81] In 1951, in an effort to reduce parking infractions of various sorts, all market staff were made special constables so they could police the metred parking on the square.[82]

While the removal of the weigh scales from Market Square in January 1957 was both overdue and inevitable, one effect of that disappearance was to further undermine the relevance of the city market. In 1900, virtually all large loads weighed at the market would have been sold on or near the square and, after 1917, small lots sold inside the building were sometimes weighed and/or checked on city scales. Over time, the association between official weighing and selling broke down. Inside the market, the retail stores and many of the farmers used their own small scales, while outside large loads were, increasingly, simply trucked in and out of the centre. As early as March 1950, when a city commissioner from Regina wrote to Commissioner Hodgson inquiring about Edmonton's use of weigh scales, Hodgson indicated that the city was considering discontinuing its weigh services.[83] Beginning in 1954, the Edmonton Chamber of Commerce began to pressure the city to move the scales, noting that they were now "off the truck routes established by City Council."[84] In August 1955, the commissioners recommended that the weigh scales be closed, suggesting that the service could be picked up by private enterprise, but council, possibly influenced by the Chamber of Commerce's reservations about private weigh scales, was unwilling to take the step.[85] Private scales, the chamber pointed out, could not issue the official weigh ticket required by the dominion government.[86] In January 1957, however, when Security Storage assured Mayor Hawrelak that "we are prepared to maintain our present weigh scale charges for a period of five (5) years," council finally decided to discontinue the scales on Market Square.[87] The disappearance of the weigh scales, necessary and unremarkable as it may have seemed at the time, eliminated one of the two primary functions around which the city market had been founded.

The opening of Edmonton's first named City Hall on 25 May 1957 on a site north of 103rd Avenue between 99th and 100th streets confirmed and gave visual expression to the separation between "hall" and "market" which had been unarticulated policy since the end of World War II. As early as April 1946, Mayor Ainlay had asked City Architect Max Dewar to prepare plans for a new city hall to be built on Market Square, but the project was denied priority on the grounds that "Edmonton would hardly have the 'nerve' to divert from housing and other vital construction the labor and material that would be needed for a new city hall."[88] When, in October 1954, the 103rd Street site was dedicated for a $2,750,000 city hall designed by Max Dewar's firm, Dewar, Stevenson and Stanley, the absence of any reference to the market in the rhetoric surrounding the project reinforced its invisibility and pointed to the certainty of its future removal from the civic centre.[89]

4.17

Margaret Oppelt enjoyed selling at the city market. Here, when she was working for one of the retail fruit stores in the 1940s, she had moved some cases of very ripe fruit outside the south door where she sold them at cut-rate prices at the end of the market day.
Courtesy of Margaret Tremblay

The withering away of the outdoor Saturday markets in the 1950s, a sure sign of institutional decline, is difficult to document and more difficult to account for. Wanda Klimke's grandfather, Jim Edwards, who came by horse and wagon from Busby on Saturday mornings in the 1930s and 1940s to sell vegetables, cream, butter, eggs, homemade soap, and live chickens when he had them, did not even apply for an inside stall, for he preferred the outdoor situation. Even in the late 1940s, Wanda could remember making the trip with her grandparents and sleeping for a few hours under the wagon before selling began on Saturday.[90] Throughout the 1930s and early 1940s, Dorothy, Walter, and Margaret Oppelt and their brothers and sisters lined up to get their favourite outdoor selling locations. The outdoor stalls had always been popular among vendors selling live animals because regulations stipulated that all such sales take place outside. Denis Hinse, son of Beaumont vendors Flore and René Hinse, was given the job of selling live poultry outdoors from the time he turned nine in 1945. Between 1945 and 1951, Denis sold chickens, ducks, and other birds on Market Square on Saturdays — mainly to oriental customers. Until 1939, when the selling of puppies on the square was officially forbidden, and even afterwards if the accounts of vendors are to be believed, many rural vendors brought litters to the market and sold them on the square to city folks looking for pets. The gradual disappearance of horses and wagons may have had something to do with the decline of outside selling, for farmers travelling by horse and wagon to attend the Saturday markets often preferred to sell outdoors. The appropriation of space on Market Square by the city for revenue parking, particularly on the east side of the building, must have cut into space available for the outdoor Saturday market. Whatever the reasons, by the late 1950s, Market Square on Saturday mornings was a much quieter and less colourful place than it had been twenty-five years earlier.

Slackening demand for outside stalls at the city market carried over to the inside of the building. The fourteen available retail spaces (six at the north end, six at the south end, and two fish stores) diminished between 1950 and 1964 as successful vendors expanded their businesses by taking over more than one space. In 1950, Superintendent McIntyre recommended on pragmatic grounds that the proprietor of stall number 6 in the south end of the building be allowed to take over the space being vacated next door, despite its being a violation of market policy to discourage monopolies.[91] When Mrs. James Jones retired in 1956, her store was taken over by neighbour and competitor Roy Heeks, proprietor of Prince Rupert Fish Market. Between 1950, when he bought Daily Meats in the south end of the Market, and 1964, Peter Lupul bought out two of his competitors, expanding into their spaces. And, in the north end, Betty Oppelt and Joe Bre-Win shared one set of three stalls while Bill Elliott and Mary Malcolm split the other three.

Though the Saturday markets remained busy, weekdays, except during bedding plant season in May and June, grew increasingly quiet, an indication of decline which either informed or reflected city policy. Between 1949 (after Ingram's departure) and 1964 (when the market was closed), the city pushed rents up and kept close track of user statistics. In December 1949, Acting Superintendent McIntyre was able to report "93 permanent stallholders occupying 184 stalls out of a total of 213 available stalls," noting that the remaining twenty-nine stalls were available on a rush basis.[92] Rental fees at all levels were pushed slowly up, with Prince Rupert Fish, for example, going from $15.50 per week in 1950 to $21.00 in 1955, while farmers who had been able to pay as little as 35 cents for a stall were held at a range between 50 cents to $2.50 per stall with no reductions during the week or in the slower winter season. Nevertheless, Saturday occupancy rates remained high, as indicated in a report prepared by the superintendent of the Land Department for the commissioners in November 1962:

> The interior section of the Market is divided into 68 greenhouse and vegetable stalls, each 7' wide, and 141 farmers' stalls, each 3' wide. The 68 greenhouse stalls are rented to 34 permanent stall holders, with the 141 farmers' stalls rented to 51 stallholders. Of the 85 permanent stall holders 53 reside within the city limits and the balance are from surrounding country points.[93]

Between 1938 (when the decision was made to move the Civic Employment Bureau to the market building) and 1964 (when the building was closed), space which could have been used by vendors was increasingly rented to nonmarket users, an informal and unexplained policy which may have undermined the market. Ingram's controversial move in 1943 to rent space at the north end of the building to the U.S. army was accompanied by a claim that, except for a short period in the summer, no vendor would be excluded on account of the army's presence. This was one of the first formal indications that demand for stalls, especially during the midweek, was declining.

In 1946, a small space in the building was rented to Swanson Lumber Company to house an employment office, conveniently located for hiring workers to supply its northern lumber camps. When Ingram tried to terminate the agreement in 1947, the company resisted: "We find these premises very useful and their location is ideal for a Personnel Office. We have tried to obtain other premises for a Personnel Office, but have had no luck in doing this and, if it is a matter of the City wanting higher rental for the premises, we are quite prepared to pay additional rent."[94] Although Ingram insisted he still wanted Swanson Lumber to leave, it remained at least through 1948; because his successor, N. J. McIntyre, in a financial report to the commissioners, included Swanson Lumber as a source of revenue ($300 per year).[95]

Signs that the market was a busy and active place, retaining and even expanding the many links it had with its various constituencies, coexisted with signs of decline. The ladies home-cooking stall, for example, remained a vital part of the market through the 1950s and 1960s. In the fall of 1953, some ladies had apparently complained to Mayor Hawrelak that the method of selecting successful occupants was faulty for he replied: "I have discussed this with Mr. Campbell and asked him to evolve some other method of making these selections, which might well be an ordinary draw at a convenient time when all the Organizations interested may be present."[96] In 1956, the stallholders, after thirty years during which the home-cooking stall had been their sole source of refreshment on Saturdays, signed a petition to allow another stallholder to sell coffee and hot dogs: "We understand Church organizations do have the Home Cooking Stall in the City Market & do appreciate there [*sic*] efforts. However, that is no reason why we should have to buy lower quality food at higher prices."[97] The charity stall persisted, however, because, in 1962, the Land Department's report to the commissioners noted that home-cooking and home-baking sale stalls "are made available at regular rental rates to local church and welfare groups each Saturday during the year. These stalls are allocated on the basis of an annual draw and appear to be a source of revenue to the various organizations utilizing these facilities."[98]

The 1940s and 1950s at the city market did not disappoint Konrad and Minnie Farkas, who decided when they married in 1938 to make their living selling chickens there. New immigrants to Canada — Konrad from Hungary and Minnie from Roumania — they met in Edmonton at the International Hotel where Minnie worked and Konrad had come to sell doughnuts. Perhaps it was Minnie's experience as a farm hand, and the fact that she had been given a cow by one of her employers, that raised in their minds the idea of developing a market-based business from an urban location. They bought a house at 10523 - 79A Avenue, acquired a few lots around it on which they grew corn for feed, and Konrad travelled to farm communities around Edmonton to purchase mature chickens. Konrad and Minnie finished these birds with a few weeks of feeding, butchered them at home with the help of their sons, John and Frank, and sold seventy to eighty chickens each week at the market. For more than twenty years, these sales constituted the family's sole income. It was not until 1950, under pressure from the city, that they abandoned their urban location and moved to a twenty-seven-acre site on 127th Street at about 147th Avenue. In 1956, Konrad was disabled by a stroke, but Minnie, helped by her sons, continued with the business until 1961.[99]

The poultry sellers, Frank Farkas remembered, were grouped together in the market in the centre of the building where they became friendly competitors. Denis Hinse, whose stall was adjacent to the Farkas's stall in the 1950s, recalled seeing Frank and his father carrying an impressive number of chickens on each arm, the birds linked together with their washed yellow feet visible and the wax paper wrapped heads hanging down.

Neither did the market, as it was in the 1940s and 1950s, disappoint Mary (Chipil) Sernowski, although her causes for satisfaction went beyond the income it afforded her. Born near Lvov, in the Polish Ukraine, on 1 September 1907, Mary's traumatic childhood and a youth spent working as an indentured labourer ended in 1928 when she contrived to emigrate to Canada. In the fall of that year, she left the train at Chipman, Alberta, and was hired as a farm worker. But life in Canada was difficult for a small woman alone, especially one who could not read, write, or negotiate a way for herself in a new country. Marriage in 1934 to Peter Sernowski, a man she didn't know but whose work as a vegetable farmer in the St. Albert area was something she could participate in, eventually led her to the city market. It was her Belgian neighbours who put the idea into her head sometime around 1940, and from the moment she began taking her produce there, nothing could keep her away. The market, she believed, in addition to giving her an income, gave her a voice and a place in the culture and, until a few months before her death in 1998, she presided over a stall there.[100]

ANNUAL POTATO SHOW

to be held in the

CITY MARKET BUILDING

Dates and further particulars to be announced later.

RULES

Entries are to be made at the Market Building, before 12 o'clock noon on the day of the Show.

Tags will be given to each exhibitor, and must be securely attached to the exhibit.

Only one entry per family allowed in each class.

All potatoes must be washed.

Exhibitors to supply own containers for the peck classes.

Paper plates will be supplied.

The decision of the judges is FINAL.

All entries FREE.

CLASSES

		1st	2nd	3rd
1.	Plate of six, round, white, named, including red-eyed varieties	$1.00	$ .75	$ .50
2.	Plate of six, round, colored, named	1.00	.75	.50
3.	Plate of six, oval, white, named (excepting Netted Gems and Carter's Early Favorite)	1.00	.75	.50
4.	Plate of six, oval, colored, named	1.00	.75	.50
5.	Plate of six, Netted Gems	1.00	.75	.50
6.	Plate of six, Carter's Early Favorite	1.00	.75	.50
7.	Collection of five named varieties, six of each	2.00	1.50	1.00
8.	Peck of any variety, white, named, including red-eyed varieties (excepting Netted Gems and Carter's Early Favorite)	2.00	1.50	1.00
9.	Peck of any variety, colored, named	2.00	1.50	1.00
10.	Peck of Netted Gems	2.00	1.50	1.00
11.	Peck of Carter's Early Favorite	2.00	1.50	1.00
12.	Plate of six, boiled, peeled, named	1.25	1.00	.75
13.	Most outstanding freak. First Prize	$1.00		
14.	Largest Potato of normal shape, named. First Prize	1.00		

For best results in both quality and quantity we recommend that you plant only certified seed potatoes. For particulars get in touch with the Dominion Government Seed Potato Inspection Department.

NOTE

Members of the Society are especially asked to give every consideration, in their dealings, to the advertisers, who through their interest and support have made possible the printing of this Prize List.

GLADIOLUS AND DAHLIA SHOW

To be held in the Market Building, Thursday, August 26th.

RULES

1. Entries must be made at the Market Building by 11 a.m. Thursday.

2. Tags, to be firmly attached to each exhibit, will be given to each exhibitor.

3. Blooms to be personally staged by exhibitor by 11:30 a.m. Thursday.

4. All spikes of Gladiolus to be named.

5. The decision of the judge to be final.

6. All entries free.

7. All blooms to become the property of the Society at the end of the show, and will be sold at auction, proceeds to go to war charities.

8. All Gladiolus Classes will be judged according to the rules of the Canadian Gladiolus Society, and blooms staged according to the color classification as set forth in their 1942 symposium. Section numbers refer to the section numbers of the symposium.

Entries Free.

Classes 1 to 9—One Entry in Each Class.

			1st	2nd	3rd
1	1 & 2	One spike, large flowered, white or cream, or blush-white, or pink with white or cream	$1.00	$ .75	$ .50
2	3, 4 & 5	One spike, large flowered, all shades of yellow, orange, apricot or buff	1.00	.75	.50
3	6 & 19	One spike, large flowered, light salmon, coral or rose, or pink with cream or yellow, Picardy barred	1.00	.75	.50
4	7, 8 & 9	One spike, large flowered, salmon, orange-salmon, or rose-salmon or salmon-rose, or medium or deep rose	1.00	.75	.50
5	10, 11, 12	One spike, large flowered, scarlet, crimson or red	1.00	.75	.50
6	13, 14, 16	One spike, large flowered, light mauve, or light mauve-pink, or medium and deep mauve or mauve-pink, or light violet	1.00	.75	.50
7	15 & 17	One spike, large flowered, purple or medium and deep violet	1.00	.75	.50
8	18	One spike, large flowered, smoky	1.00	.75	.50
9	20	Gladiolus, large flowered, named, white, light and medium colors with conspicuous dark blotch, 1 spike	1.00	.75	.50
10		Gladiolus Seedlings, grown from seed originated in the Province of Alberta. No limit to number shown by any one exhibitor, spikes to be staged in individual containers. Number of spikes to be declared when making entry. No entry fee	1.00	.75	.50
11		Basket of Gladiolus, not over 20 spikes	2.00	1.50	.75
12		Special prize for best spike in the show	1.00		

Dahlias
(Entries not limited)

		1st	2nd	3rd
1	One bloom, decorative or show	$1.00	$ .75	$ .50
2	One bloom, cactus or hybrid cactus	1.00	.75	.50
3	Four blooms, Pom Pon	1.00	.75	.50

4.18

Some market vendors exhibited their produce in the annual shows sponsored by the Edmonton Horticultural and Vacant Lots Garden Association. The 1943 prize list advertised several shows to be held in the market building, including a potato show and the fondly remembered annual gladiolus and dahlia show. Courtesy of the Edmonton Horticultural Society

Between 1939 and 1964, the market building was in demand as a venue for exhibitions, shows, and fund-raising events. In 1945, the Alberta Poultry Breeders Association held its annual show in the market building on the 4th, 5th, and 6th of December, although stallholders had voted forty-three to forty against it.[101] Despite stallholders reservations, 615 birds, including 90 turkeys and 170 pigeons, were entered by sixty-seven exhibitors and the show ended with a public auction of dressed birds and eggs.[102] More popular with stallholders were rummage sales held as fundraisers. In June 1961, for example, Mayor Elmer Roper sent to the superintendent of the Land Department a request from the Women's Committee of the Edmonton Symphony Society to hold such an event: "Would you please write Mrs. McCalla confirming exclusive use of the market Building for Tuesday and Wednesday, April 3rd and 4th, 1962."[103]

Throughout the 1940s and 1950s, one or more of the annual shows sponsored by the Edmonton Horticultural and Vacant Lots Garden Association was held in the market building each year. The annual potato show, held in the market from 1936 through 1942, had evolved by 1945 into the annual fall vegetable show. The association's annual gladiolus and dahlia show, originally sponsored by Johnston Walker Department Store and held in the store, had so expanded by 1942 that it was moved to the market. And, for several years beginning in 1946, the horticultural association held its major annual exhibition at the market rather than at previous venues such as the Edmonton Exhibition or the Riverview Pavilion. In 1946, Mayor Ainlay presented prizes "to leading entrants in one of the biggest exhibitions yet staged by the association. More than 1,000 flowers, plants and vegetables, attractively arranged, occupy the entire floor space of the main market building. A strong increase in the vegetable and novice classes was noted by officials at the show, with gladioli blooms holding the spotlight."[104]

That year, J. R. (Roy) Keeler won first prizes in nine classes, including the one for light-yellow gladiolus. Roy's wife, Bea Keeler, remembered the attractions of the market building as a venue for horticultural shows — the convenience of the stalls for arranging displays, its accessibility to entrants, and the high volumes of viewers its use guaranteed.[105]

Despite heavy use during the 1940s and 1950s, proposed repairs to the market building were ignored or reluctantly carried out. In October 1948, the MOH urged Commissioner Menzies to approve a proposal from Superintendent Ingram to provide sewer and water connections and a sink to the home-cooking booth but was refused: "As there is some prospect that the building will be demolished in a very short time, the commissioners would like to postpone any changes in the present stalls, and to assure you that proper arrangements will be made in the new market building."[106] Two years later, Superintendent McIntyre reported the appearance of a large crack in the brick work on the southeast corner of the building: "A sizeable space has developed between the frame of the large window in this section and the surrounding brickwork."[107] Although an inspection by the city architect in January 1951 suggested that significant repairs would have to be undertaken unless the building were to be demolished within a year, it was not until May 1951 that the needed $10,000 was approved for repairs and then only on the understanding that "it will be necessary to increase

4.19

Mike Tremblay, who managed day-to-day affairs at the market from the late 1950s until his retirement at the end of 1977, endeared himself to all vendors for his firm and even-handed way of conducting the market's affairs. Here, he is collecting the rent from Alexandra Belinsky at the city market on 97th Street. Courtesy of Margaret Tremblay

the rentals very considerably."[108] In September 1963, after complaints from retail vendors that they could not keep their refrigeration going, a report clearly stating that the wiring was "in a very poor and unsafe condition" was ignored and tenants were "warned not to overload the existing circuits."[109]

As the market building deteriorated and Market Square lost its visual and functional coherence as an urban space, the former Market Department disappeared as a distinct administrative unit, first reporting through and then subsumed within the rapidly growing Land Department. Ingram's appointment to the job of superintendent in 1941, a position which he added to his duties as superintendent of the Civic Employment Bureau, began this slide into administrative obscurity, confirmed by the commissioners' refusal in 1947 to raise his salary even to the level of a 'junior department.'[110] Neither was N. J. McIntyre, who took over Ingram's responsibilities for both the market and the employment bureau in 1948, able to extract a raise. In November 1950, he complained to the commissioners that "increases of varying amounts were recommended for all department Superintendents except this Department, for which no provision was made for salary increase."[111] When McIntyre resigned in April 1951, the

4.20

Rummage sales held to raise money for organizations like the Edmonton Symphony were well attended and popular even among vendors. This one was held on 7 November 1963. PAA, Wells Studio Collection 597

employment bureau was moved into the Personnel Department and the position of market superintendent was given to S. (Stan) Campbell, who supervised emergency housing for the Land Department. For eight years, Campbell carried out both roles despite his being told when taking the double job that his salary of $3,800 per annum was not eligible for the usual cost-of-living bonuses.[112] When Campbell resigned in October 1959, the running of the market was taken over by the Land Department and the position of market superintendent disappeared.[113]

In October 1959, Michael (Mike) Tremblay, known to stallholders as "the market manager," assumed most responsibilities — if not the title — of market superintendent. In 1942, when Mike returned from active service in World War II with a disability caused by shrapnel lodged in his right arm, he began to work for the city as one of the market caretakers, a title he retained even as his responsibilities increased. As late as 1961, Mike's superior in the Land Department asked Mrs. P. D. McCalla to contact two persons regarding the rummage sale she was organizing on behalf of the Edmonton Symphony Society, one of whom was, "our caretaker, Mr. Tremblay, [who] will arrange the final details."[114] Details, it seems, were Mike's strength because even vendors whose memories of the market extended as far back as the 1930s recalled his name first when asked about former managers. Renowned as a tough but fair interpreter of the rules, a diplomat who was not afraid to exercise authority, and a hard worker who kept the building spotless inside and out, it was Mike who collected rents, responded to vendors' questions and complaints, and supervised maintenance and repairs. Originally from Beaumont, Alberta, a town which supplied many vendors to the city market, Mike, in 1945, married Margaret Oppelt, herself a sometime vendor who, in addition to selling her own handicrafts, worked in several of the retail stores including the one run by her sister, Betty. Except for a brief leave in the 1970s, Mike managed the city market during its last years on Market Square, through the temporary move to the Pay'N Save building (October 1964 to April 1965) and for its first twelve years at the 97th Street location. For twenty years between 1959 and his retirement at the end of December 1977, it was probably Mike Tremblay's management skills that obscured from vendors and customers the degree to which the city had cast off its commitment to the 'market-as-public-service' and was instead struggling to find a place in its administration for the 'market-as-anachronism.'[115]

Isolated from politics, Mike nursed the market through its last years on Market Square while the city set in motion processes which would finally accomplish the long-sought redefinition of its civic centre. Although the market stood to lose both its pre-eminent site and its prominence as a civic institution, the public debate generated by the Webb and Knapp Plan (1962) and its immediate successor, the Civic Centre Development Plan, revealed how thoroughly the Edmonton City Market had insinuated itself into Edmontonians' views about urban life. Market proponents' success in extracting from the city a commitment to build and operate a new market, disappointing as the realization turned out to be, speaks to the vital role the market had played in shaping the values and aspirations of its many customers and vendors.

Even before it signed an agreement in October 1961 with Webb and Knapp (Canada) Ltd., a subsidiary of a New York-based company, to prepare, at Webb and Knapp's own expense, a civic centre plan in return for guaranteed development opportunities, council had been casting about for ways to move the market from its prime downtown site. In April 1960, Alderman Prudham, perhaps reviving an idea first suggested by Alderman Mitchell in 1957, proposed building a combined market/bus depot, but the idea expired without debate.[116] In September 1961, after it had agreed to a recommendation from the planning commission to prepare a comprehensive development plan for the downtown, council asked the commissioners to report on the feasibility of using the "old

Edmonton Motors Building" (Pay'N Save) as a temporary location for the market.[117] The plan, presented to council by Webb and Knapp on 22 March 1962, showed the civic centre reconceived primarily as a place for business high-rises buttressed by tourism (hotel) and convention facilities. The market, with no development potential to speak of, had been eliminated from the centre. Although not adopted by council, the Webb and Knapp plan was copied closely in the Civic Centre Development Plan prepared by the planning department and adopted by council at its meeting on 25 June 1962.[118] It was the omission from this internal plan of any reference to the city market which sparked public debate over the role a market could or should play in an urban centre, debate which continued up to and beyond the announcement, in January 1964, that Market Square was about to be redeveloped to contain a $3 million library and a $2.8 million underground parking garage. It seems entirely likely that the city needed to close the old and run-down market in order to gain the confidence of business in its development plan.[119]

The *Edmonton Journal* opened the debate over the city market when it published several articles in late August, one headlined, "The City Market to be Razed," and another questioning the market's notable absence from the civic centre plan: "The theme of the Civic Centre, and rightly so, may be Northern Development. But ... Edmonton is also an agricultural city, a farmer's City. Its Civic Centre should acknowledge the fact."[120]

Support for the notion that Edmonton's agricultural roots should be expressed through the retention of its city market was forthcoming. When Mrs. Jessalyn McLeod wrote to Planning Commissioner G. C. Hamilton to recommend keeping the market at the centre, just days after the *Journal* articles had appeared, she received an equivocating reply:

> The Commissioners generally agree with you regarding the value of a Farmers' Market so that fresh eggs, poultry, vegetables and goods of a like nature can be purchased direct from the producer.... However, the existing Edmonton market operation was thought to be not compatible with the type of development envisioned in the adopted Civic Centre plan which proposes that the area should be treated in a fairly formal way.[121]

When, however, the Edmonton City Market stallholders association, galvanized into action by the threat of losing the market, were able to obtain over six thousand signatures one Saturday in early September 1962 on a petition asking that the market either be retained at its "present" location or moved to another downtown location, the city's evasiveness was replaced by half-hearted commitment to a replacement project.[122] For example, the writer of a letter sent to Mayor Elmer Roper in mid-September 1962, who argued that "many large cities have retained a niche for their markets close to the main thoroughfares because the city fathers have realised that they bring life and gaiety to the all too solemn bricks and mortar," was told that the commissioners "will give earnest consideration to the provision of a site for the downtown Farmers' Market."[123]

Opinion was divided within the administration on the advisability of building a new market. In the fall of 1962, with letters supporting the retention of the market continuing to be published in the *Journal*, council embarked on a market utilization study proposed by Alderman McGugan.[124] J. R. Warner, still superintendent of the Land Department, assisted in preparing the study but delivered it along with his opinion that the market should be closed — not replaced. "In my opinion," he wrote, "a majority of the support for the market comes from those within walking distance of it. It was always a subject of complaint and probably still is from the food merchants on Rice Street who pay higher rents plus business tax."[125]

The official position of the commissioners was less straightforward. They supported the view that the existing market was incompatible with the Civic Centre Development Plan and accepted the idea that a central location for a new building would not be economically feasible. However, they did acknowledge the force of arguments in favour of keeping the market:

> The Farmers' Market has always been a part of the life of the City. Agriculture is still the most important basic industry supporting Edmonton's economy and will continue to be so in the foreseeable future. The Market then has a symbolic value, signifying an historic and honourable association with agriculture down through the years, and a recognition that farm and City are still closely linked. For many City dwellers, the weekly trip to the Market is a long-established custom — and one which is highly prized, judging by the many signature [*sic*] which were added to a recent petition protesting its closure.[126]

When, in March 1963, the Edmonton Chamber of Commerce weighed in forcefully on the side of keeping the market, the city's acquiescence was all but assured. The chamber's Civic Affairs Committee sent a report prepared by W. W. Winspear to the commissioners listing ten advantages to having a city market.[127] Naturally, the market's ability to stimulate local agricultural enterprise and its value as a consumer outlet for local products were stressed by the chamber, but as highly rated was a less tangible benefit. The market, wrote Winspear, "has symbolic value, since it suggests the integration of the city with its surrounding countryside." In early April, the president of the Chamber of Commerce wrote Mayor Roper to recommend that a farmer's market be

4.21

The civic centre concept which emerged from various planning exercises in 1962 recalled the formal proposals devised by Morell and Nichols in 1912. Here an open square and pond replace the city market and help to highlight the city hall in the centre of the photograph. Many citizens were alarmed by this plan because it neglected to specify a new market site. CEA EA-10-2717

developed on 97th Street site which, by then, was the favoured site.[128] The chamber's accompanying recommendation that the market be developed as a private enterprise, appealing as it must have been to council on philosophical grounds, could only have resulted in further delay.

Council's decision to build a new market building on the east side of 97th Street between 101A and 102nd avenues was finally made at its meeting on 27 January 1964, an adjunct to the much bigger decision made the same day to build a new library on Market Square as a formal centennial project. The market site had been selected in June 1963 after a perfunctory search for a suitable (i.e., not a central) location.[129] The development concept for the new market, which was to be built in combination with a parkade, had been suggested in October 1962 by Alderman McGugan, who anticipated that a coliseum would be built southeast of the civic centre.[130] Models for the new market building which were casually considered by council included the combined market/parking garage in London, Ontario, and a circular market being built at the time in

4.22

In October 1964, the market moved across 102nd Street into the old Edmonton Motors Building — then known as the Pay'N Save. This image of the building came from the "City of Edmonton Financial Statements and Reports for the Year Ended December 31st, 1944." Courtesy of the CEA

Coventry, England, although this latter design would scarcely have fit the selected site.[131] But, in January 1964, with the new library at the top of the civic agenda, temporary and then permanent relocation of the market became a pragmatic, not a philosophical, priority.

In 1964, as the Pay'N Save building was readied for temporary occupancy by market vendors, contradictory views about the future of the Edmonton City Market coexisted. For Alderman McKim Ross, who had voted against acquiring a site in 1963, council's decision to perpetuate the market by relocating it was the equivalent of taking a "sentimental journey from the jet to the horse and buggy age."[132] For vendors (retail, market gardener, and farmer) and for customers, the city's commitment to build a new market building meant the continuation of a way of life and of a tradition. Regrets over the loss of Market Square and its practically uninhabitable market building were balanced by anticipation of a building which would be warm, clean, and attractive. For council and for the city administration, the relocation of the market to 97th Street represented an unacknowledged confirmation of the city's altered relation to the public service it had sponsored since 1900. The Edmonton City Market on 97th Street, built as an observance to expressed opinion and as an alternative to confronting the issues raised by market supporters, was perfectly designed and sited to grow into its role as civic anachronism.

5

The 'New' City Market, 1965–2000

When the new Edmonton City Market building opened in April 1965, just two blocks east of its former location, vendors and customers hoped it would better house, and thus preserve and extend, Edmonton's market tradition, but the hope proved vain. Gone was the status that had accrued to the market by virtue of its proximity to the mayor and council, the Post Office, and the commercial heart of the city. In its short move to 97th Street, the market lost both the context within which it had been shaped as an institution and many of the constituencies from which its customers had been drawn, although the full import of these losses was not immediately evident. The path of decline followed by the market for more than twenty-five years prior to the turn of the twenty-first century was the inevitable consequence of civic policies and priorities as these were applied to Edmonton's downtown. The near obliteration of the market as a feature of Edmonton's 1962 Civic Centre Development Plan, followed by its perfunctory relocation to 97th Street in 1965, left successive councils and their administrations with the problem of finding a role for an institution which had no designated place in the civic vision. The city's failure to resituate the market within the evolving concept of the civic centre before 1998, when it was finally handed over to the Edmonton Downtown Development Corporation (EDDC) to manage, resulted first in the stagnation and then in the decline of Edmonton's downtown market tradition.

The lack of coherence and coordination that attended the design of the new city market, beginning with dramatic and arbitrary fluctuations in its budget, was an outward manifestation of the project's indeterminate status. In June 1963, when the four-block area bounded by Jasper Avenue on the south, 102nd Avenue on the north, 99th Street on the west, and 97th Street on the east (today the site of Canada Place, the Citadel Theatre, and the Sun Life Building) had been earmarked by the city as the site for a new coliseum, a scheme was developed whereby the new

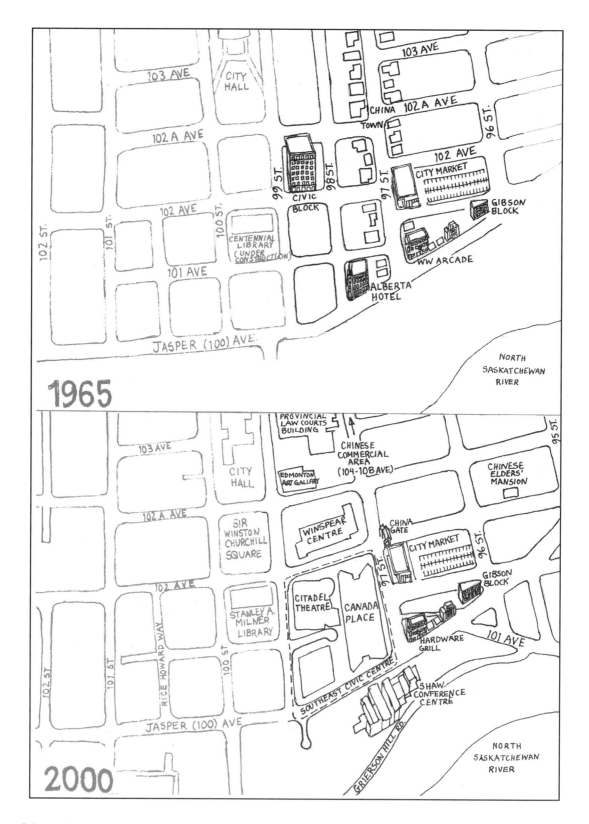

5.1

1965-2000: Urban blight, urban renewal and the market on 97th Street. Drawing by Barbara Budenz

5.2

This photograph of the 'new' market building (built 1965) was taken in 1979, six years after the provincial government began to actively promote the creation of farmers' markets. In 1978, the Edmonton City Market linked itself to the new program, an association which allowed it to display the sign and logo devised by the Department of Agriculture. PAA, *Edmonton Journal* Collection 4575/1

market would double as a three-level parking garage for the larger project. The budget figure for this "market" was estimated at $2 million, roughly a quarter of it for land acquisition while the rest was to provide, in addition to parking, twenty-five thousand square feet of covered retail and stall space and an additional ten thousand square feet of outdoor selling space.[1] But on 16 October 1963, when the electorate rejected a money by-law for the coliseum, the rationale for the market/garage combination disappeared. By January 1964, the complications and inevitable delays that would have attended trying to link the building of the market to a yet-to-be-sited coliseum, combined with the urgent need to vacate Market Square to make way for the new Centennial Library, necessitated a rethinking of the market project. By the end of January 1964, the new market was again an independent project with a budget of $250,000 and a projected combined stall and retail space totalling less than eighteen thousand square feet.[2] The design of the new market, informed primarily by the city's commitment to replace the old one, simply replicated the concept of its predecessor while failing to capture the old building's charm or its functionality.

The choice of Walter Telfer as the designer of the new market building did not enhance the status of the project. Telfer, who left the city shortly after the market opened to take a job in Ottawa with the Federal Department of Public Works, was the assistant to R. F. Duke, city architect.[3] His job — to translate the not-always-congruent interests of stallholders, council, and the city administration into an acceptable design as quickly as possible — was an awkward one. While Telfer proved competent at using the design process to promote decision-making, his relative lack of authority within the civic bureaucracy made it difficult for him to negotiate directly on changes to, or refinements of, the design. Even before the building opened in April 1965, its design and construction deficiencies began to surface, some of them with lasting consequences for the market.

Between 14 February 1964, when council approved a $250,000 budget for the new market building, and 10 August 1964, when that same council recommended the choice of Forest Construction as its general contractor for a contract price of just over $288,000, Telfer worked on the building's design with assistance from a five-person stallholders' committee and with the benefit of a critique from the MOH, Dr. Ball.[4] As early as 2 March 1964, Telfer sent an "amended sketch plan" for a market building to Commissioner Hamilton, with copies to the Land and Health departments, noting "that the size of this plan layout is considerably smaller than the previous design," an adjustment "brought about by the budget limitation of $250,000.00."[5] While Commissioner Hamilton was ready to approve Telfer's design, Dr. Ball was not. Ball proposed that washrooms be installed in the basement. He suggested terrazzo as the most appropriate material for the stalls and recommended that they be supplied with drains for easy cleaning. He also recommended that food vendors be separated from those selling plants and that a dedicated room for cleaning poultry be provided. Somewhat reluctantly, the commissioners sent a formal request to the city architect's office asking "what it would cost to implement these recommendations."[6]

Dr. Ball was not the only person to criticize the proposed design. Market stallholder Ron Krukowski, also employed by the city as a social worker, represented a group of about thirty to thirty-five stallholders who argued against the design, despite its having been approved by the designated stallholders' committee. Krukowski's complaints that the new building would be too small and that the seventy-five parking spaces allocated for customer parking were not sufficient may have been partly responsible for Telfer's return to the drawing board to produce, in early June, three new market design schemes. Scheme number three, which eliminated the retail component of the market, was not seriously considered by either the stallholders, who were committed to a continuation of the retail/farmers mix, or the city, which favoured the revenue stability assured by the retail component. The remaining two schemes differed mainly in size and therefore in budget, with the smaller one estimated at $300,000 and the larger one at $350,000. The stallholders' committee would have accepted either. Krukowski rejected both, but his suggestion that the city return to the site selection stage was not acceptable to the city or to most vendors. In the end, the Finance Committee's recommendation that council approve the larger and more expensive of the two schemes was approved, a gesture of apparent magnanimity which left both stallholders and the general public with the impression that council had fulfilled its obligation to replace the old city market with a fitting and suitable building.[7]

During the late summer of 1964, while plans were being made to vacate the old market building and move it temporarily to the Pay'N Save building across the street, Edmonton contractors were preparing bids on the new market project. Commissioner Hamilton, who informed the stallholders of the temporary relocation plans through a letter to their lawyer, M. B. O'Byrne, optimistically estimated that the new building would be ready for occupancy by 31 January 1965. On 10 August 1964, the city awarded a contract to erect the new building to Forest Construction, the lowest of eight bidders, and by 21 August the long-awaited project was underway.[8]

No group of vendors was more eager to move into the new market building on 97th Street than that made up of the many ladies' organizations which had long shared the 'charity' or 'home-cooking' stall, but no group was more betrayed by the shortcomings of the design process. In April and again in May 1964, while Telfer was working on his design, Mrs. E. A. Cote, municipal secretary of the IODE, wrote to Mayor Hawrelak in an attempt to secure a stall dedicated to the twenty-six Edmonton chapters of her organization:

> In the past Chapters [of the IODE] have rented the space which was available in the Market Building for such money raising projects as Home Baking, White Elephant and Rummage Sales, etc. We feel it would be advantageous to have a permanent stall in the new building which could be allotted to different chapters on Saturdays and would display the Chapter name and perhaps a colored Crest of the Order.

Mrs. Cote went on to ask for a copy of the market rules and to suggest that the IODE could provide "light lunches" to market patrons, but, although Mayor Hawrelak encouraged her interest and assured her of a response before the projected January 1965 opening, Mrs. Cote's enquiries seem not to have reached Telfer's drafting table where their implications for the building's electrical and plumbing systems could have been considered.[9]

Mrs. Cote was not the only member of a ladies' organization to be misled about the future of the home-cooking stall. In November 1964, as the new market building was under construction, W. A. Harvey, secretary of the Parent School Organization for Exceptional Children, wrote to the commissioners saying that her group had recently "held their annual Market Day in a booth at the Market Square" and that it was "concerned by rumors that suggest no space is being provided for a booth of this sort in the plans of the new Market Square." She pointed out that any such booth would need running water and electrical outlets.[10] Hurriedly, Mayor Hawrelak wrote to Duke, the city architect, asking him to "arrange for the installation of 220 volt outlets at a few of the booths which have communal sinks beside them so that it will be possible for charitable organizations to conduct their sales as they did in the old Market building."[11] On the same day, he wrote Mrs. Harvey assuring her there would be several booths equipped "so that your type of operation can be readily carried on."[12] Jean G. Lyne, recording secretary for the Edmonton Branch of the Consumers' Association of Canada, who wrote in December 1964 to protest that "the planners of the new Farmers' Market have decided to eliminate the stall for rummage, White Elephant, and Bake Sales," was assured by Mayor Hawrelak that she was wrong — that she had been "misinformed about charitable organizations being unable to use the new Market Building."[13]

Mayor Hawrelak's assurances notwithstanding, Miss Lyne's doubts about the future of the charity stall were well founded, as the sequence of events beginning before Christmas 1964 was to prove. In late December, architect Telfer informed Mayor Hawrelak that "it is not possible to provide 220 volt outlets as the main panel of the building is only equipped for 208 and 120 volts."[14] A few months later, when Telfer tried to obtain approval from the commissioners to spend $2,754.40 on revisions to the egg-grading room "to provide Kitchen accommodation for Ladies' Service Groups," his request was turned down.[15] Thus, despite the common understanding that health regulations which had been relaxed for the ladies' charity stall in the old market building would be fully enforced in the new one, the city failed to provide facilities that would serve the purpose. Two months after the market opened, Mrs. Wilma Harvey, who had been assured by Mayor Hawrelak that the Parent Organization for Exceptional Children would be able to participate in the operation of the charity booth but whose applications had been refused on the grounds that the stall was no longer available, wrote the commissioners to ask for an explanation.[16] Obtained from the superintendent of the Land Department, J. R. Warner, the explanation provided to the commissioners circumvented the issue of responsibility:

> Historically a small stall in which local church and public spirited organiza-
> tions could serve coffee and donuts to the Saturday market crowd has been
> provided for many years at a $3.00 charge.... This served a need and without
> getting into too great an expense was an added bit of advertising for the
> market. In attempting to provide the same or slightly improved facility in the
> new market we continue to run into the Health Departments' demands for a
> set up equivalent to a Class "B" restaurant.[17]

Mayor Dantzer conveyed a version of this explanation to Mrs. Harvey early in
July 1965, but, although he promised to "settle the matter" soon, the charity
stall was never reinstituted in the 97th Street building.[18] While this was doubtless a short-term loss to the many ladies' groups involved, the long-term loser
was undoubtedly the city market, henceforward deprived of its formal connection with a wide range of community organizations.

The omission of a stall suitably equipped for the ladies' charity groups, significant as it appears in retrospect to be, was scarcely noticed at the time by
vendors who were unhappy with other aspects of the design. A few days after
the market opened for business, the *Edmonton Journal* reported that irritation
among stallholders was growing at the new building's faults. Concrete block
walls, cement floors, and terrazzo stalls (see Figs. 5.8, 5.9) did not make for a
warm and adaptable interior and vendors complained that their quarters were
cramped and lacking in little comforts — a place to hang a coat, for instance.
Washrooms, as recommended by the MOH, had been put downstairs, but, in
addition to the many difficulties encountered trying to supervise them, the
basement location was awkward for the retail vendors who had asked that additional private washrooms be installed on the main floor. The *Journal* reporter
even noted the appearance of cracks in the walls of the new building, which
Telfer explained were "just a normal development due to shrinking and settling
of the building."[19] Two features of the 1965 market building drew the majority
of vendor complaints, however. As Krukowski had predicted, seventy-five parking stalls were not enough, a deficiency regularly aggravated by city policies
regarding their use. Less predictable was the stallholders' negative reaction to
the tall, sturdy, easily cleaned terrazzo stalls, a reaction that may have been provoked as much by the narrowness of the aisles between them and by the austere
atmosphere they generated as by their functional deficiencies.

Early in 1965, when the new market building was under construction, the
informally constituted stallholders' association questioned the city about provisions for loading and unloading produce and about the policies it intended
to apply to the parking stalls, receiving assurances that public parking would
be open all day Saturday and on evenings during bedding plant season,

5.3

In 1975, when this photograph was taken, vendors had built themselves raised wooden floors to cope with the high terrazzo stalls. PAA, *Edmonton Journal* Collection 1971/1

that vendors would be allowed to rent stalls for ten dollars per month, and that truck loading would be supplied.[20] Stallholders were not informed, however, of the city's plan to hood the metres during the week and rent them privately, thus rendering them inaccessible to casual shoppers. When the plan was put into effect, in April 1965, it drew angry complaints and then a petition signed by all vendors.[21] Immediately the city changed its policy, dedicating the seventy-five-stall lot to the market, but parking never disappeared as an issue.[22] While traffic chaos had been a feature of Saturdays at the market long before the roomy Market Square was abandoned for the 97th Street facility, the plentiful, regularly spaced and privately accessed loading doors on both sides of the old building had been much more convenient for vendors than the raised loading platform on the east side of the new building, right next to the cramped public parking lot. Throughout the 1980s and 1990s, as market patronage dwindled, vendors often pointed to the shortage of customer parking and the sometimes unfriendly and over-vigilant monitoring of the metres as the major cause of decline. And in 1998, when the EDDC took over the management of the market, a condition of the arrangement was that the city would forego its metre revenue on Saturdays, making the parking free to market customers.[23]

While vendors increasingly interpreted the city's parking policies as signs of official hostility to the market, their complaints about the terrazzo stalls pointed to bureaucratic incompetence — not malice. The stalls, designed very much as proposed to Walter Telfer by Dr. Ball, were the new building's most impressive interior visual feature. But in February 1965, just a couple of months before the new market opened, egg and poultry vendor Melvin Ash noticed two problems with them: "they were about six inches too high and not closed in underneath," he said.[24] The open design, disliked by vendors who had formerly used their understall space for a variety of purposes — the most reported of which was to tuck away sleeping babies or tired youngsters — was nevertheless favoured by the health department. The problem with stall heights was awkward since cutting down the terrazzo bases would have been costly and impractical. The city's solution, to install folding steps at the counters for a contract extra of about $2,500, was deemed ludicrous by the vendors who saw them as "a danger to life and limb."[25] Over the years, vendors devised their own solutions to the problem, equipping themselves with homemade wooden platforms and filling in the gap between the counters and the floor with a variety of storage devices, all of which posed cleaning problems that the health department had attempted by their proposals to avoid.

Stall design, like parking, remained an issue in the new city market, although over time the reviled terrazzo stalls worked themselves into the affections of the same vendors who had opposed them, turning subsequent attempts by managers to alter the layout, or tear out the stalls altogether, into mini-crises. In 1978, the new market manager, Ken Harris, over complaints from vendors, reorganized the stalls to create side aisles — his intent being to alter the customer circulation patterns which had formerly been limited by the unbroken, linear layout.[26] In 1987, when Jerry Sumka took over as manager, he determined to go one step further towards creating a flexible interior space, putting money in the budget to have the terrazzo stalls removed altogether. Vendor protests, carried first to the city administration and then to council, eventually scuppered the project, especially when a survey of stallholders revealed that ninety-eight percent were against the proposed change.[27] Nevertheless, early in 1999, a few months after the EDDC assumed responsibility for the market, the stalls were finally removed, creating a large, adaptable and easily cleaned interior space.

For customers, the market on 97th Street lacked the warmth and roominess of the old market. Narrow aisles and unbroken stretches of stalls forced customers to traverse the entire length of the building twice and made stopping to talk, especially during busy periods, practically impossible. Frank Farkas, who had sold at the old market before going into the jewellery business in Edmonton, tried shopping at the 97th Street building but found it depressing. The old market, he said, had been a place for people to meet and talk as well as to shop — impossible to do in the new building. He never returned.

But there were problems with the building's design that were felt more keenly in the city's pocketbooks than in the perceptions of vendors or customers. The flat roof, designed to be covered with one or two levels of parking in the event that the coliseum was eventually built nearby, began leaking within a year or two of the opening, a recurrent and costly problem for the city.[28] The building's electrical systems were so underdesigned that, as Telfer explained to Commissioner Hamilton just before the building opened, "the size of the

5.4

On Friday 9 April 1965, the *Edmonton Journal* published a feature page announcing the official opening of the new market the next day. The page included a rendering of the outside of the new building, a photograph of the stalls inside, and advertisements for all the retail stores moving from the old to the new market. Courtesy of the *Edmonton Journal*

wiring was not sufficiently large to give the amperage which would be required for three of the retail stores."[29] The basement washroom facilities, never perceived as adequate by the retail vendors whose request that washrooms be installed in their stores had been refused, were impossible to supervise and were easily and frequently taken over by the so-called undesirable element of the community — alcoholics, prostitutes, and drug addicts into the middle of whose neighbourhood the market had been placed.[30] While none of these deficiencies was beyond repair, as was the case in the old building, the city's ongoing but losing battle to re-establish the market as a break-even operation, created an administrative resistance to capital expenditures.

When the new market opened on 10 April 1965, complaints about the building were mingled with optimism. Vendors and customers had looked forward to resuming regular trade, and anticipatory coverage in the *Journal* stressed, through profiles of the retail vendors and selected stallholders, the theme of continuity. The *Journal* noted, for instance, that all seven retail vendors had moved from the old market: Joe Bre-Win (Bre-Win's Meats), Bill Elliott (Elliott's Fruit and Vegetables), Roy Heeks (Prince Rupert Fish Market), Betty Oppelt (Betty's Fruit Basket), Mary Oppelt (Oppelt's Fruit), Peter Lupul (Lupul's Daily Meats), and Mary Malcolm (Natural Health Centre). Stallholders, too, were carrying on traditions begun by earlier family members. Egg and poultry vendor Norman Peck described his father Thomas Peck's weekly trips to the market in 1913 from his farm north and east of Leduc — by wagon or democrat in the summer and by cutter in the winter. The Wallishes and the Blochlingers, greenhouse operators and market vendors since 1920, took stalls in the new market, as did S. Motruk, who claimed to have opened his first stall in 1925.[31]

Although not mentioned in the *Journal*'s coverage of the market opening, another sign of continuation was the move of Grace (Hinse) Kipling, egg candler, from the old to the new market building. Grace had worked at her parents' poultry stall at the city market since her childhood in the 1940s and early 1950s and, like her brother Denis, was attracted to it when she began to think of a career. But when Denis agreed to become a full partner in his parents' business on the understanding that he would eventually take it over from them, Grace looked around for a separate but complementary occupation. At the age of eighteen, which would have been in 1956, she bought the market-based egg-candling and poultry-grading business from the Hirondelle family.

Still carefully monitored by the federal government, as it had been in the days when Inspector Ennismore had been a regular presence at the market, the egg-candling and poultry grading was carried out by a private contractor who was given dedicated space in the market building by the city. Every Thursday, Friday, and Saturday, Grace, who was licensed to grade by the federal government, occupied her room in the market building where, for a fee, she graded eggs and poultry. On Thursdays and Fridays, she was patronized by farmers, many of them from Hutterite colonies, who brought their produce to Edmonton to sell wholesale, and on these days she also made trips to local butcher shops, such as Queen City Meat, to grade poultry. On Saturdays, with the assistance of a second candler to help handle the volume, she served market vendors. Conscious of the one or sometimes two government inspectors who would survey the market unannounced to check her work, she was rigorous in her grading standards. Not until the mid-1970s, when her volume of business dropped off as poultry producers were increasingly licensed to do their own grading, did Grace decide to shut down her business, thus ending a long-standing market tradition.[32]

A long-time vendor at the old city market whose name did not appear in the newspapers in 1965, but who went on to become a staunch supporter of the new market and a favourite subject of *Journal*

5.5

Mary Gordulic never spoke English with ease, but it was her favourite customers who drew her to the market every Saturday, even in her old age. The market, she said, helped her to forget her troubles. This photograph of Mary with a customer was published in the *Edmonton Journal* on 14 April 1980. Courtesy of the *Edmonton Journal*

photographers, was Mary Gordulic. Born in Czechoslovakia in August 1905, Mary made the trip to Edmonton with her small son in the spring of 1930 to join her husband, Mike, who had come ahead to work at the Black Diamond Coal Mine in Beverley. The Gordulics settled in Beverley, living in a chicken coop from April until August while they built a house on 46th Street just north of 118 Avenue. An energetic woman, who loved the soil and her kitchen in almost equal proportions, Mary's small garden expanded as she and Mike bought land near their house for Mary to farm. Although they always had at least three cows and up to thirty pigs in addition to geese, chickens, and ducks, it was the vegetable gardening that Mary most enjoyed.

Sometime in the late 1930s or perhaps the early 1940s, Mary had asked a neighbour to take some geese to the market to sell, but the neighbour refused, encouraging Mary to rent her own stall instead. Hesitant at first, Mary discovered she loved selling at the market and was soon a regular vendor selling homegrown vegetables and fruits. Although the market was merely a supplementary source of income for Mary, she took her work there seriously and spent all day

5.6

Stalwart market vendors gathered for a photograph in September 1994. Left to right, all rows, they are: Mary Sernowski, Mary-Anne Brassard, Eunice (back) and Alexandra (front) Belinsky, Grace Kipling, Flore Hinse, Kathrine Granstrom, Ray Granstrom, Betty Bre-Win, and Mary Gordulic. Courtesy of the *Edmonton Journal*

Friday in the summer picking, washing, organizing, and packing her products. She made pickles from her own beets, cucumbers, horseradish, and other veg-etables and took these to sell along with her fresh produce.

Mary preferred the old market building to the new one, partly because of the lower, roomier stalls and partly because of its friendly atmosphere. Even though her English was poor, she made friends among the other vendors and came to know many of her customers. For Mary, who otherwise stayed close to her family and the largely Slavic neighbourhood in which she lived, the Edmonton City Market and the city of Edmonton were one and the same thing. Through the market she connected with the community at large and came to value her relation to it. Thus, even though she disapproved of the high stalls and worried about the somewhat dubious location of the new market, Mary continued to sell there regularly until shortly before her death in March 1998.[33]

Mary Gordulic was one of several elderly women whose longevity and whose perseverance as market vendors earned them the respect and long-time patronage of their customers as well as the attentions of the media. In the busy,

5.7

For Lisa Frenzel, selling at the market has always been the best part about running a market-garden and greenhouse business. For many years, she and her husband, Werner, occupied an entire row of stalls at the north end of the market building. Here, she is in her familiar spot in the summer of 1995. Author's photograph

old market they would have blended into the larger scene, as Anna Triska had done before her death in 1963. But at the new and less patronized market on 97th, women like Mary Gordulic, Mary Sernowski, Marie-Anne Brassard, Alexandra Belinsky, and Flore Hinse assumed a larger-than-life profile during the 1980s and 1990s. Perplexed by the falling numbers of customers and vendors, they came to represent the standards and values that had inexplicably been lost in the move from the city centre to 97th Street.

Not all the stallholders who moved from the old to the new city market had sold there for a long time or had been brought up in a family-owned market business. Lisa and Werner Frenzel, for instance, began selling at the old market around 1960, taking vegetables Werner grew in his spare time on rented property while he worked full-time for the Jensen family of Riverdale Greenhouses, another market-based business. At first, the Frenzels had no permanently assigned stall and took whatever occasional space the manager, Mike Tremblay, could find for them. In 1963, by which time they had bought land and launched into business for themselves, they obtained their first permanent market stall, and Lisa sold full-time while Werner worked in the garden. For the Frenzels, the last few years at the old market and the first few years in the new one corresponded with the beginning of their family-based market-gardening business.

Lisa and Werner had met at a church dance in the small town in West Germany where Lisa's family, displaced Sudetens, had been relocated after World War II. Werner, who had grown up and taken horticultural training in the market town of Erfurt, determined to leave his family home after 1945 when it became part of East Germany. To this end, he had taken a job in a horticultural business near Frankfurt while he made arrangements to emigrate. In 1952, Werner finally obtained permission to emigrate to Canada, and, in 1953, Lisa left the job she had held since 1949 to join him. During their first few years in Edmonton, Werner worked for the Jensens, while Lisa first worked at the Royal Alexandra Hospital during the polio epidemic and, then, had their two children. By 1960, they had bought ten acres of land northeast of Edmonton and, somewhat reluctantly on Lisa's part, had begun their market-gardening career. She never developed the passion for gardening that motivated her husband but, like Mary Gordulic, Mary Sernowski, and others before her, Lisa always enjoyed selling at the market. Over time, Evergreen Gardens became a fixture at the new city market, occupying all the stalls at the north end which, when gladioli were in bloom, became a massive and colourful display.[34]

Lisa remembered the stallholders' discontent when they moved to the 97th Street building, especially their reservations about the location which they perceived as sinister and threatening, and she recalled their dislike of the high stalls which looked more like they belonged in a morgue than in a market. She also remembered that business at the new market was slow for a while, a memory corroborated by a story in the *Journal* about Mrs. George Dimitrov, a vegetable producer from Sherwood Park who paid eight dollars to rent four stalls on the market's opening day and took home five dollars for her efforts.[35] Lisa could not remember exactly how long it took for business to return to the levels she had developed in the old market but, by September of 1967, the *Journal* was interviewing customers who complained about the crowding and alleged bad planning on the part of the city.[36]

Although the potential disadvantages of the 97th Street location were seldom articulated immediately before or after the opening of the new market, either in the press or in correspondence between vendors and city officials, worries about the location were very much on the minds of both retail and farmer vendors, who feared that unsavoury characters hanging about would discourage long-time customers. In the end, their fears were justified. Not only did all attempts to anchor the new market in its run-down neighbourhood of 1965 fail, but as the neighbourhood continued to decay, and as properties around it were expropriated to make way for large-scale development, the market's urban context grew even more barren and disjointed. The disappearance of the Chinatown businesses and their eventual relocation too far north on 97th Street to benefit the market, the near elimination of the area's residential component, and, in 1991, the closing of Edmonton hardware store W. W. Arcade put an impossible burden on the market of creating its own context. On weekdays, retail vendors struggled to maintain an image of respectability as they battled drunks and petty thieves. On Saturdays, the bustle of the market edged out the "regulars" who asserted their claims over the territory by vandalizing the washrooms or creating scenes to test the mettle of the various market managers. If there had been any thought in 1963 that the market would be a positive influence on its new locale, these hopes evaporated as self-contained megadevelopments like the Convention Centre (opened 1983) and Canada Place (opened fall 1988) reinforced the market's isolation and its lack of connection with the community.

Despite the negative influence on the market of its urban surroundings, between 1965 and the late 1970s a newcomer to Edmonton might have been pleasantly surprised by the apparent vibrancy of the city market on a Saturday morning — by the range and quality of the produce sold there and by the bustling atmosphere that prevailed. But behind this healthy-looking exterior lay the conditions for decline. The adoption by the city of the "City of Edmonton General Plan" (1967) formalized objectives for the development of Edmonton's downtown that were inherently hostile to the market's operations, particularly its favouring of large-scale projects and its recommendation that "comprehensive design techniques" be applied to them.[37] And, in spite of the expertise and commitment Mike Tremblay brought to the market's management until his retirement at the end of 1977, regular and increasing operational deficits preoccupied the city administration which was determined that the market return to a break-even basis. While civic officials scrutinized the market's operations and attempted to restore financial equilibrium by increasing stall rental fees and decreasing hours of operation, early plans to demolish the Chinese-owned businesses on 97th Street and to redevelop the four-block section of the downtown referred to as the southeast civic centre opened the market to tentative proposals that it be absorbed into some larger project. In the background, largely unnoticed at the time but later to have implications for the context within which the market operated, lay an initiative taken by the provincial Department of Agriculture in 1973 to promote and assist in the creation of farmers' markets around Alberta.

5.8

In September 1978, when this photograph was taken, the market was still a popular destination for a committed group of customers. PAA, *Edmonton Journal* Collection 4256/1

In the early years of the new market's operation, there was no discernible decline in the Saturday trade. Long-established businesses such as Virginia Park Greenhouses (Granstroms) and Hinse Poultry Farms maintained or increased their sales. Dorothy and Jim Hurlbut, whose Ardrossan Greenhouses had by 1965 become a very large operation, continued to attend the market on Saturdays and only gave it up in 1976 because of Jim's poor health. Market gardeners and greenhouse operators whose businesses had been established in the latter years of the old market, such as the Frenzels (Evergreen Gardens), Thiels (Thiel's Greenhouses), and Wankes (South Cooking Lake Greenhouses), to name only three, became pillars of the 97th Street market, attracting and maintaining committed customers. On 5 September 1967, long-time vendor Mrs. Émile Blochlinger (Belmont Gardens) was quoted in the *Journal* as saying that it was "not unusual to sell 300 pounds of tomatoes on a Saturday." Other produce sold by Mrs. Blochlinger in 1967 was not itemized, though she could well have been selling squash for fifteen cents a pound, beans for twenty cents a pound, a one-hundred-pound bag of potatoes for four dollars, peas for twenty-five cents a pound, or corn for five cents a cob. A year later, in a *Journal* article

5.9

In May 1979, the Kuhlmann stall at the market was staffed by Anita (left) and Angela Kuhlmann. PAA, *Edmonton Journal* Collection 4575/4

which expressed the fears of Edmonton's Chinese community that their concerns were being ignored in the rush to tear down and rebuild the downtown, the market was singled out as "a tiny but relevant example of public intervention in the downtown area to preserve a human element in the midst of the inhuman concrete canyons which are rapidly coming to dominate the area."[38]

The reputation of the city market as a place to sell vegetables attracted Kuhlmann's Market Gardens and Greenhouses to take stalls there in 1972, although perhaps it was the family's commitment to maintaining a "human element in the midst of the inhuman concrete canyons" that accounted for their staying on through the hard times. Founded in 1961 by Dieter Kuhlmann, who had moved to Canada from Herford, Westphalia, in northern Germany in 1955, and by his wife Elizabeth Miller Kuhlmann, whose family had farmed in the Westlock and then the northeast Edmonton areas of Alberta after their 1926 arrival in Canada from eastern Europe, Kuhlmann's Market Gardens and Greenhouses had existed for ten years before its owners first applied for a market stall. By 1972, Dieter and Liz, along with their two young daughters, Angela and Anita, were building a thriving business on ninety acres of land northeast of Edmonton which they first rented from Liz's parents. Liz was well acquainted

5.10

Throughout the 1990s, members of the Kuhlmann family continued to serve long-time and new customers. Here, in 1996, Dorothee (Kuhlmann) Hauf is standing behind a newly stacked stall of summer produce. Author's photograph

with the market. Her father had sometimes taken his farm produce there and she had worked at the stall of her sister Martha Simon. But, until 1972, Liz and Dieter sold their produce through a combination of u–pick, which attracted many food–savvy European immigrants looking for a combination of quality and good value, and sales to wholesale customers. It was Art Simon, Angela's and Anita's cousin, who persuaded Dieter and Liz to apply for a market stall, an idea that appealed to Angela who was eager, even at the age of ten, to spend one day a week in the city. With Dieter's permission, Art negotiated with Mike Tremblay for a then difficult-to-obtain stall, initiating what became a long–term commitment to the city market.

The market turned out to be a good business move for Kuhlmann's. In the early years, they sold a large volume of produce there and received an excellent return on their sales. Dieter became one of many market gardeners who supported the provincial Department of Agriculture's initiative to pro-mote farmers' markets as a way of stimulating the small agriculture and market-gardening sector in Alberta. After 1973, in addition to selling at the city market, Kuhlmann's sold at several of the farmers' markets that sprang up around Edmonton.[39]

Between 1972 and 2000, the city market's contribution to the business done by Kuhlmann's gradually decreased for reasons difficult to determine. Perhaps, according to Liz, the decline stemmed from the decision to move the market instead of simply redeveloping it on its former site. Or perhaps, as Dieter reasoned, it had something to do with the gradual decrease, after the departure of Mike Tremblay in 1978, in the authority of the market manager. Contentious and independent-minded vendors managed to stifle the initiatives of the stream of managers who succeeded Mike by taking their objections directly to senior personnel in the administration or to members of the council. Or perhaps, family members speculated, it was the gradual closing down of businesses and shops around it which left the market isolated and lacking urban context. Urban farmers themselves, all members of the Kuhlmann family supported the Edmonton City Market as an institution worth preserving both for its historical value and for its potential to bring country and city together in a mutually sustaining compact.

But, in the years immediately before and after Kuhlmann's took their first stall at the market, the evident preoccupation of council and its administration with the market's finances complicated the issue of that institution's real and symbolic value to the community. In 1969, prompted by a request from Councillor Bateman, a report on the market's financial situation and on the strategies the city might adopt to improve it was prepared by an employee of the finance department. Compiled by W. K. Hooson, the report contained a series of recommendations which, as they were gradually adopted, came to characterize the city's reaction to the market's ongoing financial losses. Hooson recommended increasing stall rents, decreasing the hours/days of operation, and putting custodial workers on other jobs when they were not employed at the market.[40] Although the reasoning behind the recommendations was understandable, especially given Hooson's observation that most of the market's revenue was gained on Saturdays and during bedding plant season, any attempt to restrict the market's opening hours simply reduced service to the public and left the few retail vendors more exposed to the undesirable features of the area.

In 1972, the year Kuhlmann's began selling at the market, deficits again preoccupied the city. D. A. Cull, then superintendent of the Property and Building Management Division of the Department of Real Estate and Housing and the person to whom the market's manager reported, described the stalls in an interview with the *Journal* as a "dead loss" financially, but suggested somewhat tentatively that "the consensus around City Hall ... seems to be that the market's losses are justified by the services it renders to the public."[41] Later that year, the *Journal* detailed the market's financial problems as follows:

The market has operated with a deficit since it opened in 1965. That year, the loss was $8,600. Since then, the annual deficits (including cost of operations plus carrying charges) have been $12,000, $9,000, $17,000, $26,126, $24,052 and $22,465 said Property and Building Management Superintendent Doug Cull.
The estimated deficit for 1972 is $29,886.[42]

Mayor Ivor Dent, asked to comment on the figures, admitted that the market "is really not the most economical operation the city is involved in," but neither he nor others critical of the market's revenue problems questioned the statistics or strove to understand the trend they implied. With an annual carrying charge of $21,118 on a twenty-five-year loan, the market did not run an operational deficit until 1969, and during its first four years of operation had contributed significantly to paying down the debt on its new quarters.[43] The trend to higher annual deficits provided early evidence that the market was losing profile in its new location.

Despite the city's commitment to running the market as a break-even proposition, the trend towards larger annual deficits continued. In 1974 and 1975, the administration investigated alternative sites for the market, the most seriously considered of which was the soon-to-be-vacated Strathcona bus barns, but these investigations came to nought.[44] In 1975, stall rents were increased so that on Saturdays, perimeter stalls rose from two to three dollars while interior stalls went up from one to two dollars.[45] Nevertheless, in 1978, the first year of Mike Tremblay's retirement, the deficit was $49,200, a figure which confirmed, if such confirmation were necessary, the troubling status of the market as a financial burden the city was increasingly reluctant to bear.

The city market's unstable and declining revenue position throughout the 1970s was the inevitable consequence of a visible drop in the numbers of vendors and customers it attracted. As early as 1975, a *Journal* reporter noted that only eighty percent of the stalls were taken on Saturdays while less than fifteen percent were occupied during the week, a decline ascribed to a small constellation of factors which included a lack of parking and the market's noncentral location.[46] In 1978, the *Journal* reported a further decline, suggesting that in the winter only one-third of the stalls were being used on Saturdays and that the market was all but abandoned on weekdays.[47] To remedy this situation, the market's new manager, Ken Harris, was said to have initiated a $5,000 campaign to attract new business, a campaign Harris in all probability funded not from city coffers, but from a provincial grant.

In 1973, when the Alberta Department of Agriculture set up a farmers' market program, the possible effects of the initiative on the Edmonton City Market were not clear. The new program, which offered capital and advertising grants to community groups willing to establish farmers' markets in urban centres across Alberta, was intended to support small agricultural and horticultural enterprises by providing them with direct-marketing outlets. Behind the program lay the same assumption that had informed the creation of the city market seventy-three years earlier, the assumption that both city and country benefit economically and culturally when market venues exist to facilitate direct sales. In retrospect, it would seem that the province's commitment to farmers' markets might have given direction to the city's aimless search for a new role for its old market. However, this did not happen.

Between 1973 and 2000, the success of the provincial government program, which oversaw the creation of more than one hundred farmers' markets across the province and resulted in the formation of standards by which these markets were approved and regulated, was achieved with the minimal involvement of the Edmonton City Market. Under Mike Tremblay, who retired at the end of 1977, the city market did not participate in the granting program offered by the province, although this changed early in 1978 under incoming manager, Ken Harris, who immediately applied for (and received) a $5,000 advertising grant. Nevertheless, as the provincial program gradually altered the context within which the direct marketing of local produce took place in Alberta, the city market remained largely aloof from the farmers' market movement. City market managers, preoccupied with trying to run the market within the budgetary and administrative guidelines dictated by the civic bureaucracy, had little time and no officially sanctioned mandate to involve themselves in issues related to the provincial program. The Edmonton City Market, Alberta's last public market, became anomalous in its management structure since all the new markets were set up under the sponsorship of a community organization, such as a local chamber of commerce (St. Albert Market), an agricultural society (Millarville Market), or a one-of-a-kind group (the Old Strathcona Farmers' Market originally sponsored by the Strathcona Foundation).[48] Over time, a number of successful farmers' markets, many of them attracting vendors who had long sold at the city market, began to operate in Edmonton and environs, and the bustling success of some of these contrasted sharply with the dull decline of the older market.

While each new market set up in Alberta as a result of the 1973 farmers' market program grew out of, and then around, a community initiative, the city market's lack of community ties had been conspicuously obvious since it had moved to 97th Street in 1965. However, as early as 1970, Edmonton's Chinese community, itself about to be displaced from the 97th Street/Jasper Avenue area by the same civic centre zeal that lay behind the market's displacement, had expressed and demonstrated an interest in the city market.

5.11

This photograph, which appeared in the *Edmonton Journal* on 11 August 1964, was taken about a month before the old market closed. The three children seem to be imagining the transformation of the birds in front of them into something more delectable. Courtesy of the *Edmonton Journal*

Chinese patronage of the market, a patronage first directed to the egg and poultry vendors but extended to include Prince Rupert Fish Market and vegetable producers, probably began in the 1930s and 1940s — perhaps earlier — but it was after World War II, and particularly after 1947 when the Chinese gained full citizenship rights under the law, that market vendors began to cater more deliberately to Asian tastes. When, under the influence of the "City of Edmonton General Plan" (1967), which specified large-scale, comprehensively designed redevelopment proposals for the downtown, the Chinese were forced to contemplate the demolition of the many small and run-down buildings opposite the new market which then went to make up Edmonton's Chinatown, they determined to rebuild their community as a distinct entity. Between 1970 and 1979, as planning for a new Chinatown was set in motion and then progressed, the market's status in relation to this endeavour remained an open issue.

The city's opposition to redeveloping Chinatown in the area it had long inhabited (west and south of the city market) was made explicit in January 1970 when the *Journal* reported that "an extension of the present tiny Chinese area

5.12

These customers, photographed at the city market in September 1978, are intent on selecting their vegetables.

PAA, *Edmonton Journal* Collection 4256/2

around 97th Street and Jasper Avenue, was considered by city planners as too valuable land to set aside for a Chinatown."[49] That same year, Mr. K. Mah proposed to the city that two floors, a restaurant and some office space be added to the market, but apparently the planning department favoured presenting the idea to the entire Chinese community for discussion before approving a development project. Not until 1974 was another proposal sent to the planning department which included the market as part of a Chinatown redevelopment project. But no action was taken by the city on this scheme.[50]

Between April 1977, when an Edmonton Chinatown Planning Committee was struck under the chairmanship of Dick Wong, and April 1979, when the committee produced its plan, the possibility that the market would be included in the larger project was favourably entertained by the city. Early in the planning process, several aldermen were reported as suggesting that "the city market be purchased and redeveloped," but Stephen Iu, architectural consultant to the Chinatown committee, recommended against this approach, preferring coexistence to takeover: "We don't want to push those people out."[51] When the elaborately detailed Chinatown plan was produced in 1979, showing the area east of the market to 95th Street and south to Jasper comprehensively redeveloped according to a design scheme by Iu & Ross Architects, the market, renamed on the drawings "City Market Mall," was depicted occupying the western margins of the proposed new development — neither annexed to nor entirely detached from it.[52] In the end, the Wong report was not implemented as a comprehensive development and, despite the erection of the massive Harbin Gate (1987) over 102 Avenue next to the market, intended to be the main entrance to Chinatown, the Asian business community gravitated to properties further north along 97th Street, leaving the gate, a few institutional buildings such as the Chinese Elders' Mansion, and the city market behind.

By the end of the 1970s, the city was no closer to solving its chronic problems with the market than it had been at the beginning. As redevelopment plans for the area continued to dominate the civic agenda, including Chinatown, the much anticipated Convention Centre to be built south of Jasper Avenue, and then the gigantic federal government building, Canada Place, the market's unpretentious physical attributes and the desolation of its stalls came to be regarded as a civic embarrassment. In May 1979, a month after the Chinatown Plan was produced, the Department of Real Estate and Housing proposed setting up a steering committee — to be comprised primarily of senior civic bureaucrats — to study the city market. While the deficit problem was cited as the major reason for the study, the terms of reference proposed were broad, including a mandate to examine the "role of the Farmers' Market concept within the context of urban social development."[53] Although this proposal was never implemented, its broad terms of reference were incorporated a couple of years later into the mandate of HLA Consultants when they prepared a study for the Department of Real Estate and Housing in 1982. This report, which guided civic policy *vis-à-vis* the market throughout the 1980s and 1990s, recommended a radical reinterpretation of the role and function of the Edmonton City Market.

The years 1977 to 1979 saw the retirement of four long-time retail vendors whose departures, preceded by those of Bill Elliott, Mary Oppelt, and Roy Heeks, truly marked the end of the transition era. Bill Elliott had been the first of the original seven retail vendors to leave, and his departure was followed by the retirement of Mary Oppelt, in 1969, and the closing of Oppelt's Fruit. Early in the 1970s, Roy Heeks sold Prince Rupert Fish Market to Val Lampa who continued to serve customers there throughout the 1970s and well into the 1980s before the business declined, was sold again, and eventually closed. In 1971, Joe Bre-Win had closed his butcher shop but remained a major presence at the market by combining his store space with that of his wife Betty so that the two of them could work together to run Betty's Fruit Basket. From 1971 to just before 1978, four retail stores dominated the space formerly divided

5.13

Val Lampa (holding the fish) was the new owner of the Prince Rupert Fish Market in August 1976 when this photograph was taken for an article in the *Edmonton Journal*. PAA, *Edmonton Journal* Collection 2649/2

among seven: Betty's Fruit Basket, the Natural Health Centre, Prince Rupert Fish Market, and Lupul's Meats.

At the end of October 1977, Peter Lupul sold his business to Dominic Andreana and retired. Lupul, who had run his shop from the dilapidated south end of the old city market from 1950 to 1964, had welcomed the move to 97th Street. In the new building, he paid four hundred dollars per month for 1,100 square feet, and this was, in his opinion, a fair rent for premises which were clean and well organized in contrast to his former situation. Although business initially improved after the move to 97th Street, it also changed. By 1977, Lupul had many more non-English-speaking customers than he had dealt with at the old market, some of whom wanted to barter and many of whom wanted cuts he seldom displayed. He was not unhappy to retire because, although the business had more than satisfied his career aspirations and provided him with a good living, he did not see it as a future for either of his children.

In 1978, Mary Malcolm, whose husband, Laurie, had died in 1971, decided to sell her health-store business, which by then had expanded to several locations outside the market. Mary missed her husband's participation and she found the new market rougher than the old one and less congenial. When the buyer of her business decided not to retain the market location, the health store there was closed, although the space was quickly snapped up by Denis Hinse and converted to a poultry store.

Then, in 1979, Betty and Joe Bre-Win sold Betty's Fruit Basket to Albert and Fatima Fayad and became the last of the original seven retailers at the new market to retire. Betty and Joe had never entirely adapted to the new location. "We had a lot of rough customers," said Betty, "and I got worn down trying to keep my eye on them all the time." Perfectionists both, the Bre-Wins created magnificent displays of polished and stacked fruit. On Saturday mornings,

5.14

Mary Malcolm was photographed with one of her customers after the Natural Health Centre moved to the new market on 97th Street, probably in the late 1960s. Courtesy of Mazelle Nohr

a small, wiry, white-haired and dapper Joe, usually wearing an open neck shirt and an immaculately tailored blazer, stood at the entrance to the shop greeting customers and managing the traffic with expansive arm gestures. Inside, Betty supervised a staff of young women, usually comprised of nieces and members of the local Asian community, and together they kept the stalls brimming with produce and dealt with the lines of customers waiting at the cash register. During the week, by contrast, Joe kept a baseball bat tucked down beside the cash register, "just to keep law and order."[54]

In 1978, the year Mary Malcolm retired and Ken Harris took over from Mike Tremblay as manager, Dick and Carolyn De Klerk took their first stall at the market to sell vegetables. The De Klerks had been living and working as teachers in Edmonton when they decided to act on an idea they had talked about several years earlier while at university — farming organically in a community living situation. In 1978, they rented land from Jennie and Clarence Visser, whose son Doug, with his wife, Evelyn, was soon to become a vegetable vendor at the market too.[55] While the De Klerks looked for a suitable property to buy, they worked their rented land and sold the harvest at the market. In

5.15

Not long before she sold her store in 1978, Betty Bre-Win was photographed speaking to a classroom of children from Alex Taylor School. She was naming and describing the origins of the fruit in the store. At the end of the visit, each child was given a bag and some fruit to take away. Betty enjoyed these visits, which were regularly scheduled by the teachers. Courtesy of Betty Bre-Win

1979, they bought approximately one hundred acres south of Leduc, which they named Eyot Creek Farms, and built a house there.

Over the next few years, Eyot Creek became home to seven adults as the De Klerks were joined by Dick's sister, Jan, by Corrie and Frank Blenke, and by Joanne and Ted Koopmans, all of whom worked full-time at Eyot Creek and raised their children there.[56] In addition to growing vegetables without fertilizers or pesticides, the group at Eyot Creek began, in 1981, to maintain a herd of thirty-five to sixty dairy cows, selling the milk to Palm Dairies. Some time in the early 1980s, Jan, perhaps drawn to it by her Dutch background, began to experiment with cheesemaking. She produced a gouda-type cheese from unpasteurized milk which Dick began taking, along with the vegetables, to sell at the city market. One thing led to another and, by the early 1990s, cheese had become Eyot Creek's main product. By 1997, Dick's vegetable stall at the market had been converted to a stall selling variously flavoured and aged Gouda-type cheeses made in an artisanal fashion from unpasteurized milk.

Farmers' markets were, from the beginning, the primary outlet for produce from Eyot Creek Farms because the time and care taken by the De Klerks, Blenkes, and Koopmans to produce the food they sold yielded its best returns

5.16

In 1996, the year before Eyot Creek Farms decided to sell only cheese at the city market, Mischa Koopmans was selling both organically grown vegetables and cheese. Author's photograph

in direct exchanges with interested and responsive customers. In addition to the city market, Eyot Creek sold for varying periods of time at the Capilano, Leduc, Mill Woods, and Wetaskiwin markets. By the late 1990s, they had settled on three — the Edmonton City Market, the Old Strathcona Farmers' Market, where Carolyn began selling in 1996, and the St. Albert Farmers' Market.[57]

The De Klerks' first twenty-two years as regular vendors at the city market coincided with the most confusing and demoralizing period in that institution's long history. While a series of city-appointed managers kept their noses glued to the bottom line in a futile struggle to keep costs down and revenues up, civic politicians, senior bureaucrats, consultants, and other groups given a role in determining the future of the city market, redefined and repackaged the public market concept for the city. The "Old Towne Market" plan, which emerged between 1977 and 1987 and then dominated civic thinking regarding the market until the late 1990s, saw the city market reconceived as the centrepiece of an urban restoration and renewal project — something well outside the farmers' market concept being promoted by the provincial government. Although announcements regarding the Old Towne Market project appeared intermittently in the newspapers, the scheme seemed remote from, and largely irrelevant to, those who frequented the market, either as vendors or customers. More relevant on a day-to-day basis were changes in the market's urban context. The opening of the Convention Centre in 1983 and Canada Place in 1988, followed

5.17

Market shoppers often have several destinations in mind when they shop. W. W. Arcade hardware store, shown here in a photograph from 1976, was a favourite destination for customers of the Edmonton City Market. CEA, EA-245-224

by the closing of W. W. Arcade in 1991, were felt at the market like hammer blows. Business continued to fall throughout the 1980s and 1990s and the more it declined the more operational resources the city withdrew. By 1998, Jerry Sumka, who had begun his long tenure as manager in April 1987 full of enthusiasm, was reduced to 'minding the shop' as he spent up to sixty percent of his time on "other assignments." By 1998, also, the Old Towne Market bubble had burst. In July 1998, when the council approved the EDDC's proposal to take over responsibility for managing the Edmonton City Market, the only alternative would have been closing it, an alternative even the embattled vendors of the 1980s and 1990s opposed.[58]

Among the most embattled of the city market vendors were those who took over its once vital retail component from the original seven. Although the Fayads, assisted largely by their five children, maintained high standards at Betty's Fruit Basket and did excellent business, particularly in the first half of the 1980s, the general malaise affecting the market gradually undermined their trade. In 1987, they sold Betty's Fruit Basket to Joe and Cheryl Madaski who, a few years later, sold to Patrick Bong. Throughout most of the 1990s, Betty's Fruit Basket was gradually converted to a small convenience-store operation, selling a few vegetables and dry goods to neighbourhood residents.

Dominic Andreana, who bought Lupul Meats in October 1977, renaming it Ital-Canadian Meats, did well at first but was also affected by the market's declining fortunes. Dominic's volatile personality brought him into conflict with successive market managers and other vendors over matters relating to the running of the market, and he decided to relocate to the Italian commercial centre on 95th Street. The closing of Ital-Canadian Meats in December 1986 left the city market without a retail butcher for the first time since 1916.

The gradual demise of Prince Rupert Fish Market, which had sold continuously at the city market since 1919, was protracted and difficult to watch. When its last owner closed the doors in April 1996, due to bankruptcy, another long-time market tradition was over. Only Hinse Poultry Farms, strictly speaking not a retailer because it never acted as a middleman for products outside its own operation, maintained a viable, if diminished, business during the 1980s and 1990s, partly due to patronage from the local Asian community.[59]

A substantial group of stallholders who had moved from the old to the new market continued to operate their stalls throughout the period of decline. Flore Hinse, for example, who maintained her market stall even when her son Denis took over one of the retail store spaces, continued to sell until well into the 1990s, assisted by her daughter Laurette who took over the stall herself when Flore retired. Other elderly women, some with family members to support them and some without, continued to attend as long as they were physically able. The Granstroms of Virginia Park Greenhouses ended a presence which had begun in 1929 when they gave up their stall at the market in June 1993. But the Thiels of Thiel's Greenhouses, the Wankes of South Cooking Lake Greenhouses, the Frenzels of Evergreen Gardens, the Rasimus family of 3R Greenhouses, and the Van Dorssers of Birchdale, were among those whose memories of the old market remained a factor in their commitment to the new one.

Not all regular vendors after 1965 had memories of the old market to sustain their commitment to the new one. Pearl Chamaschuk (doll clothes and home baking), Eyot Creek (vegetables and cheese), Pat Francis (honey), Otto Holzbauer (dried and fresh mushrooms, wild rice, prepared foods), Robert Kublik (honey), Kuhlmann's (vegetables and bedding plants), Lois Noble (baking), the Veermans (vegetables and bedding plants), and the Vissers (vegetables) were only some of those who had never sold at the old city market but whose regular and long-term appearance each Saturday morning gave the market on 97th its specific character and a measure of stability.

5.18

In 1997, Otto Holzbauer reluctantly decided to close his stall at the city market. The day this photograph of Otto and Ann Tong was taken was to have been their last day there. However, after a short absence, they decided to re-open the Mo-Na Mushroom stall, much to the satisfaction of their customers. Author's photograph

Despite the numbers of vendors who maintained a long-term presence at the city market during the 1980s and 1990s, there were many more who came and went, staying for periods that varied from a few weeks to a few months to a few years. The trend turned into a spiral, with vendors leaving for lack of customers and customers leaving for lack of vendors.[60]

One vendor whose regular presence at the city market on 97th Street did as much as any to attract and sustain customers throughout the 1980s and 1990s was Otto Holzbauer. Otto moved to Edmonton in 1976 with his wife, Rita, and four children (aged thirteen to twenty-one). He was almost fifty years old at the time, and his working career had been spent mainly in the building and decorating trades. Canada, however, seemed a good place to indulge two other of Otto's skills, a knowledge of mushrooms, gained attending the Trade and Forestry School at Grazen, Czechoslovakia, in 1941, and a knowledge and love of cookery he had learned from his mother. The idea to establish a business around the harvesting and selling of mushrooms and other wild products, such as berries and wild rice, came to him during his first few years in Canada when

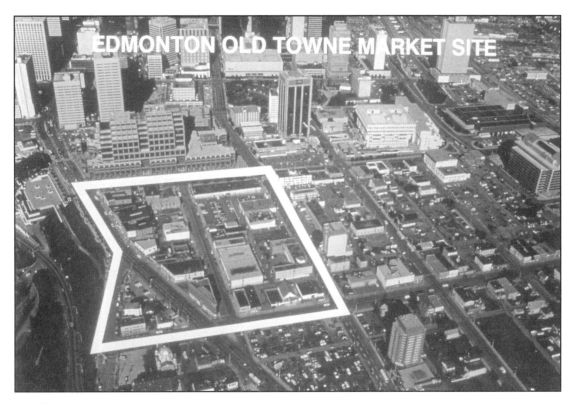

5.19

This aerial photograph designating the "Old Towne Market Site" as it was defined by the EDDC clearly shows 97th Street as the eastern boundary of the highrise portion of Edmonton's "downtown." The market is the long, low building in the top, right-hand corner of the site. The site contains many of Edmonton's oldest buildings and the EDDC continues to promote an approach to re-development aimed at preserving and re-vitalizing Edmonton's architectural and historical heritage. Courtesy of the EDDC

he took visiting European friends to the mountains and into the forests. Mo-Na Food Enterprises Ltd. (the name is short for Mother Nature) was incorporated in May 1980 and, by Christmas of that year, had obtained an export licence. In January 1981, Otto took a stall at the city market.

The city market played a small but important role in the business development of Mo-Na Mushrooms, and Otto's regular attendance, usually assisted by Ann Tong, attracted and supported a strong customer following. For Otto, the market provided an opportunity to talk to his Canadian customers about what they liked and how they used the products they bought from him. Every week, he brought a new array of prepared foods to the market, handing out samples and soliciting reactions. Without the city market, Otto's venture from raw to prepared products would have been difficult to accomplish. Without Mo-Na Mushrooms, the city market would have missed one of its most energetic and flamboyant vendors of the 1980s and 1990s.[61]

Disappointed, perplexed, and sometimes angry about the city market's falling fortunes in the 1990s, vendors such as Otto Holzbauer, many of whom acted for periods of time on the Downtown City Market Association, tried to explain the decline and made tentative efforts to bring about a reversal.[62] In 1994, acting on the assumption that the city's lack of vested interest in the fortunes of the market was the main reason for decline, a group of vendors under then president Steve Madsen worked on a plan whereby the Downtown City Market Association would assume direct fiscal and management responsibilities for the city market. This initiative, which happened to coincide with a much more elaborate project being promoted by the EDDC to demolish the 97th Street Market and to replace it with a new facility to be built as part of an Old Towne Market redevelopment project, divided vendor opinion. Eventually, the vendor management notion was dropped in favour of awaiting the outcome of the Old Towne Market plan.

The Old Towne Market plan, although strictly speaking not a civic initiative but rather one developed and promoted by the EDDC, grew out of attempts by two city departments to revive the fortunes of the city market by giving it a new role in civic life. As early as 1977, when the planning department commissioned Bell Spotowski Architects to carry out the *Southeast Civic Centre Urban Design Study*, the city was open to that report's recommendation that the market be expanded and redeveloped as part of a new Chinatown — a recommendation considered for, but ultimately excluded from, the 1979 Chinatown Plan. Nevertheless, two features of Bell Spotowski's report as it pertained to the city market informed subsequent civic thinking — first, the notion that the market should be expanded rather than contracted, and second, the preference for private over public ownership. Although these ideas had the status of mere suggestions in the Bell Spotowski study, they were elaborated and formalized in the much more specific "Edmonton City Market Study" completed by HLA Consultants for the Department of Real Estate and Housing, in 1982.

The "Edmonton City Market Study" (1982), the most detailed and extensive study ever commissioned by the city in an effort to address its ongoing problems with the viability of its public market, made several recommendations that were to radically alter all subsequent policy decisions regarding it. HLA's research, which included a thorough review of the market's history and operations as well as a study of comparable markets in both Canada and the United States, led to a series of related conclusions. First, HLA concluded that a "demand analysis" indicated a need for a "farmers' market" in the downtown. Secondly, they pointed to the inadequacy of the existing facility and to the underutilization of the site. Thirdly and most importantly, after selecting Granville Island Market in Vancouver and Pike Place Market in Seattle as appropriate models, HLA recommended that the city have the 97th Street site redeveloped as a "festival market" and operated as a private venture — not a public service. Despite potential confusion over terms such as "public market," "farmers' market," and "festival market," the HLA report was favourably received by the Department of Real Estate and Housing which was ready, in 1983, to act on it by beginning to solicit developer proposals when Mayor Laurence Decore pre-empted such action by appointing a task force to study all development in the "Heart of the City."[63]

HLA's terminology and approach to the future of the city market were adopted and expanded by the mayor's "Task Force on the Heart of the City" before being incorporated into its "A Blue Print for the 21st Century," released in August 1984. In that document, the "festival market" was renamed the "international festival market" and the models proposed included Ghiradelli Square in San Francisco, Faneuil Hall in Boston, and Harborplace in Baltimore:

> Single-handedly, these downtown development projects, with their distinctive architecture, unusual settings, special mix of shops, restaurants and entertainment and unique urban style, rekindled sparks of life in their cities and, in turn, became celebrations of the vibrancy and diversity of city life.... The same opportunity exists in Edmonton with the present City Market.[64]

The new role for the Edmonton City Market, as envisioned by the task force, was to be the catalyst for urban redevelopment in the depressed and run-down area north of Jasper Avenue between 96th and 97th streets. Conceived as a project "achievable through the cooperation of the City and the landowners and an imaginative developer," the task of replacing the city market with an international festival marketplace was earmarked for a then non-existent entity — the Edmonton Downtown Development Corporation.

The EDDC, founded as a nonprofit corporation in 1986, was itself the product of the 1984 Task Force Report. The task force recommendation that a downtown development corporation be formed was based on the assumption that a mechanism was needed to bring together the needs and interests of all three levels of government with those of private enterprise, particularly in order to conceive and coordinate major development projects. Other cities had successfully founded such entities, and the task force believed that one was required in Edmonton. Although "A Blue Print for the 21st Century" did not say so, it was generally assumed that the newly formed EDDC would take on several of the projects recommended in it, including and especially the conversion of the city market to an international festival marketplace which would revitalize the east Jasper Avenue area.[65]

In the hands of the EDDC, which commissioned the architectural firm of Chandler Kennedy Architects to carry out a study of the east Jasper and city

5.20

This concept plan (Kasian Kennedy, 1992) for the re-development of the Old Towne Market site was proposed as a replacement for the existing market building. Courtesy of the EDDC

market area, the concept of an international festival market was transformed by 1987 into the Old Towne Market plan, a comprehensive scheme to rejuvenate the irregular block bounded by 97th Street on the west, 96th Street on the east, Jasper Avenue on the south, and 102nd Avenue (Harbin Road) to the north. Budgeted at just short of $160 million dollars and intended to include, in addition to a "public market," "specialty retail outlets, restaurants, a children's market, artists' studios, loft offices, an arts and culture complex, a cinema complex, performing arts venues, two hotels and two levels of underground parking," the Old Towne Market project was intended to attract developer interest and would have led, eventually, to the demolition of the "new" city market and the withdrawal of the city from the provision of market services.[66] However, despite dogged persistence on the part of Armin Preiksaitis, president of the EDDC from its founding until his departure in 1995, to realize the Old Towne Market scheme, a rejuvenated city market failed to materialize. Even the updating of the Chandler Kennedy plan by Kassian Kennedy Architecture, Interior Design and Planning in 1992, and the formation of an Old Towne Market Corporation in March 1993 as an implementation mechanism for the project failed to attract and retain a developer. By 1998, by which time the Old Towne Market Corporation had been dissolved, the orthodoxies of city planning had changed, and the notion that a megaproject such as the Old Towne Market scheme was an appropriate way to achieve urban renewal had few champions, even within the city and the EDDC.

The collapse of the Old Towne Market project, though unimportant to most vendors and customers who had always viewed it with skepticism, could only have spelled doom for the city market. Saturdays in 1997 and early 1998 were, for vendors and customers, little more than gloomy and depressing exercises in habit, or loyalty, or both. Although the market gardeners continued to do well during bedding plant and harvest seasons and Hinse Poultry Farms continued to sell out to their many loyal customers, particularly at Chinese or western holidays, most vendors cut their sales staff to the minimum and many customers either stopped coming or were lured away to other farmers' markets in the city. The then part-time manager, Jerry Sumka, knew the market's days were numbered but was temperamentally disinclined to turn this knowledge into an issue. Only the intervention of the EDDC, this time with a low-budget, pragmatic approach to assuming management responsibilities, could have saved the city market from closure after almost one hundred years of continuous operation.

5.21

On 31 July 1999, vendors at the Edmonton City Market attempted to re-create the market as it might have been in the 1940s. Many former vendors visited for the day, the Provincial Museum of Alberta loaned artifacts recalling the 1940s, and vendors like Leslie and Ron Prins dressed for the part. Author's photograph

In the summer of 1998, when the EDDC went to council to present and defend its "Proposal to Revitalize the City Market," its motivation for doing so was still rooted in the idea that the market had a role to play in downtown Edmonton. Its approach to defining that role, however, had changed. Replacing the emphasis on capital-intensive development designed to draw tourists and locals together in an international marketplace that had characterized the Old Towne Market project was a new emphasis on community involvement and community building, with the market playing a time-honoured role mediating the interests of country and city to the benefit of both partners. In October 1998, the EDDC began a three-year mandate, endorsed by the Edmonton City Council, to manage the Edmonton City Market.

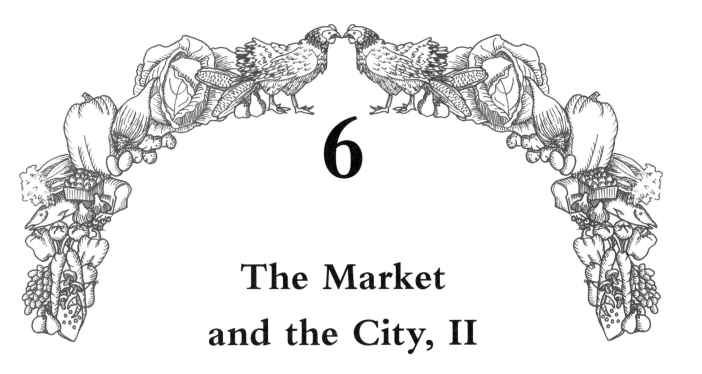

6

The Market
and the City, II

When W. W. Winspear articulated his "Thoughts Relating to [a] Proposed New Farmer's Market" in a report submitted by the Edmonton Chamber of Commerce to the city administration in March 1963, he expressed mild surprise that the Edmonton City Market had persisted so vigorously as a civic institution:

> There is a natural inclination to feel that with the ascendency of super markets, the day of the farmers' public market must be coming to a close. There does not, however, seem to be any indication that there is much fall in the rentals of stalls in our market.

In fact, Winspear could not find much to criticize about the city market, except perhaps that it was run by the city, for his predisposition in favour of private enterprise, combined with his judgment that the market was financially viable, led him to question the need for public sponsorship. What Winspear saw when he looked at the market and reflected on the matter of whether it should be kept or closed, was an institution that contributed to the economic and cultural strengths of the city. He believed the market encouraged market-garden enterprises, drew people to the centre who then supported surrounding businesses, and offered consumers direct access to local producers. He also reflected on the market's "symbolic value," a value derived from the role it had played in the "integration of city with surrounding countryside." For Winspear, the cultural benefits conferred on the city by the market derived also from its social and celebratory aspects. He saw the market as a potential tourist attraction and, because of the street traffic it drew, he believed it would "enhance and encourage the development of the CivicCentre [sic]."[1]

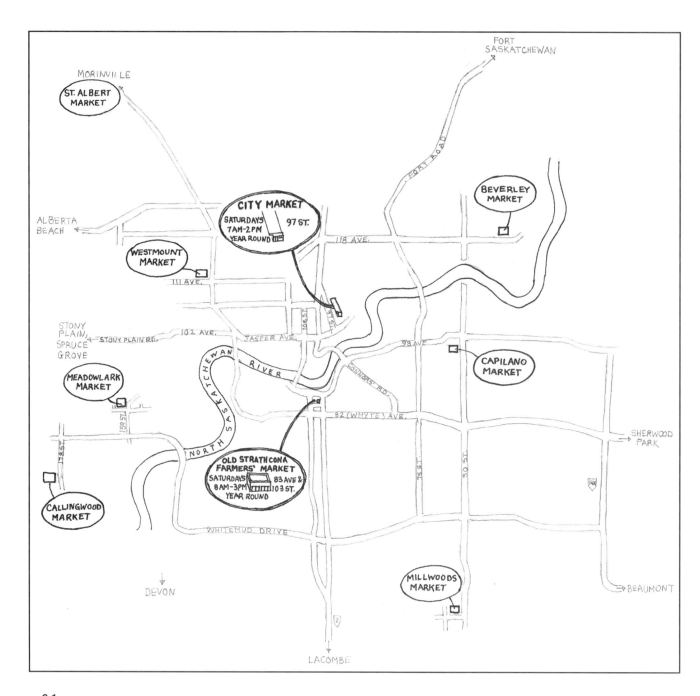

6.1

2000: Farmers' markets in and around Edmonton. Drawing by Barbara Budenz

Winspear's assessment of the benefits to the city of retaining its market recalls arguments made earlier in the century by the market's first promoters and provokes questions about the role produce markets have played, do and will play in the culture and economies of urban places. In April 1900, Philip Heiminck had insisted that "there is no greater impetus to the growth of any town than a well established market,"[2] and his views were echoed eleven years later by an *Edmonton Bulletin* reporter:

> A good market, with moderate fees charged and reasonable conveniences afforded is the best means the city has of holding trade against the competition of other towns.... It is the strongest inducement the city can offer for getting the farmers of the district to produce the dairy, poultry and other products needed by the townsman and for making the farmer a frequent visitor to the city and a more liberal patron of the city stores.[3]

Between December 1900 and October 1964, the Edmonton City Market consistently drew farmers and urban dwellers to its central Rice Street location, proving that, in Edmonton at least, Heiminck had been right in predicting that a market would be an economic and a cultural asset to the city. During these same years, however, other urban centres across Alberta had failed to establish markets rooted deeply in the lives of their communities.

Calgary passed its first by-law "to Establish a Public Market and Weigh Scales" in 1885, with the market to be located between Byers Blacksmith Shop and Drinkwater Street (2nd Street East) while the weigh scale was located at the corner of McTavish Street and Stephen Avenue.[4] Between 1885 and 1914, the Calgary Public Market was moved several times — not a difficult task as it was usually held in the open air protected at most by a rudimentary shelter. In 1914, largely due to the persuasive efforts of Alderman Annie Gale — whose membership in the Consumers' League gave support to her lobby for a new covered market — the city of Calgary built a "handsome civic brick and sandstone Calgary Public Market" on 2nd Avenue and 3rd Street East.[5] That same year, a report in the *Macleod Spectator* suggests that business at the Calgary market was brisk, but, by 1918, Mrs. Gale, this time acting as advisor to the mayor and council, "found little or no business doing" there, and she recommended that the city change its market policy.[6] Although the Calgary Public Market probably did not close until about 1930, in 1919 the vacated Calgary City Post Office at 709 - 2nd Street next to the city hall was renovated by a group of citizens, many of them Jewish, to become a privately operated market. In 1953, this market also closed and the building was appropriated for another use.[7] From 1953 until after the province of Alberta introduced a farmers' market incentive

6.2

Sod turning for city market shed, Calgary, 1908. GA, NA-2399-5

program in 1973, no public or quasi-public market in Calgary served the citizenry with local produce — a vivid contrast to Edmonton's market tradition which gradually shut out private ventures, coalescing instead around the large and vigorous Rice Street (Edmonton City) Market.

The opening of a livestock and farm produce market in Irvine, Alberta, in 1906, was advertised and reported in the *Medicine Hat News*, but, although the first day's business was promising, the endeavour seems to have foundered in a matter of months.[8] In March 1914, a produce market opened in Macleod, Alberta, but by September of the same year, a letter in the *Macleod Spectator* reported that "the attendance of farmers at the Macleod Public Market during the past two months has not been as large as was expected by the market committee."[9] In September 1909, a writer to the *Claresholm Review* promoted the founding of a public market with the argument that "there is only one way of keeping the trade and that is by showing very practical appreciation of the fact that the business life of the town is dependent on the farmers."[10] It is worth noting, however, that, despite the commonly held views of the reporter for the *Claresholm Review*, public markets founded early in the settlement period failed

6.3

This photograph of the Calgary Public Market was likely taken shortly after it opened in 1914 — the same year that Edmonton opened its new (and rapidly abandoned) building on 101st Street and 107th Avenue. (See Fig. 2.13) The neo-classical facade of the Calgary Public Market suggests a civic status which it may, in fact, never have enjoyed. GA, NA-644-5

or floundered in most communities in Alberta and the consequences of these failures, economic and social, remain open to speculation.

In 1963, when Winspear prepared his report, the Edmonton City Market may have been the only public market operating in Alberta. Almost certainly it was the biggest and most culturally prominent of any that existed. Is it possible, as Winspear suggested in his report, that the market served a civic purpose in the 1960s comparable to the one Heiminck had envisaged for it in 1900 and that this purpose was as valuable in 1963 as it had been more than half a century earlier? What kinds of stories drawn from its history could possibly illustrate the role played by the Edmonton City Market in the simultaneous production of a civic culture and a local economy?

In 1919, when sixteen-year-old Robert Simonet arrived in Edmonton accompanying his eighteen-year-old sister, Marguerite, who had decided to marry an Edmonton-based Canadian soldier she had met in France, Heiminck had not yet died and the newly housed city market was busy enough that the open shed had been filled in with brick walls and two fish stores had just been added to complete the range of products sold there. Despite his youth, it

6.4

All who knew or met Robert Simonet reported that he liked nothing better than to spend time in his greenhouses. By the time this photograph was taken, probably some time in the mid-1960s, he had achieved international renown for his achievements in plant breeding. Courtesy of Janine Dunn

would only be a few years before Simonet would rely on the market to earn a living while he pursued a complementary career as a plant breeder. Working with plant varieties suitable to Edmonton's climate and growing conditions and catering to contemporary tastes, Simonet earned an international reputation in a local context where the market featured as a key cultural institution — a showcase for local products, a meeting-ground for local producers, an opportunity to make money growing and selling produce, a place to observe and assess customer demand, and a place to make contacts with fellow vendors who were potential customers for his newly developed plant varieties.

Simonet, whose widowed mother ran a tobacconist store in Paris to earn a living, was brought up by his grandmother in the town of Vimpelles, south of Paris along the Seine. Perhaps it was the grandmother who nurtured her grandson's interest in plant breeding for she was a keen gardener: family members suggest Robert may have had his own small garden at her home in Vimpelles.

Whatever the cause of his passion, Simonet arrived in Edmonton with little more than a few books and a determination to make his living in an occupation related to the growing and breeding of plants, despite his lack of formal training in horticulture.

Not long after Simonet arrived in Edmonton, he began to work for Peter Juchli, a bachelor who raised vegetables in the Bonnie Doon area and sold them at the city market. Perhaps taking his cue from Juchli, Simonet became an urban gardener/farmer, renting vacant land on or near 83rd Avenue and growing vegetables. At the same time, he pursued his studies by any means available, making use of the public and the University of Alberta libraries and staff to further his knowledge of plant genetics. In 1929, he married Lillian Herard of Edmonton and in 1930, close to the beginning of the Great Depression, he and Lillian bought five acres in King Edward Park (near Bonnie Doon) at 7529 - 81st Street and began to earn their living selling vegetables at the market.

Robert and Lillian did not have children but, like many couples selling at the city market, they relied on extended family to assist them in the garden and with the market selling. Robert's older sister Georgette had also moved to Edmonton, from France in the 1920s, and a crop of nieces and one nephew born to his two sisters in the 1920s would later all help with their uncle's business. The nephew, Marc Gielen, eventually took over the market-gardening side of his uncle's business and continued to sell at the city market. Around the time Robert and Lillian began selling full time at the market, Mme Simonet left Paris to join her children in Edmonton, and she entered enthusiastically into the role of chief salesperson at her son's market stall.

While Mme Simonet, assisted by her grandchildren, revelled in the sociability of the Saturday markets and was sought out by well-off customers from the west end of the city for her Parisian French and for her tailoring skills as well as for the quality of her son's produce, Robert kept close to the garden and greenhouses, creating new hybrids and hardy varieties of fruits, vegetables, and flowers. Some thought Simonet began his 1930s quest to "crack the code" of the hybrid double-flowering petunia after seeing a fellow vendor selling ones grown from Japanese seed, but his niece Janine Dunn who knew him well, could not corroborate that story.[11] In any case, shortly before World War II broke out in 1939, rendering the Japanese seed unavailable, Simonet solved the puzzle that had absorbed him for several years, a discovery which alleviated his financial dependence on the market because he became the sole producer of double-flowering petunia seed in the western world, selling it throughout Canada and the United States as well as in Europe.

Vendors at the market and market gardeners around Alberta proudly sold Simonet's double-flowering petunias as well as other of his discoveries such as Alta Sweet turnips, a hybrid strawberry developed from a wild Alberta strawberry plant crossed with a less hardy but large-fruited domestic variety, and strawberry rhubarb which was particularly valued for cooking. Writing in the gardening column of the *Globe and Mail*, in 1998, Lois Hole of Hole's Greenhouses remembered driving out to "Bob" Simonet's place east of Sherwood Park with her husband, Ted, in the 1960s to buy their strawberry and petunia seeds and to tour around the greenhouses.[12] Hole celebrated Simonet's work as both "a very important contribution to the war effort" and a great contribution to his country. Too shy and retiring to seek celebrity status, Robert Simonet worked steadily to produce new cultivars. Those that met his standards, developed in response to local tastes and bred to thrive in local growing conditions, moved quickly into production in market gardens around Edmonton to be celebrated in the gardens and on the dinner tables of the citizenry.[13]

Although it is unlikely that Simonet relied on the city market for his livelihood for much more than a decade, it is equally unlikely that the market was simply a backdrop to a career that culminated in national and international recognition. Simonet's arrival in Edmonton in 1919 coincided with a period of growth and consolidation for the market. Urban agriculture was increasingly practised in the years before and after 1919, promoted aggressively by the Edmonton Horticultural and Vacant Lots Garden Association which rented vacant land in populated areas on behalf of the city. Many of these urban farmers became vendors at the city market, including several from the southeast (Bonnie Doon, King Edward Park) area where Simonet settled. Through the market, local agriculture was institutionalized as an urban concern, a partnership which served Edmontonians, including Simonet, especially well throughout the lean 1930s. Although the Edmonton City Market never became a way of life for Simonet as it did for many market gardeners, there is little doubt that it mediated the interests and abilities of this self-taught scientist, providing him with a congenial way to make a living and a channel through which his interests and discoveries quickly became part of the community's wealth and culture.

If Heiminck's confidence in the ability of the city market to stimulate agricultural enterprise was exemplified in the story of Robert Simonet, Winspear's 1963 prediction that preserving the market would continue to serve the economic interests of market gardeners and their customers finds proof in a number of stories, including that of Rudolf (Rudi) Thiel, his wife, Annalotte, and their children, Rudy and Horst. Thiel's Greenhouses, begun in 1960 and thereafter a regular presence at the city market, drew on the old market's reputation, accessibility, and customers during its early years. Once established, Thiel's contributed to the vitality and reputation of the new market building on 97th Street, maintaining a year-round vendor status and establishing a large and faithful clientele.

6.5

When the Thiel family arrived in Canada in 1954, they went first to a farm near Cooking Lake, Alberta, where this photograph was taken. Courtesy of Rudolf Thiel

When Rudi, Annalotte, and their two young boys arrived in the Edmonton area from Germany, in 1954, he a trained farm worker and she a practised cook, they owned practically nothing; rather they owed money to the Lutheran society which had sponsored their emigration and advanced their passage. Rudi, who had a less theoretical interest in plant genetics and reproduction than Simonet, had brought with him some tomato seed from a favoured variety, but it would be several years before he had an opportunity to grow tomatoes from that seed and sell them at the market. That chance came in 1960, when he first managed to obtain an occasional stall at the Edmonton City Market, two years after a combination of happy accident and calculated risk had ended in his buying six acres of land north of Edmonton in the town of Bruderheim.

Unlike Robert Simonet, Rudi Thiel enjoyed selling at the market. By 1962, he was trying to grow vegetables not commonly sold there, some in the greenhouse he had built by fitting pieces of salvaged glass into hand-made wooden frames and some outside. To appeal to his European customers, for instance, he grew root celery. While still selling in the old market building, Rudy grew some perfect green peppers, and Horst, who would have been a teenager at the time, remembered the day Mary Oppelt emerged from her retail store at the south end of the old building and needed a great deal of convincing before she would believe that the peppers had been grown in Edmonton, even in a greenhouse. Thiel's Greenhouses sold petunias grown from Simonet's double-

6.6

By 1960, the Thiel family had moved to their own acreage in Bruderheim. Rudi Thiel built this greenhouse largely with salvaged materials and then went into the business of growing and selling vegetables for a living. Courtesy of Rudolf Thiel

flowering petunia seed, and Horst, who earned a B.Sc. (1970) majoring in horticulture at the University of Alberta, knew the renowned plant breeder and, like Lois Hole, went to see him at the Sherwood Park acreage to which he had moved in the 1950s.

Without the city market, it is unlikely that Thiel's Greenhouses could have grown after 1960 into the thriving business that made it an attractive career prospect for both sons, with Horst entering the business in 1973 and his brother Rudy following in 1981. The market brought Thiel's in touch with a large number of potential customers, many of whom bought year round from their market stall and some of whom began to take the hour's drive to the greenhouses to purchase their bedding plants direct. In the early years, the market generated eighty percent of Thiel's retail earnings, a percentage which gradually diminished to about ten percent in 2000 as the business expanded its greenhouse sales, increased its retail sales outlets by opening garden centres in Vegreville and Fort Saskatchewan and, perhaps more important, as the city market slid further and further into decline, failing to maintain and develop its former following.[14]

But Thiel's Greenhouses was just one of many greenhouse operations founded in the 1960s and 1970s that sought its customers and custom at the city market. Greenhouse businesses run by the Frenzel, Kuhlmann, Veerman, Visser, and Wanke families also became regular vendors at the city market

6.7

Thiel's Greenhouses grew to be a large operation, as this aerial photograph, taken around 1990, illustrates.
Courtesy of Rudolf Thiel

6.8

Market-gardening in and around the City of Edmonton has been popular since the end of the fur trade. This
aerial photograph, taken in 1936, shows Belmont Market Garden in the midst of a large farming area. CEA,
EA-160-244

in the 1960s, 1970s, and even 1980s, joining long-standing vendors such as the Blochlinger, Granstrom, Oppelt, Panasiuk, Rasimus, and Wallish families, who, in earlier decades, had found the market equally useful as a stepping stone to independence and financial security. With sixty major greenhouse businesses within a one-hundred-mile radius of Edmonton in 2000, a much larger number than exist around Calgary or in any other populated area in Alberta, one must at least speculate about the role played by the Edmonton City Market in promoting and sustaining a 'greenhouse culture.'[15]

Market gardening and greenhouse operations may have been the most numerous and the most visible of the family-based businesses to emerge from the crucible of the Edmonton City Market, but they were not the only agricultural enterprises to have been formed there. From the market's earliest years, poultry and eggs were always in high demand on Rice Street. Mrs. Lou Hyndman, Sr., recalling her girlhood in Edmonton and her regular Saturday morning trips to the market with her mother in the 1920s, said it was her mother's preference for capon at Sunday dinner that accounted for their weekly trips to the market from Strathcona. The city market, according to Mrs. Hyndman's mother, was the only good source at the time of fresh local capon.[16] When Mary Svekla made her first trip to the market in the 1950s, it was a fresh chicken she was after and she bought it from a Mrs. Powell, possibly the daughter of Mary Triska. Members of the Asian community in Edmonton were major buyers of poultry at the market but had a decided preference for live birds. Even vendors who did not maintain an outside stall kept enough live chickens in their trucks to supply the needs of regular Asian customers.

About the time Robert Simonet's mother began attending the market on her son's behalf, Flore Hinse, motivated by the need to expand her young family's income, decided to start a small business there selling butter she made from milk from her mother's cows and eggs bought from her mother's farm neighbours. Perhaps, in the beginning, she thought it would be a temporary activity, a way of supplementing the small income her husband earned as a labourer until he earned more. She travelled at first from Beaumont with the Magnan family from Looma, returning with them at the end of the day. Over time, Flore stopped selling butter and expanded the egg and poultry side of her business, drawing in her husband to help when the project grew beyond her ability to handle alone. By the time Robert Simonet's economic dependence on the market had ceased and he was hiring local women to do the delicate and tedious cross-pollinating and seed harvesting in his greenhouses, Flore and her husband René had settled on the market as the locus of their career, travelling in and out from Beaumont each Saturday to sell chickens and eggs to their market customers. Thus defined, Hinse Poultry supplied the needs of a family of eight throughout the 1930s, 1940s, and 1950s.[17]

The poultry vendors, many of whom were clustered in the centre aisles of the old market building, offered more choice to their customers in the 1930s, 1940s, and 1950s than would have been immediately apparent to a casual buyer. Konrad and Minnie Farkas, for example, did not raise their own birds but finished them with home-grown grain and occasionally with milk. As did other vendors, they slaughtered their birds at home the day before they were to be sold, but, unlike some other vendors, they presented them beautifully, making sure that their yellow feet were washed as clean as the bodies. Only the Antmans, according to Frank Farkas, brought capons to the market in the 1950s, and they may also have been among the first to experiment with hormones because Frank remembers that the Antman's chickens were always much bigger than any others.[18] And then, there were barnyard-raised chickens sold from time to time by vegetable vendors such as Mary Sernowski who brought them only when they were surplus to her own need. Marie-Anne (Magnan) Brassard sometimes raised turkeys, geese, and ducks in addition to chickens. She was very particular about her killing technique, preferring to cut their

6.9

Taken on a Friday in the mid-1950s, this photograph shows Hinse chickens ready to go to market the next day. Wrapping the heads of newly killed birds in wax paper was routine practice for the poultry vendors. Courtesy of Grace Kipling

throats and hang them rather than cutting off their heads. Flore Hinse began, like Minnie and Konrad Farkas, buying chickens from farms around Beaumont. She went on, however, to raise the birds she sold and, when she could not fully supply the demand of her customers, began to contract with neighbours to get an assured supply of additional birds. This was the business she and René found almost too much to handle on their own in the mid-1950s, leading them to make a proposal to their son Denis, which he decided to accept.

In 1955, after four years of hard study at Collège St. Jean where he planned to take his Bachelor of Arts and become a teacher, Denis Hinse was presented with

6.10

This photograph shows Flore Hinse (foreground) and her husband René (with his back to the camera) selling chicken at the old city market around 1955. Courtesy of Grace Kipling

a choice — to continue his studies or to go into business with his parents. Denis knew and liked his parents' business and had enjoyed selling at the city market since childhood. He had particularly enjoyed his dealings with Asian customers, joking with them on the square and making efforts to learn enough Cantonese phrases to keep a conversation lively. Between 1955, when he decided to join his parents in the poultry business, and 1966, when he formally took over the business from his parents, Denis sold from a second family stall, developed his own style of selling, and cultivated a clientele that was a little different from the one that faithfully patronized his mother. During the years of his informal apprenticeship, Denis formed definite ideas about how to raise high-quality poultry and about how to sell it. An openness to his oriental customers and a willingness to accommodate their tastes by saving for them parts of the birds rejected by most Caucasians, led to an expansion of the wholesale side of the business as Denis began to sell directly to restaurants and small businesses in Chinatown. By 1966, the year he built his own processing plant and began to hire staff outside his extended family, he was ready to take his mother's business to a new level of size and complexity.

Between 1966 and 2000, Hinse Poultry Farms retained many of the features defined for it by Flore and René, although the addition of the processing plant introduced a new set of logistics and a new set of business and development opportunities. As before, the business remained family owned and managed, with Denis's son Gerry taking over major ownership and management responsibilities in the 1990s. Denis's wife, Marie, his sisters Angèle, Laurette, and Grace, his son Victor, daughter Denise, and her children, along with many other family members sold at the city and, from 1986, at the Strathcona markets. Staff hired outside the family to work in the processing plant increased from five in 1966 to approximately eighteen full-time workers. Sales to restaurants, which began with Flore's determination never to bring a chicken home at the end of a market day, expanded to include more

6.11

Denis Hinse always joked and laughed with his customers when he could. Here Denis is selling at the old market some time around 1955. Courtesy of Grace Kipling

restaurants and several higher-end retail stores in both Edmonton and Calgary. The practice of contracting out production to Beaumont-area farmers, begun by Flore as a way of ensuring adequate supply, was continued as a preferred alternative to mass production. Processing, which had been simple in Flore's day when all birds had been sold 'New York dressed' (plucked but intact), became more complex. By 2000, it was rare to sell a 'New York dressed' bird. Instead, whole birds were eviscerated to be sold with, or without, the giblets. In response to changing consumer tastes, which favoured more processing, Hinses began first to sell poultry cuts and then introduced value-added products such as smoked and fresh boneless turkey rolls, ground chicken, chicken sausage, and even chicken pepperoni. And, finally, while for Flore the term "market" was reserved for the only one she knew, the Edmonton City Market, Hinse Poultry took on another Saturday market in 1986 when it became a vendor at the Old Strathcona Farmers' Market.

A major factor in the longevity of Hinse Poultry Farms as a local, market-based business, was Denis's decision to build a processing plant in 1966, because it was not long afterwards that regulations were introduced requiring poultry vendors to have their birds processed in a provincially inspected plant. The Hinse plant, one of only five (in 2000) in the province not run by the giant Lilydale company, began processing birds for a host of small producers, many of whom were selling at other farmers' markets around the province.[19] Beginning in the 1980s, the processing plant became the site of testing and experimentation carried out by the University of Alberta Department of Agriculture, a collaboration which lasted until 2000 when the university completed its own facility. Collaboration of another sort — with a Vietnamese family interested in developing a particular kind of sausage for the oriental market in Alberta — was a natural outgrowth of Denis's city market contacts and has been a long-standing sideline of the plant's operations.

The Edmonton City Market was critical to the conception and definition of Hinse Poultry Farms as a local, family-run business and the market's continuation, along with the continuation of the Old Strathcona Farmers' Market, remain essential if the business is to continue at something approximating its present scale. Through the city market, Hinse Poultry gained a substantial following and developed the customer service ethic that has sustained it through almost seventy years of continuous operation. Direct sales at farmers' markets, as for greenhouses, are the mainstay of Hinse Poultry, generating a higher percentage of profit than can be made selling wholesale. Without the existence of farmers' markets, it is unlikely that Hinse Poultry could exist to expand the variety of product and range of choice to Edmonton's growing urban population.[20]

In 1973, when Hugh Horner, then Minister of Agriculture for the province of Alberta, announced a program to promote and assist the formation of farmers' markets in Alberta, his intention was to support the development of agricultural enterprises such as Thiel's Greenhouses and Hinse Poultry Farms by providing more outlets for direct sales.[21] Produce markets had become all but extinct in Alberta, the major exception being the Edmonton City Market, which was still a popular civic institution and perennially unable to accommodate the numbers of vendors waiting to get in.[22] The Alberta Market Gardeners' Association, some of whose members had sold at the city market and were familiar with its benefits to local agricultural producers, was fully behind the program which provided capital and advertising grants along with a variety of assistance and support to fledgling markets. Government vegetable and fruit specialists were also strong supporters of the new program, realizing the importance of direct-marketing outlets for small producers and the benefits they stood to gain from customer feedback.

Between 1973 and 1989, while the Edmonton City Market was moving from a state of mild disorientation into one of severe decline, the Alberta farmers' market program achieved its major goals. Over one hundred farmers' markets of varying size sprang up across the province, including several in Edmonton and environs. Alberta Health collaborated with Alberta Agriculture to establish a policy for food and safety regulations, and a farmers' market section based on that policy was written into the Public Health Act. In 1989, a fully elaborated set of guidelines for farmers' markets in Alberta was adopted by the Minister of Agriculture and Rural Development, allowing his department to reduce its staff and to cease providing direct material support to markets.

Since 1989, Alberta Agriculture's relation to farmers' markets has changed. No longer does it supply grants, promotional items, or free advertising. Rather, it administers the process by which farmers' markets are "approved," a term which indicates conformance to the guidelines. It initiates and carries out reviews and alterations to its policies, health regulations, or guidelines. And, through its part-time Farmers' Market administrator, it offers advisory services to groups and agencies wanting to start new markets or having operational difficulties with existing ones.[23]

The formation of the Old Strathcona Farmers' Market in 1983 and its rapid rise to become both an economic and a cultural force in its community, serves as one illustration of how the farmer's market program has worked in Alberta.[24] Beyond that, the Old Strathcona Farmers' Market's popularity among customers and the role it has played in launching a number of successful small businesses, recall the pre-1965 days of the Edmonton City Market and send us back to questions raised earlier in this chapter about the role produce markets have, do, and will play in the culture and economy of urban life. What, one is tempted to ask, when contemplating the historic reversal of the city market's decline and the corresponding rise of the Strathcona market, is the successful formula for creating a market that is a vital rather than a superficial element of its community?

When the Old Strathcona Foundation, an organization dedicated to fostering a revitalization of the Strathcona area of the city, decided, in 1983, to sponsor a farmers' market under the aegis of the Alberta Agriculture program, its primary goal was to bring street traffic to the heart of the historic centre of Strathcona. A market, thought Elaine Warwick, who spearheaded the initiative for the foundation, was consistent with that organization's wish to emphasize local culture and local production, and it was a project which could be referred back to its historical origins when, in 1909, the former city of Strathcona built a market building and installed new scales on the very outdoor site (northeast corner of 104th Street and 83rd Avenue) chosen by the foundation for its first outdoor summer market.[25]

The first stage in the Strathcona market's coming of age was reached in 1986 when the Old Strathcona Foundation turned over the job of managing the market to a legally structured not-for-profit corporation run by the vendors. It was also in 1986 that arrangements were made to lease the old bus barns on 83rd Avenue and 103rd Street from the city, making it possible for the Old Strathcona Farmers' Market to operate year round. Despite many growing pains, most of these expressed as squabbles among the vendors involved in its management, the Strathcona market flourished and grew, generating enough revenue through stall rents to be able to plow some of its profits back into the restoration and upkeep of the old building.

In 1994, prompted by the city of Edmonton, which held the lease on the bus barns, the Old Strathcona Farmers' Market was reconstituted as a not-for-profit society to give it a more open and democratic structure. Also in 1994, Jim O'Neill was hired as the market's full-time manager, and, in 1996, a renegotiated twenty-year lease agreement was signed with the city of Edmonton for the bus barns. Run by a twelve-member board of directors, with day-to-day practical arrangements being made by four committees responsible for finance, vendors, facilities, and buskers, the Old Strathcona Farmers' Market has drawn thousands of customers most Saturdays during the 1990s and has begun to generate a substantial record as a starting ground for small agricultural-and craft-based businesses.[26]

Despite obvious and significant differences in the origins, affiliations, and management structures of the Edmonton City Market and the Old Strathcona Farmers' Market, there is one important point on which a comparison yields insights. The years during which the Edmonton City Market flourished were years when it embodied a popularly held and powerful civic idea, the interdependence of country and city. What customers bought, along with their turnips and their capons, was the satisfaction of representing the countryside on their tables and celebrating its bounty through their purchases. Similarly, the Strathcona market's success can be traced back to the power and efficacy of an idea, the ability of local production to transform the quality of urban life. Determined to guide Strathcona's revitalization away from the model of anonymous international mall culture, the Old Strathcona Foundation's initiatives, which also included the Fringe Theatre Festival and the renovation of the Princess Theatre, tapped into Edmontonians' mall fatigue and their reaction against the formal, monolithic, and hostile-to-pedestrian manner in which Edmonton's downtown had been developed. Local enterprises, it would seem, find farmers' markets a congenial outlet for their products only when these markets reflect, through their sites, architecture, management, and surroundings, an informing idea which brings customer and vendor onto common ground.

By October 1998, when the City of Edmonton gave over the management of the market to the Edmonton Downtown Development Corporation (EDDC), the city market had long lost the excitement that emanates from a produce market in full celebratory mode. The country had not entirely deserted its former home at the city market, with many long-time vendors retaining their stalls well into the 1990s and even to 2000, while many newer vendors, such as Kuhlmann's Market Gardens and Greenhouses (began selling 1972), the De Klerks from Eyot Creek (began selling in 1978), and Otto Holzbauer of Mo-Na Mushrooms (began selling January 1981), represented a continuation of the important and various role the country has to play in urban life. And there were customers who continued to patronize the city market, primarily to search out the best of locally grown produce. Joyce Pearson for example, whose job with Northwestern Utilities' Blue Flame Kitchen (1960-98) had given her countless opportunities to promote the city market during her working career, remained an enthusiastic shopper throughout the most dreary of the city market's days.[27] But thirty-three years after the city market had been displaced from the geographical centre of the city around which its identity had been created, the few remnants of urban life that surrounded the new market building in 1965, especially Chinatown and businesses like W. W. Arcade, had been all but blotted out to make way for monolithic buildings, leaving the market without an urban context — derelict and in a kind of cultural no-man's-land.

Changing urban tastes have, against all common sense, as Winspear noted in his 1963 report for the Edmonton Chamber of Commerce, not undermined the role farmers' markets have the potential to play in city life. In fact, informed by powerful ideas such as the interdependence of country and city, the ability of local production to transform urban life and, more recently, the perceived need to create an economic model which features the concept of sustainability, the numbers of farmers' markets in Alberta, in Canada, and across North America are increasing.[28] The Edmonton City Market stands to benefit from this trend, but only if it can recapture its role of mediating and commingling rural and urban culture.

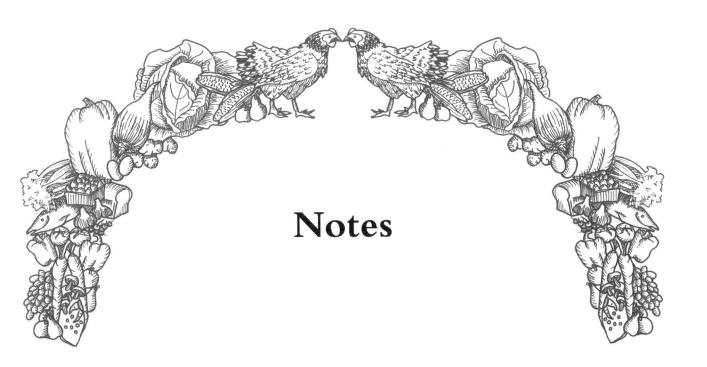

Notes

Chapter 1

1. *Edmonton Journal*, 4 March 1962.
2. Mary Svekla, interview with author, Edmonton, Alberta, 13 August 1993.
3. Mary Sernowski, interviews with author, St. Albert, Alberta, 3 and 14 December 1992, 20 January 1993.
4. *Edmonton Bulletin*, 6 April 1900.
5. John M. Camp, *The Athenian Agora: Excavations in the Heart of Classical Athens* (London: Thames and Hudson, 1986), 14, 172.
6. This condensed version of a complicated process relies on many newspaper articles and archival records which will be cited in the more detailed treatment of the 1914 market in Chapter 2.
7. The actual figure, $3,781.88, appears in the "City of Edmonton Financial Statements and Reports for year ending December 31, 1916," CEA.
8. Peter Lupul, interviews with author, Edmonton, Alberta, 9 and 22 September and 4 October 1993.
9. Howard Saalman, *Medieval Cities*, Planning and Cities Series, General Editor, George R. Collins (New York: George Braziller, 1968), 37.
10. *Edmonton Journal*, 19 September 1962.
11. *Edmonton Journal*, 4 September 1962.

12. Westward Ho chapter of the Imperial Order of the Daughters of the Empire and Children of the Empire (now known as the Imperial Order Daughters of the Empire or IODE) to His Worship the Mayor and City Council, 15 February 1911, M.S. 209, File 127, CEA. The Beaverhill chapter wrote to the mayor and city council on the same day.

13. *Edmonton Bulletin*, 31 January 1911.

14. Morell and Nichols, landscape architects, "A Report on City Planning," 1 November 1912, CEA.

15. Mrs. Mabel Dean to Alderman Findlay, 10 (illegible) May 1926, R.G. 11, City Commissioners correspondence, CEA.

16. Paul Zucker, *Town and Square: From the Agora to the Village Green* (New York: Columbia University Press, 1959), describes the historical configurations of market spaces and explains them as responses to secular and religious forces in European society (75).

17. "We claim and firmly believe that a town especially of the size of ours without a market has little right to demand even the title of a village that aspires to prosperity." A letter written by Philip Heiminck and published in the *Edmonton Bulletin*, 6 April 1900.

18. Marion MacRae and Anthony Adamson, *Cornerstones of Order: Courthouses and Town Halls of Ontario, 1784-1914* (Toronto: Clarke, Irwin, 1983), 213.

19. City historical pamphlet on the market published in 1996.

20. MacRae and Adamson, *Cornerstones of Order*, 76.

21. Stephen A. Otto, Unpublished paper, "First City Hall (1834-45)," 1986.

22. MacRae and Adamson, *Cornerstones of Order*, 72-73.

23. Otto, "First City Hall (1834-45)", 10.

24. Market Committee Minutes, 1876-1882; Market, License & Health Committee Minutes, 1883-1908; Market Committee Reports, 1874-1893, City of Winnipeg, Archives and Records Control.

25. M. Ross Waddell, *The Exchange District: An Illustrated Guide to Winnipeg's Historic Commercial District* (Winnipeg: Winnipeg Heritage Corporation, n.d.), 22-23; Don Aiken, "The Real Market Square," *Winnipeg Real Estate News* (26 January 1996), suggests that Market Square in Winnipeg continued to be the site of political meetings, particularly through the 1930s (3).

26. This sketch, owned by the author, was never converted to a painting.

27. Commissioner Hodgson, City of Edmonton, to Commissioner Gillespie, City of Red Deer, 10 July 1946, R.G. 11, Class 44, File 11, CEA.

Chapter 2

1. A detailed description of the construction, plan, and exterior appearance of the new town facility can be found in the *Edmonton Bulletin*, 17 July 1893. This building has been replicated and can be toured at Fort Edmonton.

2. At the town council meeting held 26 May 1893, K. A. McLeod moved and J. Goodridge seconded a motion that the Town Hall and Market Committee be instructed to bring in a report at the next meeting recommending a suitable position for a Market Square. This motion was carried. At the council meeting of 7 June 1893, the Town Hall and Market Committee reported "that in their opinion it is unnecessary to purchase a Market site," CEA.

3. James H. Marsh, ed. in chief. *The Canadian Encyclopedia 2000*, World Edition (Toronto: McClelland and Stewart, 1999), s.v. "Rupert's Land," by Shirlee Anne Smith, notes that the legal transfer of Rupert's Land to the Crown took effect 1 December 1869 but the Red River Rebellion effectively delayed the transfer until the middle of July 1870.

4. *Edmonton Bulletin*, 4 August 1888.

5. *Toronto Mail*, 1 October 1892.

6. John Patrick Day, "Donald Ross, Old-Timer Extraordinaire," in *Edmonton: The Life of a City*, edited by Bob Hesketh and Frances Swyripa (Edmonton: NeWest Press, 1995), 34-35. Information on Donald Ross can also be found in Tony Cashman, "Donald Ross, Our First Hotelman," in *The Best Edmonton Stories* (Edmonton: Hurtig Publishers, 1976), 96-99; R. G. Ironside and S. A. Hamilton, "Historical Geography of Coal Mining in the Edmonton District," *Alberta Historical Review*, vol. 20, no. 3 (Summer 1972): 6-16; and Allan Shute and Margaret Fortier, *Riverdale: From Fraser Flats to Edmonton Oasis* (Riverdale: Tree Frog Press, 1992), 358-59.

7. *Edmonton Bulletin*, 3 January 1903.

8. *Edmonton Bulletin*, 12 September 1902.

9. Donald Ross to Council of the Municapality [*sic*] of the Town of Edmonton, 19 July 1904, R.G.8, Class 10, File 62, CEA.

10. Roger Vick, "Klondyke Gardens: The Early Years," *Kinnikinnick*, vol. 6, no. 5 (February 1989), 127-32.

11. *Edmonton Bulletin*, 10 December 1898.

12. *Edmonton Bulletin*, 4 May 1889.

13. Various correspondence, R.G. 8.3, Class 1, File 4 and M.S. 209, File 6, CEA.

14. For example, Town Clerk A. S. Randall wrote to P. Heiminck Esq., 26 March 1897, as follows: "I have the honor to acknowledge receipt of your esteemed favors of the 12th, 13th & 24th Inst. I am instructed to inform you that the Council cannot, at the present time, consider the proposition as made in yours of the 12th Inst., for a Market site," R.G. 8, Class 4, File 1, p. 175, CEA.

15. Edmonton City Council Meeting Minutes, CEA.

16. Edmonton City Council Meeting Minutes, 3 July 1897, CEA.

17. Title search 177-M-81, as named on 26 August 1935 when all the various titles making up Block X were cancelled and renamed.

18. Edmonton Town Council Meeting, 11 April 1900. The by-law was announced in the *Edmonton Bulletin*, 16 April 1900, and town members were invited to vote on 11 May 1900.

19. R.G. 8.3, Class 1, File 14, CEA.

20. *Edmonton Bulletin*, 13 September 1922.

21. *Toronto Mail*, 1 October 1892, M.S. 68, CEA.

22. J. G. MacGregor, *Edmonton: A History*, 2d ed. (Edmonton: Hurtig Publishers, 1975), 123.

23. The Heiminck block was built before Edmonton's real-estate crash of 1912. In 1920, part of it was rented for an expansion of the Johnstone Walker store, and in 1948 the building disappeared entirely as an independent entity when it was incorporated into the store.

24. R.G. 8, Class 3, File 10, CEA.

25. John C. Bown, city solicitor, to the City Councillors and the Mayor, 19 April 1910, R.G. 11, City Commissioners correspondence, CEA; City Solicitor Thomas E. Garside to the City Commissioner, 7 September 1939, Newspaper clippings file on the City Market, CEA.

26. Copy of receipt issued to Isabella Heiminck by the Town of Edmonton for fifty dollars "being full payment for fence about the land leased by the Town for the purpose of a market ground," 21 September 1900. Mr. Heiminck signed the receipt for his wife, R.G. 8.1, Class 6, File 62, CEA.

27. *Edmonton Bulletin*, 28 December 1900.

28. "City of Edmonton Annual Report for eleven months ending 31st October 1908," CEA.

29. "Municipality of the City of Edmonton, Alberta, Financial and Departmental Reports for year ending October 31st 1909," CEA.

30. "City of Edmonton Annual Report for eleven months ending 31st October 1908," CEA.

31. Edmonton City Council Meeting Minutes, 27 November 1900, CEA. On 24 January 1903, when his salary was forty dollars per month, Ernest Grierson wrote to the Chairman of the Market Committee requesting a raise to sixty dollars per month, and by September of the same year, he had asked that the salary be raised to seventy-five dollars per month, R.G. 8, Class 5, File 2, CEA.

32. The vendor uproar regarding the implementation of vendors fees was reported in the *Edmonton Bulletin*, 4 February 1911. Annual Reports and Financial Statements

of the Town and then City of Edmonton, 1901-11, CEA. The names of these reports vary slightly from year to year.

33. "Municipality of the City of Edmonton, Alberta, Financial and Departmental Reports for year ended October 31, 1910," CEA.

34. Tony Cashman, *Abraham Cristall, 1868-1944: The Story of a Simple Man* (no publisher, no date), 28. Not surprisingly, Abe Cristall was vigorously opposed to prohibition.

35. Kathrine Granstrom, Rita (Arends) Granstrom, and Ray Granstrom, interviews with author, Edmonton, Alberta, 3 and 29 December 1993.

36. *Edmonton Bulletin*, 21 October 1910.

37. Vick, "Klondyke Gardens: The Early Years."

38. *Edmonton Bulletin*, 11 October 1910.

39. Results of plebiscite, R.G. 8, Class 24, File 1, CEA.

40. 15 February 1911 and 26 March 1911, M.S. 209, File 127, 128, CEA.

41. Municipality of the City of Edmonton, Alberta, Financial and Departmental Reports for year ended October 31st, 1910, CEA.

42. Edmonton City Council Meeting Minutes, 5 April 1910, CEA. The same day council received another delegation supporting the removal of the market to 101st Street.

43. *Edmonton Bulletin*, 26 March 1910.

44. Edmonton City Council Meeting Minutes, 17 May 1910, CEA.

45. "City of Edmonton, Alberta, Eighth Annual Financial and Departmental Report for year ended October 31st, 1912," CEA.

46. *Edmonton Bulletin*, 31 January 1911.

47. Edmonton City Council Meeting Minutes, 28 February 1911, CEA.

48. *Edmonton Bulletin*, 1 February 1911.

49. Edmund Herbert Dale, "The Role of Successive Town and City Councils in the Evolution of Edmonton, Alberta, 1862-1966," Ph.D. thesis (University of Alberta, 1969), 141, hereafter shortened to "Dale, [page number]." Dale refers to C. L. Gibbs as "Alderman" but in fact, although Gibbs had run and lost in the aldermanic race of 1910, he did not become an alderman until 1928, a post he retained until his sudden and unexpected death in 1934. Joseph Rek, *Municipal Elections in Edmonton, 1892-1998: summary of results with short biographies of mayors and councillors* (Edmonton: Edmonton Public Library, 1998), 121-22, says Gibbs was born in England in 1877 and that he established the firm Barnes and Gibbs Architects in Edmonton in 1907, later becoming a teacher at the Edmonton Technical School.

50. C. L. Gibbs, "A Civic Centre for Edmonton," *Saturday News*, 18 March 1911, 9 and 12. Civic Centre clippings file, CEA.

51. Morell and Nichols, landscape architects, "A Report on City Planning for the City of Edmonton," November 1912, CEA. The section on the market assumes that it will be moved to 101st Street: "Foreseeing the need of establishing in Edmonton market facilities where various food products could be brought daily and supply the City continuously with garden and farm products, the City has already acquired a site for a central market called the Market Square, located between First Street and Queens Avenue, north of the land opposite Nelson Avenue."

52. By-law no. 485 was approved by council 4 March 1913 "for the creating of a debt in the sum of $2,712,193.34 for the purchase of lands for the establishment of a civic centre." On 28 March, the money by-law was defeated. On 29 March 1913, the *Edmonton Daily Bulletin* ran the headline, "Not Yet' Say Citizens on Civic Centre."

53. Mayor G. Armstrong to City Council, 14 August 1912, M.S. 209, File 146, CEA.

54. Edmonton City Council Meeting Minutes, 21 January 1909, CEA.

55. Minute Book of the Market Committee from the date of the first election after amalgamation of Edmonton and Strathcona, CEA.

56. Diana Lynn Bodnar, *The Prairie Legislative Buildings of Canada* (M.A. thesis, University of British Columbia, 1979), 24–26. Jeffers held the position of City Architect from 1 February 1912 until the position was abolished in 15 November 1913. When the city reinstituted the position on 10 February 1914, Jeffers was reinstated as City Architect. See also, Michael Payne, "Edmontonians and the Legislature" in *Edmonton, The Life of a City*, edited by Bob Hesketh and Frances Swyripa (Edmonton: NeWest Press, 1995), 104–15.

57. It is not clear whether Wheeler was assigned to the project to carry out the plans prepared by Jeffers or whether Jeffers withdrew in anticipation of the abolishment of the office of City Architect. The Annual Financial and Departmental Report for the year ending 31 December 1913 contains a detailed description of the design. It notes that "under the direction of Mr. A. W. Wheeler, Lic. R.I.B.A., revised drawings were made, specifications prepared, tenders called for and contracts were awarded."

58. *Edmonton Bulletin*, 11 November 1912.

59. *Edmonton Capital*, 15 February 1913.

60. Minute Book of the Market Committee from the date of the first election after amalgamation of Edmonton and Strathcona, CEA. At meeting number seven of the Market Committee, held 11 July 1913, Jeffers's design was discussed and approved in principle. On 15 July 1913, the same plan was approved by council. Consideration given to a return to Rice Street is recorded in the minutes of the meeting held 20 June 1913.

61. "City of Edmonton, Alberta, Ninth Annual Financial and Departmental Report for fourteen months ended December 31st, 1913," CEA.

62. *Edmonton Journal*, 22 September 1914.

63. Edmonton City Council Meeting Minutes, 13 October 1914, CEA.

64. Parks and Markets Committee Minutes, 1914, uncatalogued, CEA.

65. *Edmonton Bulletin*, 24 December, 1914.

66. *Edmonton Bulletin*, 6 January 1916.

67. *Edmonton Bulletin*, 26 January 1916.

68. *Edmonton Bulletin*, 12 June 1916.

69. *Edmonton Bulletin*, 19 June 1916.

70. "City of Edmonton, Financial Statements and Reports for the year ending December 31st, 1916," CEA.

Chapter 3

1. *Edmonton Bulletin*, 12 April 1916.

2. *Edmonton Bulletin*, 19 June 1916.

3. Edmonton City Council Meeting Minutes, 17 October 1916 and 24 October 1916.

4. Edmonton City Council Meeting Minutes, 31 October 1916, 14 December 1916, 19 December 1916, and 19 June 1917.

5. *Edmonton Bulletin*, 28 October 1910.

6. "City of Edmonton, Alberta, Eighth Annual Financial and Departmental Report for year ended October 31st 1912," CEA.

7. Annual financial statements published by the city of Edmonton show that between 1924 and 1939, the years the market was managed by Edgar Kendall, annual expenditures for the market ranged between $7,000 and $9,000, while revenues ranged from about $12,000 to $16,000.

8. John (Jack) McMann, interview with author, Edmonton, Alberta, 5 October 1994.

9. Mabel Dean to Alderman Findlay, 10 (illegible) May 1926; G. E. Mantle, secretary to Mrs. Mabel Dean, containing reaction of Superintendent Edgar Kendall to her letter of the previous month, 9 June 1926, R.G. 11, City Commissioners correspondence, CEA.

10. Market Superintendent Edgar Kendall to Mayor Bury, 1 August 1928, R.G. 11, City Commissioners correspondence, CEA. This could have been Wm. J. C. Carswell, proprietor of Carswell's Market Hardware at 9902 - 102 Avenue, but there were other Carswells in the city at the time.

11. Superintendent Kendall to Mayor Bury, 1 August 1928; Mayor Bury to Building Inspector J. R. Huntbach, 1 August 1928; J. R. Huntbach to Mayor Bury, 2 August 1928; Bury to Huntbach, 9 August 1928, R.G. 11, City Commissioners correspondence, CEA.

12. Report from Sergeant Major Riddell to Chief Constable Shute, 5 July 1938; Forwarded report from Chief Constable Shute to the Commissioners, 7 July 1938; Commissioners to J. Munro, 8 July 1938, R.G. 11, City Commissioners correspondence, CEA.

13. Edgar Kendall to Mayor A. U. G. Bury, 19 March 1928, R.G. 11, City Commissioners correspondence, CEA.

14. Commissioners to A. W. Haddow, 24 October 1928; Haddow to Commissioners, 27 October 1928; Commissioners to Haddow, 1 November 1928, R.G. 11, City Commissioners correspondence, CEA.

15. Superintendent Edgar Kendall to Mayor A. U. G. Bury, 26 August 1929, R.G. 11, City Commissioners correspondence, CEA.

16. *Edmonton Journal*, 3 October 1930.

17. D. R. Fraser to Chief Constable Shute, 22 February 1934, R.G. 11, City Commissioners correspondence, CEA.

18. Commissioners to Edmonton City Council, 26 February 1934, R. G. 11, City Commissioners correspondence, CEA.

19. Commissioners to A. W. Haddow, 30 April 1934; Haddow to Commissioner Mitchell, 9 May 1934, R.G. 11, City Commissioners correspondence, CEA.

20. Superintendent Kendall to Mayor Bury, 6 December 1927, R.G. 11, City Commissioners correspondence, CEA.

21. In 1929, vendors complained to Mayor Bury about flies in the building and asked for screens. An investigation by Building Inspector Martland, however, revealed that, while screens for the clerestory windows existed, they were not being used because of their darkening effect (Martland to Bury, April 1929). On 4 September 1931, MOH R. B. Jenkins wrote to Kendall saying that "complaints have been received regarding the presence of flies in excess in and about market buildings." The issue came up again in 1937 and this time Dr. Jenkins was more aggressive, giving Kendall only fourteen days from 22 June 1937 to comply with a notice to screen windows "in compliance with Section 260 of the Food and Drink Regulations." Screens, however, were not in the budget. Commissioner Gibb wrote Martland 14 September 1937 asking him to be sure to put $234.50 in the 1938 estimates for screens. R.G. 11, City Commissioners correspondence, CEA.

22. Edmonton City Council Meeting Minutes, 28 November 1916.

23. Superintendent Edgar Kendall to Mayor Bury, 1 May 1928, R.G. 11, City Commissioners correspondence, CEA.

24. Superintendent Kendall to Mayor Bury, 2 February 1928, R.G. 11, City Commissioners correspondence, CEA.

25. Mayor Clarke to Superintendent Kendall, 9 January 1935; Kendall to Mayor Clarke, 10 January 1935, R.G. 11, City Commissioners correspondence, CEA.

26. Superintendent Edgar Kendall to Commissioner Mitchell, 13 March 1933, R.G. 11, City Commissioners correspondence, CEA.

27. Betty (Oppelt) Bre-Win, interviews with author, Edmonton, Alberta, 7 October and 9 December 1993 and 16 February 1994.

28. N. P. Finnemore to Commissioners, 30 March 1932, R.G. 11, City Commissioners correspondence, CEA.

29. Betty (Oppelt) Bre-Win, interviews with author, Edmonton, Alberta, 7 October and 9 December 1993 and 16 February 1994.

30. Flore (Bilodeau) Hinse, interviews with author, Beaumont, Alberta, 20 and 26 April 1993.

31. Marcel Juchli, letter addressed to author, received 3 October 1994, followed by telephone interview 14 October 1994.

32. Edmonton City Council Meeting Minutes, 20 May 1919.

33. The City financial statements for 1919 record an expenditure of $1,443.02 for an "extension" to the market building and a separate expenditure of $7,479.60 for a fish market. It must have been at this time that the sides of the farmers' hall were bricked to create a year-round covered shelter.

34. H. Mandlis to the Commissioners, 5 April 1927, R.G. 11, City Commissioners correspondence, CEA.

35. Mayor Bury to Building Inspector Martland, 12 May 1927; Martland to Bury, 25 May 1927, R.G. 11, City Commissioners correspondence, CEA.

36. Mayor Bury to Building Inspector Martland, 6 November 1928; Mayor Bury to Superintendent Edgar Kendall, 6 November 1928; Martland to Bury, 19 November 1928; Bury to Martland, 21 November 1928, R.G. 11, City Commissioners correspondence, CEA. The project cost was $382.

37. Commissioner R. J. Gibb to John Martland, 28 April 1937; Building Inspector's Office (Huntbach) to Commissioners, 20 May 1937; Commissioners to Huntbach, 21 May 1937, R.G. 11, City Commissioners correspondence, CEA.

38. Roy Heeks, interview with author, Edmonton, Alberta, 15 December 1993; telephone conversation with Clive Heeks (Roy's son), 24 May 1994.

39. *Edmonton Daily Capital*, 2 October 1914.

40. *Edmonton Bulletin,* 15 June 1916.

41. *Edmonton Bulletin*, 18 March 1916.

42. *Edmonton Bulletin*, 22 July 1918.

43. Robert Wallish, telephone interview with author, 12 March 1994; letter from Robert Wallish to the author, 4 July 1994; Reg Dockstader, interviews with author, Edmonton, Alberta, 24 March and 18 May 1994.

44. Miss Gladys Maddock to Mayor Bury, 24 September 1928, R.G. 11, City Commissioners correspondence, CEA.

45. Miss Gladys Maddock to Mayor Bury, 24 September 1928; Mayor Bury to Miss Maddock, 25 September 1928; N. P. Finnemore to Mayor Bury, 24 September 1928; Mayor Bury to N. P. Finnemore, 25 September 1928; Mr. G. B. O'Connor of Griesbach, O'Connor and O'Connor to Mayor Bury, 25 September 1928; Mayor Bury to Greisbach, O'Connor and O'Connor, 27 September 1928; Griesbach, O'Connor and O'Connor to Mayor Bury, 3 October 1928; Mayor Bury to Griesbach, O'Connor and O'Connor, 6 October 1928; N. P. Finnemore, Edmonton Market Gardeners and Florists' Association, to Mayor Bury, 9 October 1928; Mayor Bury to N. P. Finnemore, 13 October 1928, R.G. 11, City Commissioners correspondence, CEA.

46. Joe Bre-Win, interviews with the author, Edmonton, Alberta, 7 October and 9 December 1993 and 16 February 1994.

47. Commissioners' Report to the Aldermen, 10 October 1924, R.G. 11.1, Class 1, File 24, CEA.

48. *Edmonton Journal*, 5 July 1941.

49. Superintendent Kendall to Mayor Knott, 5 July 1932, R.G. 11, City Commissioners correspondence, CEA.

50. Superintendent Kendall to Mayor Knott, 10 August 1933, R.G. 11, City Commissioners correspondence, CEA.

51. Superintendent Kendall's report to Commissioner Mitchell responding to the Whiston Report, 12 February 1935, R.G. 11, Class 229, File 2, CEA.

52. Mark E. Tookey to the Commissioners, 13 November 1926, R.G. 11, City Commissioners correspondence, CEA. In 1926, the city spent almost $4,000 for new scales and scale house and an additional $1,534.50 to widen the intersection. A. W. Haddow to D. Mitchell, City Commissioner, 25 January 1926, R. G. 11, City Commissioners correspondence, CEA.

53. Mayor Bury to E. Tookey, 7 December 1929, R.G. 11, City Commissioners correspondence, CEA.

54. Superintendent Kendall to Mayor Bury, 23 September 1929, R.G. 11, City Commissioners correspondence, CEA.

55. Mayor Bury to Superintendent Kendall, 27 April 1928, R.G. 11, City Commissioners correspondence, CEA.

56. Samuel Lee to Commissioners, 18 April 1934; Commissioners to Samuel Lee, 24 April 1934, R.G. 11, City Commissioners correspondence, CEA.

57. Commissioners' Reports to the Aldermen of the City of Edmonton, 26 December 1923 and 19 December 1924, R.G. 11.1, Class 1, Files 14 and 26, CEA.

58. Flore (Bilodeau) Hinse, interviews with the author, Beaumont, Alberta, 20 and 26 April 1993.

59. Superintendent Kendall to Mayor Knott, 11 April 1933, R.G. 11, City Commissioners correspondence, CEA.

60. Edmonton City Council Meeting Minutes, 19 March 1924, CEA.

61. J. Henry (spelled Henri in other correspondence with the City) to Commissioners, 22 August 1927, R.G. 11, City Commissioners correspondence, CEA.

62. F. E. Moroney to the Mayor, 29 April 1929, R.G. 11, City Commissioners correspondence, CEA.

63. Max Baader to the Mayor, 25 January 1932, R.G. 11, City Commissioners correspondence, CEA.

64. Robertson, Winkler and Hawe to the Commissioners, 27 October 1927, R.G. 11, City Commissioners correspondence, CEA.

65. Mayor Bury to Robertson, Winkler and Hawe, to the attention of Mr. Winkler, 5 November 1927, R.G. 11, City Commissioners correspondence, CEA.

66. Chow Kwo-Hsien, consul-general for China to Mayor Bury, 16 November 1927, R.G. 11, City Commissioners correspondence, CEA.

67. Marcel Aldry and Henri Valentin to Superintendent Kendall, 24 November 1927, R.G. 11, City Commissioners correspondence, CEA.

68. Superintendent Kendall to Mayor Bury, 12 December 1927, R.G. 11, City Commissioners correspondence, CEA.

69. H. A. Bannard to Mayor Bury, received 21st December 1927, R.G. 11, City Commissioners correspondence, CEA.

70. Superintendent Kendall to Mayor Knott, 3 January 1933, R.G. 11, City Commissioners correspondence, CEA.

71. Kathrine Granstrom, Rita (Granstrom) Arends, and Ray Granstrom, interviews with the author, Edmonton, Alberta, 3 and 29 December 1993.

72. Superintendent Kendall to Mayor Knott, 3 July 1933, R.G. 11, City Commissioners correspondence, CEA.

73. Superintendent Kendall to Mayor Bury, 24 August 1928, R.G. 11, City Commissioners correspondence, CEA.

74. Louise Berger (with daughter Yvonne Hoekstra and son Andy Berger), interviews with author, Edmonton, Alberta, 15 November and 13 December 1994.

75. Ronald C. Neal, secretary treasurer of the Edmonton and District Market Gardeners and Florists' Association to Mayor Knott, 6 April 1933, R.G. 11, City Commissioners correspondence, CEA.

76. Mayor Joseph A. Clarke to John Chapman, butcher, 11 May 1935, R.G. 11, City Commissioners correspondence, CEA.

77. Superintendent Kendall to Mayor Bury, 2 Feb 1928, R.G. 11, City Commissioners correspondence, CEA.

78. Superintendent Kendall to Mayor Knott and Commissioners, 3 July 1933, R.G. 11, City Commissioners correspondence, CEA.

79. It is not clear to me whether the city paid the egg candler directly or whether the candler was authorized by the city to operate from the market and to charge for her candling services. The latter model definitely applied from the 1950s to 1970s, as will be seen in Chapter 5.

80. City Commissioners to R. H. Ennismore, provincial egg inspector, 8 May 1926; R. H. Ennismore to City Commissioners, 10 May 1926; Commissioners to R. H. Ennismore, 18 May 1926; Commissioners to Dr T. H. Whitelaw, MOH, 9 June 1926, R.G. 11, City Commissioners correspondence, CEA.

81. P. E. Poirier to Ennismore, 10 January 1927; R. H. Ennismore, senior egg inspector for Alberta to P. E. Poirier of Milner, Carr, Dafoe and Poirier, 11 January 1927; Lord to Whitelaw, 17 January 1927, R.G. 11, City Commissioners correspondence, CEA.

82. R. H. Ennismore to the Mayor, 24 September 1929, R.G. 11, City Commissioners correspondence, CEA.

83. Superintendent Kendall to Commissioner D. Mitchell, 1 October 1929, R.G. 11, City Commissioners correspondence, CEA.

84. Letter from City Secretary Mantle to Edgar Kendall, 25 September 1926, R.G. 11, City Commissioners correspondence, CEA.

85. Mrs. Stanley Uren, secretary, United Farm Women of Alberta to Mayor Clarke, 5 December 1935; Mayor Clarke to Mrs. Uren, 7 December 1935, R.G. 11, City Commissioners correspondence, CEA.

86. James Babcock, Hattonford, Alberta, to the Mayor, 30 September 1926; G. E. Mantle to Babcock, 18 October 1926, R.G. 11, City Commissioners correspondence, CEA.

87. Fred Wagner to Mayor Douglas, 17 Feb 1930; Mayor Douglas to Fred Wagner, 21 February 1930, R.G. 11, City Commissioners correspondence, CEA.

88. François and Yvette Morin, interview with the author, Edmonton, Alberta, 20 July 1994.

89. R.G. 11, Class 2, File 10, CEA. The advertisement read as follows:
    Citizens are patronizing the City Market in increasing numbers. No other public market offers such opportunities for supplying your household requirements in the matter of farm products of excellent quality.
    The latest addition to the building offers the fullest protection against variable weather conditions and patrons are also assured of the best service. E. Kendall Supt. City Commissioners.

90. Joe Bre-Win, interviews with the author, 7 October and 9 December 1993, 16 February 1994, Edmonton, Alberta.

91. Manager of the Edmonton Poultry Association to the Commissioners, 26 October 1926, R.G. 11, City Commissioners correspondence, CEA.

92. Edgar Kendall to the Mayor, 4 February 1929, R.G. 11, City Commissioners correspondence, CEA.

93. Acting MOH to Superintendent Kendall, 12 January 1940, R.G. 11, City Commissioners correspondence, CEA.

94. R. C. Neal, secretary treasurer of the Edmonton and District Market Gardeners and Florists' Association, to the Mayor, 14 February 1935, R.G. 11, City Commissioners correspondence, CEA.

95. Mayor Bury to Superintendent Kendall, 19 April 1928, R.G. 11, City Commissioners correspondence, CEA.

96. W. J. Cardy, president of the Edmonton Horticultural and Vacant Lots Garden Association, to the Commissioners, 16 September 1936, R.G. 11, City Commissioners correspondence, CEA.

97. John Blue to Commissioner Mitchell, 29 Oct. 1936, R.G. 11, City Commissioners correspondence, CEA.

98. C. S. Longman, field crops commissioner, to Commissioner Mitchell, 11 February 1937, R.G. 11, City Commissioners correspondence, CEA.

99. *Edmonton Journal*, 19 December 1932.

100. *Edmonton Journal*, 21 December 1932.

101. The meeting was held at 7:15 p.m. on Market Square. A set of notes signed by O. Wilchiuski (illegible), describes the events, R.G. 11, Class 160, File 7, CEA.

102. Edmonton City Council Meeting Minutes, 28 December 1925.

103. Dale, 231-34.

104. Edmonton City Council Meeting Minutes, 15 September 1926.

105. List of clubs invited to appoint representatives to the Edmonton Town Planning Committee, R.G.11 Class 25 File 1, CEA.

106. *Edmonton Journal*, 30 June 1932.

107. Mrs. A. Morris to Mayor Knott, probably August 1933, R.G. 11, City Commissioners correspondence, CEA. The quotation in the text exactly transcribes a handwritten letter which, in its punctuation, conveys the writer's anguish at having to admit her indigence.

108. Norman Finnemore to the Commissioners, 24 March 1932, R.G. 11, City Commissioners correspondence, CEA.

109. Joe Bre-Win, interviews with the author, 7 October and 9 December 1993, 16 February 1994, Edmonton, Alberta. Although I have not verified to my satisfaction Joe's claim that the relief tickets could not be redeemed, the circumstance is entirely likely. Throughout the 1930s, senior officials from the Imperial Bank of Commerce wrote frequently to city commissioners threatening to limit credit despite the consequences to the city, R.G. 11, Class 18, Files 5-15, CEA.

110. Commissioners to Kendall, 22 August 1932; Mayor Knott to Kendall, 13 September 1932; Harry Mandlis to Commissioners and Mrs. Jones to Commissioners, 13 December 32; Kendall to Commissioners, 15 December 1932; Commissioners to Kendall, 18 December 1932, R.G. 11, City Commissioners correspondence, CEA.

111. Superintendent Kendall to Mayor Knott, 20 September 1933, R.G. 11, City Commissioners correspondence, CEA.

112. In his account of the evening trips to the countryside to buy an animal directly from a farmer, Joe Bre-Win thought the streetcar went as far west as 142nd Street. In fact, its route went north along 127th Street to 127th Avenue in the 1930s. See, Colin K. Hatcher and Tom Schwarzkopf, *Edmonton's Electric Transit: The Story of Edmonton's Streetcars and Trolly Buses* (Toronto: Railfare Enterprises Limited, 1983).

113. Mayor Douglas to Superintendent Kendall, 11 June 1930, R.G. 11, City Commissioners correspondence, CEA.

114. Mayor Knott to Superintendent Kendall, 10 June 1932, R.G. 11, City Commissioners correspondence, CEA.

115. E. Kendall to Mayor Knott, 7 June 1933; Mayor Knott to E. Kendall, 8 June 1933, R.G. 11, City Commissioners correspondence, CEA.

116. Mr. B. Caswell to Commissioner Mitchell, 29 Feb 1932, R.G. 11, City Commissioners correspondence, CEA.

117. Ronald C. Neal, secretary treasurer of the Edmonton and District Market Gardeners and Florists' Association, to Mayor Knott, 60 April 1933, R.G. 11, City Commissioners correspondence, CEA.

118. Mayor Knott to A. W. Haddow, 21 March 1932, R.G. 11, City Commissioners correspondence, CEA.

119. J. Martland to D. Mitchell, City Commissioner, 16 December 1932, R.G. 11, City Commissioners correspondence, CEA. Martland estimated a cost range of $5,500 to $7,500.

120. Commissioners to J. Martland, 27 January 1933, R.G. 11, City Commissioners correspondence, CEA.

121. Kendall to Commissioners, 17 February 1933, R.G. 11, Class 38, File 15, CEA.

122. A. Farmilo, general secretary of the Edmonton Trades and Labor Council, to Commissioners, 7 March 1933, R.G. 11, City Commissioners correspondence, CEA; Edmonton City Council Meeting Minutes, 27 March 1933.

123. Minnie (illegible) Bowen to the Mayor and Commissioners, 11 March 1933, R.G. 11, City Commissioners correspondence, CEA.

124. Mitchell to Martland, 6 April 1933, R.G. 11, City Commissioners correspondence, CEA.

125. Commissioners to J. Martland, 30 June 1933, R.G. 11, City Commissioners correspondence, CEA.

126. The successful tenders included: D. H. Fraser & Co (Lumber supply, $540.82); W. H. Clark & Co Ltd (Millwork, $761.55); Tomlinson and Lymer (Electrical, $332.50); Templeman Bros. (Plumbing, $969); and Freeze Maxwell Co (Sheet Metal, $549.00).

127. A. E. Sibun to Commissioners, 14 March 1933, R.G. 11, City Commissioners correspondence, CEA.

128. Commissioners to J. Martland, 25 April 1933; Mayor Knott to Martland, 3 and 5 June 1933, R.G. 11, City Commissioners correspondence, CEA.

129. Commissioners to Martland, 29 June 1933, R.G. 11, City Commissioners correspondence, CEA.

130. Brewin [sic] to Commissioners, 2 August 1933, R.G. 11, City Commissioners correspondence, CEA.

131. Joe Gaudio to Commissioner Mitchell, 11 July 1933, R.G. 11, City Commissioners correspondence, CEA.

132. Tighe & Wilson to Mr. Garside, city of Edmonton legal department, 24 August 1933, R.G. 11, City Commissioners correspondence, CEA. The other four successful applicants were: H. Holland, butcher; J. Gaudio, grocer; J. W. Sharp, fruits; and N. G. Seng, fruits.

133. *Edmonton Journal*, 2 September 1933.

134. Geneva Close, interviews with author, Edmonton, Alberta, 3 and 25 June 1999.

135. Janine Dunn, interviews with author, Edmonton, Alberta, 24 July and 25 September 1995 and 25 January 1996.

136. Lang Jae Ly to City 22 January 1937; J. Paterson, superintendent of land department to Lang Jae Ly, 5 February 1939, R.G. 11, City Commissioners correspondence, CEA.

137. Edmonton City Council Meeting Minutes, 26 June 1939. Council discussed a variety of issues pertaining to the future development of the civic centre.

138. Thomas E. Garside to City Commissioners, 7 September 1939, R.G. 11, City Commissioners correspondence, CEA.

139. Alderman D.A. Grout to Commissioners, 1 June 1938, R.G. 11, City Commissioners correspondence, CEA.

140. Alderman Grout to the City Commissioners, 12 August 1938, R.G. 11, City Commissioners correspondence, CEA.

Chapter 4

1. Joseph Rek, *Municipal Elections in Edmonton, 1892-1998*, gives the population as 90,419 in 1939 and 371,265 in 1965 (4).

2. John Martland to Commissioners, 12 March 1940; Purchasing Agent to Commissioners, 17 April 1940, R.G. 11, City Commissioners correspondence, CEA.

3.   John Turner to Commissioner Gibb, 11 February 1941; Gibb to Turner, 12 February 1941, R.G. 11, City Commissioners correspondence, CEA.

4.   Contract sent 8 March 1941 by G. M. Reid, Sunwapta Broadcasting Co. Ltd., to J. Hodgson, City Commissioner, R.G. 11, City Commissioners correspondence, CEA.

5.   Kendall to Commissioners, 14 May 1941, R.G. 11, City Commissioners correspondence, CEA.

6.   Geneva Close, interviews with author, Edmonton, Alberta, 3 and 25 June 1999.

7.   Joe Bre-Win, interviews with author, Edmonton, Alberta, 7 October and 9 December 1993 and 16 February 1994.

8.   Superintendent Kendall to Commissioners, 10 June 1941, R.G. 11, City Commissioners correspondence, CEA.

9.   *Edmonton Journal*, 4 July 1941, reported on Ingram's amalgamated appointment suggesting that it was the "first in a series of moves being considered by commissioners with a view to effecting economies in the civic administration."

10.   C. J. Ingram to Commissioners, 4 July 1941, R.G. 11, City Commissioners correspondence, CEA.

11.   Ingram to Commissioners, 18 July 1941, R.G. 11, City Commissioners correspondence, CEA.

12.   Ingram to Commissioners, 27 November 1947; Commissioners to Ingram, 9 December 1947, R.G. 11, City Commissioners correspondence, CEA. As he had resolved when he took office in July 1941, Ingram improved the accounting system for the city market, having found it to be "incomplete, obsolete and unworkable." Thereafter, he provided brief monthly financial statements to the commissioners, tracking revenue and expenditures against the yearly estimates and clearly separating out costs associated with operating the comfort stations.

13.   Varied correspondence, M.S. 209, File 141 and R.G. 11, Class 10, files 1-6, CEA.

14.   Ingram to Commissioners, 18 July 1941, R.G. 11, City Commissioners correspondence, CEA.

15.   Ingram to Commissioners, 23 March 1942, R.G. 11, City Commissioners correspondence, CEA.

16.   Peter Juchli, former vendor at the city market, to Mayor Fry, 10 October 1941; and Mrs. Finnemore to Ingram, 14 March 1942, R.G. 11, City Commissioners correspondence, CEA. Both vendors praised the changes.

17.   Ingram to Commissioners, 18 May 1942, R.G. 11, City Commissioners correspondence, CEA.

18.   Ingram to Commissioners, 18 July 1941, R.G. 11, City Commissioners correspondence, CEA.

19.   Ingram to Commissioners, 1 August 1941, R.G. 11, City Commissioners correspondence, CEA.

20. Ingram to Commissioners, 16 August 1941, R.G. 11, City Commissioners correspondence, CEA.

21. Ingram to Commissioners, 6 February 1942; Commissioner Gibb to Ingram, 3 March 1942, R.G. 11, City Commissioners correspondence, CEA.

22. G. M. Little to Mayor Fry, 30 April 1942, R.G. 11, City Commissioners correspondence, CEA.

23. Ingram to stallholders, 14 March 1942, R.G. 11, City Commissioners correspondence, CEA.

24. Mrs. N. P. Finnemore to Ingram, 21 March 1942, R.G. 11, City Commissioners correspondence, CEA.

25. Ingram to Commissioners, 31 August 1942; Commissioner Gibb to Ingram, 5 September 1942, R.G. 11, City Commissioners correspondence, CEA.

26. Petition dated 6 May 1944; Ingram to Commissioners, 11 May 1944; Commissioner Gibb to Ingram, 30 May 1944, R.G. 11, City Commissioners correspondence, CEA.

27. Ingram to Commissioners, 1 February 1944; Commissioner Hodgson to Misener, 3 February 1944, R.G. 11, City Commissioners correspondence, CEA.

28. Tisdale to City, 16 June 1942; Gibb to Tisdale, 18 June 1942; Tisdale to Gibb, 20 June 1942, R.G. 11, City Commissioners correspondence, CEA.

29. Mayor Fry to Donald Gordon, administrator, Wartime Price & Trade Board, 12 September 1942, R.G. 11, City Commissioners correspondence, CEA.

30. Mayor Fry to Geo. E. Shortt, director of Commercial and Institutional Rationing, 20 October 1942, R.G. 11, City Commissioners correspondence, CEA.

31. Mayor W. T. Henry to Jack Ramsey, 16 February 1943, R.G. 11, City Commissioners correspondence, CEA.

32. *Edmonton Journal*, 17 June 1943.

33. Commissioner Hodgson to Ingram, 25 March 1942; Ingram to Commissioners, 3 April 1943, R.G. 11, City Commissioners correspondence, CEA.

34. A. Russell, city clerk, to Norman Finnemore, 5 April 1943; Finance Committee minutes for Wednesday 7 April 1943, R.G. 11, City Commissioners correspondence, CEA; *Edmonton Journal*, 8 April 1943.

35. Ingram to Commissioners, 31 March 1942; Little to Commissioner Gibb, 6 April 1942, R.G. 11, City Commissioners correspondence, CEA.

36. Albushie to Mayor Fry, 29 April 1944; Commissioner Gibb to Ingram, 4 May 1944; Ingram to Commissioners, 8 May 1944, R.R. 11, City Commissioners correspondence, CEA.

37. Betty (Oppelt) Bre-Win, interviews with author, Edmonton, Alberta, 7 October 1993, 9 December 1993 and 16 February 1994.

38. Petition dated 2 March 1942; John Martland to Commissioners, 6 December 1941, R.G. 11, City Commissioners correspondence, CEA. The building was estimated by Martland at $161,954.

39. *Edmonton Journal*, 12 March 1942.

40. Edmonton City Council Meeting Minutes, 23 March 1942.

41. City Solicitor to Mayor W. T. Henry, 2 February 1943, R.G. 11, City Commissioners correspondence, CEA.

42. Mayor to N. P. Fenimore [*sic*], 17 March 1943, R.G. 11, City Commissioners correspondence, CEA.

43. Ingram to Commissioners, 13 February 1946, R.G. 11, City Commissioners correspondence, CEA.

44. Dewar to Commissioners, 22 April 1946, R.G. 11, City Commissioners correspondence, CEA.

45. Commissioner Hodgson to Ingram, 26 April 1946, R.G. 11, City Commissioners correspondence, CEA.

46. Pat Brennan, interview with author, Edmonton, Alberta, 15 August 1994.

47. Bill Elliott, interviews with author, Lacombe, Alberta, 2 and 18 August 1994.

48. As soon as the war ended, the federal government must have been negotiating with city officials because, at its meeting of 26 November 1945, Edmonton City Council approved a plan "to lease the ground floor of a new Market building to the Federal Department of Public Works." This odd idea failed to materialize.

49. Edmonton Town Planning Commission Report on the Civic Centre, 15 April 1947, Clippings File on Planning Civic Centre, CEA.

50. Dale, 422-23.

51. *Edmonton Journal*, 4 and 5 June 1948.

52. Edmonton City Council Meeting Minutes, 16 June 1948; *Edmonton Journal*, 17 June 1948.

53. *Edmonton Journal*, 27 September 1949.

54. Edmonton City Council Meeting Minutes, 3 October 1949, CEA.

55. Edmonton City Council Meeting Minutes, 12 December 1949; J. Martland of Martland and Aberdeen to the City Commissioners, 7 December 1949, R.G. 11, City Commissioners correspondence, CEA; *Edmonton Journal*, 13 December 1949.

56. *Edmonton Journal*, 6 January 1950. An article in the *Edmonton Journal*, 1 February 1949, reported that Cecil Burgess was leaning towards the idea of moving the federal building westwards "in the neighborhood of the provincial buildings." On 29 July 1950, the *Edmonton Journal* reported that the "dominion government has officially agreed to a change in site for Edmonton's new, $4,500,000 federal building — from the market square to the city's newly zoned government centre area — city commissioners announced Friday, following an 80-minute secret session of council in the mayor's office."

57. N. P. Finnemore, Chairman of the Edmonton City Market Committee to City Commissioners, 10 March 1948, R.G. 11, City Commissioners correspondence, CEA. Finnemore broaches the subject of the rumoured move of the city market and conveys the concern of stallholders.

58. Commissioner Hodgson to Mr. Finnimore [*sic*], 11 March 1948; Commissioner Hodgson to Dr. Little, MOH, copy to Ingram, 22 October 1948, R.G. 11, City Commissioners correspondence, CEA.

59. Edmonton City Council Meeting Minutes, 21 February 1949; *Edmonton Journal*, 22 February 1949.

60. The city's annual financial statements before 1965 show that the retail component of the city market consistently generated an annual revenue lower than, but close to, the annual revenue generated by stall rentals. In 1949, for instance, $5,746 was collected in retail rents and $6,484.31 in stall rents. In 1950, $5,682 was collected in retail rents and $6,412.50 in stall rents. W. K. Hooson's "Report on the Study of the Stall Fees — City Market Building" (1969) shows that in 1965, $17,760 was collected in retail rents and $17,645 in stall rents; in 1966, $17,760 was collected in retail rents and $19,520 in stall rents and, in 1967, $17,760 was collected in retail rents and $19,835 in stall rents.

61. Commissioner J. Hodgson to the chairman and members of the Utilities Committee, Edmonton City Council and copied to Mayor H. D. Ainlay, 14 September 1949, R.G. 11, City Commissioners correspondence, CEA.

62. Bylaws Committee Report No. 4, 6 January 1950, CEA.

63. Winifred M. Scott to Mayor Parsons, 11 January 1950, R.G. 11, City Commissioners correspondence, CEA.

64. Dorothy (Oppelt) Hurlbut, interview with author, Sherwood Park, Alberta, 6 April 2000.

65. Peter Lupul, interviews with author, Edmonton, Alberta, 9 and 22 September and 4 October 1993.

66. *Edmonton Bulletin*, 3 August 1950.

67. *Edmonton Journal*, 15 July 1950; Dale, 424–25.

68. *Edmonton Journal*, 29 July 1950, reported that the "dominion government has officially agreed to a change in site for Edmonton's new, $4,500,000 federal building — from the market square to the city's newly zoned government centre area."

69. *Edmonton Journal*, 5 May 1954.

70. Mary Malcolm, interviews with author, Edmonton, Alberta, 16 and 26 May 1994.

71. Ingram to Commissioners, 21 May 1942; Commissioners to Ingram, 26 May 1942, R.G. 11, City Commissioners correspondence, CEA.

72. A. Lawrence to Ingram, 30 August 1948; Commissioners to Ingram, 21 September 1948, R.G. 11, City Commissioners correspondence, CEA.

73. Between 1929 and 1951, Bagley and McManus occupied a brick building on the southwest corner of Market Square.

74. Ingram to Commissioners, 9 October 1945, R.G. 11, City Commissioners correspondence, CEA.

75. For example, Commissioner D. B. Menzies to Mr. E. W. Ayre, Alberta Motor Association, 30 April 1957; Commissioner J. M. Tweddle to Paul A. Land, Junior Chamber of Commerce, 30 April 1958; Commissioner J. M. Tweddle to Mr. S. J. Baker, executive secretary, Canadian Legion, R.G. 11, City Commissioners correspondence, CEA.

76. N. J. McIntyre to Commissioners, 14 November 1950; Commissioners to McIntyre, 17 November 1950, R.G. 11, City Commissioners correspondence, CEA.

77. Tony Cashman, *A History of Motoring in Alberta*, 3d ed. (Edmonton, 1990), 53, 82, and 93.

78. Edmonton City Council Meeting Minutes, 15 September 1953, record a decision by council to authorize the commissioners to arrange a temporary location for Queen City Meat, either in a temporary building on Market Square or in the market building. An account appeared in the *Edmonton Journal*, 11 September 1953.

79. Anne Allison, daughter of Pearl and John Manzewich, who began selling at the city market in the mid to late 1930s, believes the last person to have taken a horse to Market Square was Peter Kuziek. In a telephone conversation with the author, 2 August 2000, Anne described him taking his wagon, hitched to his horse, Honey, and that it was a year or two after 1953.

80. Ingram to Commissioners, 2 August 1947, R.G. 11, City Commissioners correspondence, CEA.

81. McIntyre to Commissioners, 13 September 1949, R.G. 11, City Commissioners correspondence, CEA.

82. Commissioner D. B. Menzies to N. J. McIntyre, 18 January 1951, R.G. 11, City Commissioners correspondence, CEA.

83. City Commissioner, Regina to Commissioner Hodgson, Edmonton, 27 March 1950; Hodgson's response, 29 March 1950, R.G. 11, Class 44, File 15, CEA.

84. D. F. Martlett, Executive Secretary of the Edmonton Chamber of Commerce, to the Mayor Council, 27 October 1954, R.G. 11, City Commissioners correspondence, CEA.

85. Edmonton City Council Meeting Minutes, 3 August 1955.

86. D. F. Martlett to the mayor and commissioners, 31 August 1955, R.G. 11, City Commissioners correspondence, CEA.

87. R. E. M. Potter to Mayor Hawrelak, 8 January 1957, R.G. 11, City Commissioners correspondence, CEA.

88. *Edmonton Journal*, 25 April 1946.

89. *Edmonton Journal*, 8 October 1954, included a photograph of the design model. The proposed city hall was described as being "the first step in developing the civic square."

90. Wanda Klimke, telephone conversations with author, Edmonton, Alberta, April and May 2000.

91. McIntyre to Commissioners, 15 November 1950, R.G. 11, City Commissioners correspondence, CEA.

92. McIntyre to Commissioners, 28 December 1949, R.G. 11, City Commissioners correspondence, CEA.

93. Between 1950 and 1955, fees for stallholders and for the retail stores rose regularly. Such raises were usually introduced by the market superintendent and approved by the commissioners. J. R. Warner, superintendent of the Land Department to the Commissioners, 21 November 1962, R.G. 11, City Commissioners correspondence, CEA.

94. R. W. Swanson to Commissioner Hodgson, 8 January 1947, R.G. 11, City Commissioners correspondence, CEA.

95. Revenue breakdown provided by Acting Superintendent McIntyre to the Commissioners, September 1949, R.G. 11, City Commissioners correspondence, CEA.

96. Mayor Hawrelak to Mrs. David McAra, 18 November 1953, R.G. 11, City Commissioners correspondence, CEA.

97. Stallholders to the Market Superintendent, 6 January 1956, R.G. 11, City Commissioners correspondence, CEA.

98. Report from J. R. Warner to the Commissioners, 21 November 1962, R.G. 11, City Commissioners correspondence, CEA.

99. Frank Farkas, interview with author, Edmonton, Alberta, 7 May 2000.

100. Author interviews with Mary Sernowski, St. Albert, Alberta, 3 and 14 December 1992, 20 January 1993.

101. City Administration to stallholders, 27 September 1945; Commissioner Gibb to Superintendent Ingram, 2 October 1945, R.G. 11 City Commissioners correspondence, CEA.

102. *Edmonton Journal*, 4 December 1945.

103. Mayor Roper to J. Warner, 28 June 1961, R.G. 11, City Commissioners correspondence, CEA.

104. *Edmonton Journal*, Wednesday, 21 August 1946.

105. Beatrice (Bea) Keeler, telephone interview with author, April 2000.

106. Dr. G. M. Little to Commissioner Menzies, 21 October 1948; Commissioner Hodgson to Dr. Little and to Superintendent Ingram, 22 October 1948, R.G. 11, City Commissioners correspondence, CEA.

107. N. J. McIntyre to Commissioners, 17 November 1950, R.G. 11, City Commissioners' correspondence, CEA.

108. R. F. Duke to Commissioners, 17 January 1951, R.G. 11, City Commissioners correspondence, CEA; Edmonton City Council Meeting Minutes, 28 May 1951; *Edmonton Journal*, 28 and 29 May 1951.

109. J. R. Warner, superintendent of the Land Department, to Commissioners, 24 September 1963; Commissioner J. M. Tweddle to Warner, 11 October 1963, R.G. 11, City Commissioners correspondence, CEA.

110. Ingram to Commissioners, 27 November 1947; Commissioners to Ingram, 9 December 1947, R.G. 11, City Commissioners correspondence, CEA.

111. N. J. McIntyre to City Commissioners, 17 November 1950, R.G. 11, City Commissioners correspondence, CEA.

112. Commissioner Hodgson to F. C. Ockenden, city comptroller, 2 May 1951; Commissioner Menzies to Comptroller Ockenden, 10 May 1951, R.G. 11, City Commissioners correspondence, CEA.

113. Commissioner Tweddle to J. R. Warner, superintendent of the Land Department, 1 October 1959, R.G. 11, City Commissioners correspondence, CEA.

114. J. R. Warner to Mrs. P. D. McCalla, 30 June 1961, R.G. 11, City Commissioners correspondence, CEA.

115. Margaret (Oppelt) Tremblay, interview with author, Edmonton, Alberta, March 1999.

116. *Edmonton Journal*, 30 May 1957 and 12 April 1960.

117. Edmonton City Council Meeting Minutes, 13 March 1961; City Clerk G. S. Docherty to Commissioners, 26 September 1961, R.G. 11, City Commissioners correspondence, CEA. The Planning Advisory Commission advised the Edmonton City Council at its meeting on 6 January 1961 to appoint a Downtown Design Committee on which the planning commission was represented. It was the Downtown Design Committee that presented the recommendation to City Council at its 13 March 1961 meeting to prepare "a comprehensive plan of the area in order to ensure orderly and comprehensive development."

118. Edmonton City Council Meeting Minutes, 17 August 1961; 29 August 1961; 19 March 1962; 9 April 1962; 28 May 1962; and 25 June 1962. For an overall account of these two plans see Dale, 430-33 and 457-59. Dale provides a summarized account of the litigation which followed when Webb and Knapp claimed that their plan had been appropriated and their agreement with the city violated, 437-39.

119. Edmonton City Council Meeting Minutes, 27 January 1964; Dale, 457-59.

120. *Edmonton Journal*, 23 August 1962.

121. Mrs. Jessalyn McLeod to Commissioner Hamilton, 28 August 1962; Commissioner Hamilton to Mrs. McLeod, date illegible, R.G. 11, City Commissioners correspondence, CEA.

122. *Edmonton Journal*, 30 August 1962, reported on a meeting held by the stallholders association, claiming that the group was reacting to "the news that Edmonton City Market will be one of the first buildings to go when work starts on a new Civic Centre next spring." The five elected members of the association were: Jack Templeman (president), Bill Panasiuk, Walter Oppelt, Peter Lupul and Melvin Ash.

123. Mrs. J. I. Johnston to Mayor E. Roper, 19 September 1962; Mayor Roper to Mrs. Johnston, 12 October 1962, R.G. 11, City Commissioners correspondence, CEA.

124. Edmonton City Council Meeting Minutes, 22 October 1962.

125. J. R. Warner to Commissioners, 21 November 1962, R.G. 11, City Commissioners correspondence, CEA.

126. Commissioners Report to Council, 26 November 1962, R.G. 11, City Commissioners correspondence, CEA.

127. Report dated 11 March 1963, R.G. 11, City Commissioners correspondence, CEA.

128. R. N. Harvey, president of the Edmonton Chamber of Commerce to Mayor Elmer E. Roper, 11 April 1963. Letter submitted to Council on 22 April 1963, R.G. 11, City Commissioners correspondence, CEA.

129. Edmonton City Council Meeting Minutes, 24 June 1963.

130. Edmonton City Council Meeting Minutes, 22 October 1962.

131. Edmonton City Council Meeting Minutes, 24 November 1962 and 11 February 1963.

132. *Edmonton Journal*, 25 June 1963.

Chapter 5

1. *Edmonton Journal*, 8 June 1963; Commissioners' Report No. 35, 24 June 1963, CEA.

2. Mayor Hawrelak quoted in the *Edmonton Journal*, 31 January 1964; the $250,000 was approved as part of the capital estimates at the city of Edmonton council meeting, 14 February 1964, CEA; Commissioners Report Number 29, 8 June 1964. The budget for the market building was increased to $350,000 prior to calling tenders.

3. A small article in the *Edmonton Journal*, 25 June 1965, reported that "Walter Telmer [*sic*], assistant city architect, is leaving for an architect's job with the federal department of public works in Ottawa."

4. The existence of the stallholders' committee is referred to in Commissioners' Report Number 29, 8 June 1964, CEA, and in an article in the *Edmonton Journal*, 6 June 1964.

5. W. Telfer, assistant city architect to Commissioner Hamilton, 2 March 1964, R.G. 11, City Commissioners correspondence, CEA.

6. Dr. G. H. Ball, MOH to Commissioner Hamilton, 3 March 1964; Commissioner Hamilton to Mr. R. F. Duke, city architect, 4 March 1964; Commission Board secretary to Mr. R. F. Duke, 6 March 1964, R.G. 11, City Commissioners correspondence, CEA.

7. Walter Telfer sent the three schemes to Commissioner Menzies, 3 June 1964, R.G. 11, City Commissioners correspondence, CEA; *Edmonton Journal*, 6, 9, 16, 18 and 30 June 1964; Edmonton City Council Meeting Minutes 8, 22 and 29 June 1964, CEA.

8. Commissioner G. C. Hamilton to Mr. M. B. O'Byrne of Ogilvie, O'Byrne & Gallant, Barristers & Solicitors, 29 July 1965; Commissioner D. B. Menzies to Mr. R. F. Duke, 5 August 1964, lists the eight tenders received, R.G. 11, City Commissioners correspondence, CEA. Forest Construction was the lowest bidder, but the contract price was negotiated downward by the city to reflect substitutions. The final contract price was $288,169.

9. Mrs. E. A. Cote, municipal secretary of the IODE, to Mayor Hawrelak, 5 April 1964; Letter from Mayor Hawrelak to Mrs. Cote, 9 April 1964; letter from Mrs. Cote to Mayor Hawrelak, 31 May 1964; letter from Mayor Hawrelak to Mrs. Cote, 31 July 1964, R.G. 11, City Commissioners correspondence, CEA.

10. W. A. Harvey, secretary of the Parent School Organization for Exceptional Children, to the Commissioners, 16 November 1964, R.G. 11, City Commissioners correspondence, CEA.

11. Mayor Hawrelak to Mr. R. F. Duke, city architect, 23 November 1964, R.G. 11, City Commissioners correspondence, CEA.

12. Mayor Hawrelak to Mrs. Harvey, 23 November 1964, R.G. 11, City Commissioners correspondence, CEA.

13. Jean G. Lyne, recording secretary for the Edmonton Branch of the Consumers' Association of Canada to "His Honor the Mayer" [*sic*], 16 December 1964; Mayor Hawrelak to Miss Jean G. Lyne, 21 December 1964, R.G. 11, City Commissioners correspondence, CEA.

14. W. Telfer, assistant city architect to Mayor Hawrelak, 22 December 1964, R.G. 11, City Commissioners correspondence, CEA.

15. W. Telfer to Commissioner Hamilton, 17 March 1965; Commissioners to R. F. Duke, city architect, 6 April 1965, R.G. 11, City Commissioners correspondence, CEA.

16. Mrs. Wilma Harvey to the Commissioners, 17 June 1965, R.G. 11, City Commissioners correspondence, CEA.

17. J. R. Warner to the Commissioners, 25 June 1965, R.G. 11, City Commissioners correspondence, CEA.

18. Mayor Dantzer to Mrs. Wilma Harvey, 8 July 1965, R.G. 11, City Commissioners correspondence, CEA.

19. *Edmonton Journal*, 15 April 1965.

20. B. Huffman, traffic engineer, to Mr. P. Lupul of Lupul's Daily Meat, 19 January 1965; Mayor Dantzer to J. D. A. Macdonald, City Engineer, 27 May 1965, R. G. 11, City Commissioners correspondence, CEA.

21. G. S. Docherty to Peter Lupul, 22 June 1965, R.G. 11, City Commissioners correspondence, CEA. The petition, dated 3 June 1965, and signed by Peter Lupul of Lupul's Daily Meat Market, Roy A. Heeks of Prince Rupert Fish Market, Mrs. Mary Oppelt of Oppelt's Fruit, W. Elliott of Elliott's Fruit, Mrs. W. L. Malcolm of Natural Health Centre Ltd., Betty V. M. Oppelt of Betty's Fruit Basket, J. Bre-Win of Bre-Win's Meat Market, and Mr. L. Sitch for the Stallholder's Committee, was sent to the city and submitted to council on 21 June 1965.

22. *Edmonton Journal*, 8 April and 11 June 1965.

23. Edmonton Downtown Development Corporation, "Proposal to Revitalize the City Market" (25 March 1998).

24. *Edmonton Journal*, 17 February 1965.

25. W. Telfer to Commissioner Hamilton, 17 March 19656; Commissioners to R. F. Duke, 6 April 1965, R.G. 11, City Commissioners correspondence, CEA; *Edmonton Journal*, 10 April 1965.

26. Ken Harris, interview with author, Edmonton, Alberta, 3 May 2000.

27. Jerry Sumka, interview with author, Edmonton, Alberta, 27 April 2000.

28. Jerry Sumka, interview with author, Edmonton, Alberta, 27 April 2000; Policy, Planning and Control Branch, Real Estate and Housing Department, City of Edmonton, "Proposal to Establish a Farmers' Market Steering Committee" (May 1979), CEA.

29. W. Telfer, assistant city architect to Commissioner G. C. Hamilton, 29 March 1965, R.G. 11, City Commissioners correspondence, CEA.

30. W. Telfer to Commissioner Hamilton, 17 March 1965; Commissioners to R. F. Duke, city architect, 6 April 1965, R.G. 11, City Commissioners correspondence, CEA. Telfer had asked for a contract extra to "install washrooms and fixtures at the locations where the plumbing was roughed in in the retail stores."

31. *Edmonton Journal*, 9 April 1965.

32. Grace (Hinse) Kipling, conversations with author. On 31 July 1999, Grace returned to the city market to demonstrate egg-candling for an event associated with Historic Edmonton Week.

33. Mary Gordulic, interviews with author, assisted by her daughter, Minnie Chovanec, Edmonton, Alberta, 28 March and 13 June 1994.

34. Lisa Frenzel, interviews with author, Edmonton, Alberta, May 2000.

35. *Edmonton Journal*, 10 April 1965.

36. *Edmonton Journal*, 5 September 1967.

37. The "City of Edmonton General Plan" (1967) was adopted under Mayor V. M. Dantzer. Technically, land to the east of 97th Street was not defined as a part of the downtown, though it was designated as a "core area expansion zone." The maps prepared to accompany this document show a new coliseum on the site west of 97th Avenue between Jasper Avenue on the south and 102nd Avenue on the north.

38. *Edmonton Journal*, 20 November 1968.

39. Dieter and Elizabeth Kuhlmann, Angela (Kuhlmann) Kruk, Anita (Kuhlmann) McDonald and other members of the family, interview with author, Edmonton, Alberta, 23 May 2000. Also involved in the family-owned business are Dale Kruk and Doug McDonald.

40. The City of Edmonton Finance Department, "A Report on the Study of the Stall Fees — City Market Building," July 1969, compiled by W. K. Hooson, 4-5, CEA. The report suggests that the retail space (5,386 square feet) continue to be rented at $3.50 per square foot, saying that this figure "lies within the $2.00 to $5.00 per sq. ft. estimates which were quoted for property which is located in the market area." The 12,076 square feet allocated to stall space is divided into 278 three-foot stalls. Rents in 1969 varied from $1.00 to $2.00 on Saturdays and from 50 cents to $1.00 on weekdays.

41. *Edmonton Journal*, 21 August 1972.

42. *Edmonton Journal*, 14 October 1972.

43. The City of Edmonton, Real Estate and Housing Department, "Edmonton City Market Study," 1982, prepared by HLA Consultants, CEA.

44. "Edmonton City Market Study," 1982, CEA.

45. *Edmonton Journal*, 9 August 1975.

46. *Edmonton Journal*, 9 August 1975.

47. *Edmonton Journal*, 18 May 1978. The very low figures suggested in this article clash with reports of vendors and managers who report higher figures.

48. The term "public market" can be confusing because all markets seek patronage from the public at large. Here, it is used to refer to any market that is sponsored and managed by a local government and supported by tax revenue. Traditionally, public markets have combined limited retail sales with a space available to local producers to sell direct to their consumers. The Alberta farmers' market program is designed to facilitate direct sales — hence the term "farmers' market." The guidelines established by the province for farmers' markets stipulate a limit to

the percentage of goods not produced locally that may be sold in any accredited farmers' market.

49. *Edmonton Journal*, 7 January 1970.

50. "Edmonton City Market Study," 1982, by HLA Consultants, in a section titled "A Brief History of the Farmers' Market Since 1962," CEA.

51. *Edmonton Journal*, 2 June 1977 and 1 September 1977.

52. *Chinatown Plan*, April 1979, CEA.

53. Policy, Planning and Control Branch, Department of Real Estate and Housing, "Proposal to Establish a Farmers' Market Steering Committee," May 1979, CEA.

54. Joe laughed and joked about the baseball bat but was adamant about its usefulness. According to Joe, he gave the bat to the Fayads as a gift when he and Betty turned over the business. When the Fayads tried to refuse it, telling him they did not play baseball, Joe assured them that they would soon learn.

55. The Vissers, Riverbend Gardens, began selling at the city market in 1981.

56. Dennis and Ruth Vriend spent a short period at Eyot Creek, leaving in the spring of 1981 to begin their own market-gardening business. Corrie and Frank Blenke took up residence at Eyot Creek in 1980. Jan De Klerk moved there in 1982. The Koopmans moved to Eyot Creek in 1983, although they left from 1987 to 1991 to do community development work in Indonesia.

57. Dick De Klerk, Joanne and Ted Koopmans, and Frank Blenke, interview with author, Eyot Creek Farms, 16 June 2000.

58. Jerry Sumka, interview with author, Edmonton, Alberta, 27 April 2000, and Ken Harris, interview with author, Edmonton, Alberta, 3 May 2000. The managers of the city market following Mike Tremblay's retirement were: Ken Harris (January 1978 through December 1979), Kathryn Fournier, Bev Clarke, Robert Ryerson, Cheryll Ryll, and Jerry Sumka (April 1987-October 1998).

59. Retail rents (per month) in 1981, as reported by HLA in "Edmonton City Market Study," 1982, were as follows: Betty's Fruit Basket ($785), Prince Rupert Fish ($886.25); Ital-Canadian Meats ($701.87), Hinse Poultry ($503.75), and Market Dairy Bar ($278), CEA.

60. HLA Consultants, in "Edmonton City Market Study," 1982, give 1981 stall rental prices as: weekdays with shelving $2.00/day, without shelving $1.50/day, weekends with shelving $4.00/day, without $2.25/day.

61. Otto Holzbauer, interviews with author, Edmonton, Alberta, 13, 20, and 27 May 1999.

62. From time to time, associations of vendors were formed at the city market, usually to deal with specific issues or threats to the market's existence. The Edmonton City Market Association was the first officially constituted vendors' association and was registered under the Alberta Societies Act on 23 March 1992.

63. *Edmonton Journal*, 17 August 1982, reported that the Department of Real Estate and Housing, in conjunction with HLA Consultants, recommended that the current market be replaced by an eight-storey building. It went on to say that developer proposals would be solicited. Correspondence addressed to Armin Preiksaitis, president of the EDDC, 18 September 1986, suggests that in September 1983 the Real Estate and Housing Department had designed a City Market Proposal Call designed to gauge developer interest in a multi-use development that would have included a market component, Old Towne Market Files of the EDDC.

64. "A Blue Print for the 21st Century," Final Report: Mayor's Task Force on the Heart of the City (1984), 50.

65. "A Blue Print for the 21st Century," 27 and 48-49.

66. Edmonton Downtown Development Corporation, Annual Report, 1987-88.

Chapter 6

1. Winspear's report was submitted to the city administration on 11 March 1963. The information upon which the author based his opinion that the market was a viable financial operation, probably supplied to him by the Land Department, was contained in the "City of Edmonton Financial Statement and Reports for the Year ended December 31, 1961," which showed that revenues from retail stores and farmers' stall rents covered the market's operating expenses and those of the "comfort station" leaving a net profit of $4,611.

2. *Edmonton Bulletin*, 6 April 1900.

3. *Edmonton Bulletin*, 1 February 1911.

4. By-law no. 20 was passed 11 February 1885. By-law no. 98, also to establish a public market, was passed 5 March 1889, and, on 31 May 1898, By-law no. 309 "To Establish A Public Market and a Weigh Scale" was passed, CCA.

5. Jack Peach, "Calgary's public market dream began long before Eau Claire," *Calgary Real Estate News*, 21 March 1997.

6. *Macleod Spectator*, 17 September 1914; Report from Annie Gale, market advisor to Mayor and Council, City of Calgary, 15 July 1918, Box 129, File 899, CCA.

7. Harry M. Sanders, "City Hall Market Home to Many Jewish Vendors," *Discovery: The Journal of the Jewish Historical Society of Southern Alberta*, vol. 10, no. 2, Spring 2000, 1-2.

8. *Medicine Hat News*, 3 May 1906.

9. *Macleod Spectator*, 17 September 1914.

10. *Claresholm Review*, 30 September 1909.

11. Roger Vick, "Alberta Plantsman, Robert Simonet," *Kinnikinnick*, vol. 2, no. 8 (November 1979), says that Simonet's desire to break the code of the double-flowering petunia was sparked by seeing some which had been grown from

Japanese seed and were being sold by Mr. Bannard, Simonet's neighbour at the market (203).

12. Lois Hole, "Cracking the code of double-flowering petunias," *Globe and Mail*, 13 June 1998.

13. Janine Dunn, interviews with the author, Edmonton, Alberta, 24 July and 25 September 1995 and 25 January 1996.

14. Rudi and Annalotte Thiel and Horst Thiel, interviews with author, Bruderheim, Alberta, 4 June 2000.

15. Dr. Mohyuddin Mirza, greenhouse crops specialist, Horticultural Unit, Plant Industry Division, Industry Development Sector, Alberta Agriculture, Food and Rural Development, telephone conversation with author, 7 June 2000.

16. Mrs. Lou Hyndman, Sr., interview with author, Edmonton, Alberta, October 1999.

17. Flore (Bilodeau) Hinse, interviews with author, Beaumont, Alberta, 20 and 26 April 1993.

18. Frank Farkas, interview with author, Edmonton, Alberta, 6 May 2000.

19. Dan Morris, regional supervisor for Edmonton North Food Safety Division, Regulatory Services Branch for Meat Inspection, Alberta Agriculture and Rural Development, telephone conversation with author, 15 August 2000, confirmed that approximately eighty percent of the poultry processing done in the province of Alberta in 2000 was carried out at three plants run by Lilydale. Independent producers must have their poultry processed in a provincially inspected facility. In 2000, in addition to the three Lilydale plants, there were four small independently run plants in the province, of which the Hinse plant in Beaumont was one. A fifth plant run by The Poultry Company was being operated in Edmonton. The number of facilities licensed to slaughter poultry varies from time to time.

20. Denis Hinse, interviews with author, Edmonton, Alberta, 29 April, 6 May, and 13 June 2000. The poultry business run by the Hinse family was officially named Hinse Poultry Farms in 1966, the year the plant was built.

21. In 1993, the Department of Agriculture changed its name to Alberta Agriculture and Rural Development. Since 1994, the official name of the ministry has been Alberta Agriculture, Food and Rural Development — often shortened in this chapter to 'Alberta Agriculture.'

22. In the early 1970s, according to information gathered by Alberta Agriculture prior to the commencement of its program in 1973, there were only four farmers' markets in the province. These were in Edmonton, Lethbridge, Medicine Hat, and Calgary.

23. Information on the farmers' market program was received from Simone Demers Collins, Farmers' Market administrator for Alberta Agriculture and Rural Development since 1992, by letter to the author and in meetings. The benefits

of the program to small agricultural businesses, especially market gardeners and greenhouse operators, have been corroborated in my conversations with market vendors.

24. At least two other farmers' markets created in response to Alberta Agriculture's program, the Millarville Farmers' Market and the St. Albert Farmers' Market, have grown to become large and community-defining institutions. Millarville, a flourishing and immensely popular summer market open from June to early October on the site of the famous Millarville Race Track, represents a continuation of the race-meet atmosphere but, according to its manager, Jackie Lacey, has stimulated the creation of several small but flourishing agricultural and craft enterprises. The gigantic outdoor St. Albert Market offers vendors in the Edmonton area yet another outlet for their products. Many small agricultural businesses attend several of the markets in the Edmonton area.

25. On 29 May 1907, the burgesses of the newly incorporated city of Strathcona passed *By-law no. 189*, allowing council to raise $12,000 to purchase Block 25 "A" as a market site. The minutes from the meetings of the Strathcona City Council, 1907-09, chart the progress of the project. On 17 November 1908, Alderman Tipton recommended that money be put in the following year's estimates "for putting the market site in condition, and the erection of suitable buildings for market purposes." On 29 April 1909, council agreed to erect a new market building on the site as speedily as possible. At the meeting on 8 June 1909, council voted to raise $2,000 for a market building, $300 for new scales, $250 for an office for a weighmaster and market superintendent and $100 to grade the site. It seems that the facilities were operational by October 1909 because at the meeting on the 12th of that month council agreed to take an old stove from the police station to the new market building and to hire a team and "have the litter around the Market Site cleared up", R.G.100.1, Class 9, File 145, CEA.

26. Information on the Old Strathcona Farmers' Market gathered with the assistance of Wanda Klimke, Jim O'Neill, Ruth Vriend, and Elaine Warwick.

27. Joyce Pearson, interview with author, Edmonton, Alberta, 30 May 2000.

28. In Alberta, the number of farmers' markets has remained stable for several years at between 110 and 120. These are listed every year in a pamphlet put out by Alberta Agriculture, Food and Rural Development. In 1998, the Department of Human Ecology at the University of Alberta and Alberta Agriculture, Food and Rural Development, published a report based on a two-year study of the assumptions behind the Farmers' Market program, specifically the assumption that the program would benefit both consumers and small producers. The study was designed, carried out, and written by Joyce Lencucha, Marian Williams, Linda Capjack, and Valerie M. Gross and is called "Farmers' Markets in Alberta: A Direct Channel of Distribution." Its five conclusions support the historical argument implied in

this chapter — that farmers' markets do contribute to local (rural and urban) economic development. Other provinces in Canada are interested in this issue.

In 1999, the School of Rural Planning and Development, University of Guelph, published a report called "Community and Economic Impact of Farmers' Markets in Ontario," in which an attempt was made to quantify overall sales at Ontario's 127 farmers' markets ($487.7 million) and jobs (27,000) as well as to assess the spin-off benefits to communities.

An article in the *Globe and Mail*, 11 September 1999, "Farmers' markets sprout across the U.S.," quoted the United States Department of Agriculture as reporting that the number of farmers' markets had increased from two thousand to three thousand in a few years, with an overall 1999 sales figure of about $1 billion. The article speculated that the trend to farmers' markets constitutes a small but significant threat to large-scale agribusiness.

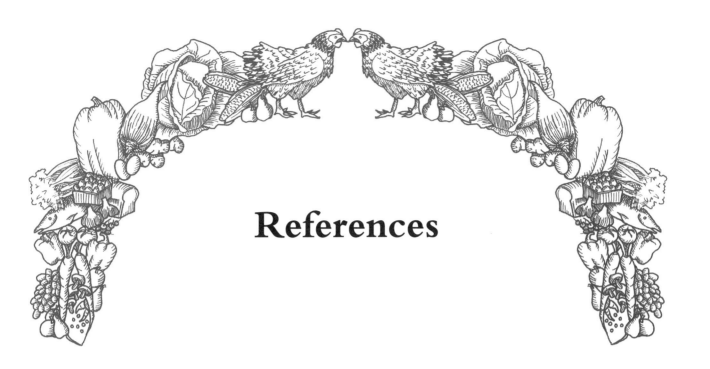

References

List of Interviewees

The following list includes the names of several individuals who were interviewed while this book was being researched and written. Many of these interviews were recorded in the form of short personal histories and have been accessioned by the CEA. They can be found there under the accession number, A95-205.

Andrew, William T. (Bill)
Berger, Louise (Marletaz)
Brassard, Marie-Anne (Magnan)
Brennan, Pat
Bre-Win, Betty (Oppelt)
Bre-Win, Joe
Close, Geneva
De Klerk, Dick, with Ted and Joanne Koopmans and Frank Blenke
Demers Collins, Simone
Dockstader, Reg
Dunn, Janine
Elliott, Bill
Farkas, Frank
Frenzel, Lisa (Heimrath)
Gordulic, Mary, with Minnie Chovanec

Granstrom, Kathrine, with Ray and Rita (Granstrom) Arends

Harris, Ken

Heeks, Roy, followed by assistance from Clive Heeks in clarifying some of the details

Hinse, Denis

Hinse, Flore (Bilodeau)

Holzbauer, Otto

Hurlbut, Dorothy (Oppelt)

Hyndman, Mrs. Lou Sr.

Juchli, Marcel

Kipling, Grace (Hinse)

Klimke, Wanda

Kuhlmann, Dieter, Elizabeth, Angela (Kuhlmann) Kruk, Anita (Kuhlmann) McGregor

Lacey, Jackie

Lupul, Peter

Malcolm, Mary

McMann, John (Jack)

Moore, Mary

Morin, Yvette and François, with Doris Morin and Alice Gingras

Pearson, Joyce

Sernowski, Mary (Chipil)

Sumka, Jerry

Svekla, Mary (Chibree)

Thiel, Rudolf, Annalotte, and Horst

Tremblay, Margaret (Oppelt)

Van Dorsser, Gerard (Gerry)

Wallish, Robert

Sources

Note on Primary Sources

The CEA holds the public records used for this book, including standard sources such as council meeting minutes and annual financial reports. The majority of the correspondence relating to the Edmonton City Market has not been fully catalogued and is collected in R.G. 11 under the title, City Commissioners Correspondence. This collection was invaluable to my research, but it does not contain all the correspondence records related to the market because the practice of storing records varied from time to time and from administration to administration. Many records seem to have disappeared. Recent correspondence has not yet been archived. In addition to public records, the CEA has a collection of published and unpublished works on local history, including two unpublished theses referred to in this book: Diana Lynn Bodnar, "The Prairie Legislative Buildings of Canada," M.A. thesis (University of British Columbia, 1979); and Edmund Herbert Dale, "The Role of Successive Town and City Councils in the Evolution of Edmonton, Alberta, 1862-1966," Ph.D. thesis (University of Alberta, 1969).

Local newspapers have been an invaluable resource. Those consulted most frequently are the *Edmonton Bulletin* (December 1880-January 1951) and the *Edmonton Journal* (November 1903 to the present). The Alberta Legislature Library holds an excellent collection of Alberta newspapers, some of which were surveyed for evidence of whether markets existed in various communities.

Note on Secondary Sources

My attempts to extend the research for this book on the Edmonton City Market to secondary sources led to some interesting forays into complementary material and resulted in several wild goose chases. I was surprised, for example, to see that the city market did not figure as a topic in any of the standard histories of Edmonton. Indeed, the market tradition in Canada has so far attracted the interest of few published scholars (see articles by Sean Gouglas and W. Thomas Matthews in the list of further reading below for exceptions). General interest in the subject is suggested by the publication of a very brief and cursory survey of public markets by Linda Biesenthal with photographs by J. Douglas Wilson, *The Public Market Tradition in Canada* (Toronto: Peter Martin Associates Limited, 1980).

Although my research suggested that the Edmonton City Market has played a mediating role in the creation of a local economy between 1900 and 2000, I was unable to find any economic studies of Alberta which shed theoretical light on this notion. The books of Jane Jacobs, however (three of which appear on the list of further reading below), supply a valuable theoretical framework within which the role played by produce markets in their local economies can be situated. Jacobs represents the economy as a complex network of one-on-one transactions, each of which has a ripple-out effect. This representation, along with her focus on the city as the unit within which economies can best be understood, allows us to see the role produce markets can play in the economic mainstream as opposed to thinking of market transactions as a subspecies of the economy.

The disciplines of architecture and urban planning are most likely to treat the subject of public or produce markets, both from a historical and from a contemporary perspective. This trend is likely to continue, particularly as the methods of the social historian are adopted by architectural historians and by historians of the city. A recent study of the British Market Hall by James Schmiechen and Kenneth Carls (1999) is an excellent example.

A topic I do not develop in this book, but which suggested itself in the research, is the relationship between immigration history and the Edmonton City Market. On the surface, it would seem that the market offered new immigrants an opportunity to launch a small business despite a lack of investment capital — unless, of course, a particular group was excluded from taking stalls at the market, as the Chinese may have been in the 1920s. I was reluctant to suggest this, however, as I could not find the kind of data in local histories of particular ethnic groups to support the impressions I formed.

Below are two lists. The first contains works consulted in this book, published and unpublished. The second is a list of some of the books I read and found stimulating and helpful in my efforts to understand the role played by the Edmonton City Market in the local culture.

Works Consulted

Aiken, Don. "The Real Market Square," *Winnipeg Real Estate News* 26 January 1996.

Camp, John M. *The Athenian Agora: Excavations in the Heart of Classical Athens.* Series: New Aspects of Antiquity, General Editor, Colin Renfrew. London: Thames and Hudson, 1986.

Cashman, Tony. *Abraham Cristall, 1868-1944: The Story of a Simple Man.* No publication information.

———. "Donald Ross, Our First Hotelman." In *The Best Edmonton Stories.* Edmonton: Hurtig Publishers, 1976.

———. *A History of Motoring in Alberta.* 3d ed. Edmonton: Alberta Motor Association, 1990.

Dale, Edmund Herbert. "The Role of Successive Town and City Councils in the Evolution of Edmonton, 1862-1966." Ph.D. diss., University of Alberta, 1969.

Day, John Patrick. "Donald Ross, Old-Timer Extraordinaire." In *Edmonton: The Life of a City,* edited by Bob Hesketh and Frances Swyripa, 31-39. Edmonton: NeWest Press, 1995.

Hatcher, Colin K. and Tom Schwarzkopf. *Edmonton's Electric Transit: The Story of Edmonton's Streetcars and Trolly Buses.* Toronto: Railfare Enterprises Limited, 1983.

Hesketh, Bob and Frances Swyripa, eds. *Edmonton: The Life of a City*. Edmonton: NeWest Press, 1995.

Hole, Lois. "Cracking the code of double-flowering petunias," *Globe and Mail* 13 June 1998.

Ironside, R. G. and S. A. Hamilton. "Historical Geography of Coal Mining in the Edmonton District," *Alberta Historical Review* 20 (Summer 1972): 6-16.

MacGregor, J.G. *Edmonton: A History*. 2d ed. Edmonton: Hurtig Publishers, 1975.

MacRae, Marion and Anthony Adamson. *Cornerstones of Order: Courthouses and Town Halls of Ontario, 1784-1914*. Toronto: Clarke, Irwin, 1983.

Marsh, James H., ed. in chief. *The Canadian Encyclopedia 2000*, World Edition, on CD-ROM. Toronto: McClelland and Stewart, 1999. S.v. "Rupert's Land," by Shirlee Anne Smith and "Page, John Percy," by Cathy MacDonald.

Otto, Stephen A. "First City Hall (1834-45)." Unpublished paper, c.1986.

Payne, Michael. "Edmontonians and the Legislature." In *Edmonton: The Life of a City*, edited by Bob Hesketh and Frances Swyripa, 104-15. Edmonton: NeWest Press, 1995.

Peach, Jack. "Calgary's public market dream began long before Eau Claire," *Calgary Real Estate News* 21 March 1997.

Rek, Joseph. *Municipal Elections in Edmonton, 1892-1998: summary of results with short biographies of mayors and councillors*. Edmonton: Edmonton Public Library, 1998.

Saalman, Howard. *Medieval Cities*. Planning and Cities Series. George R. Collins, general editor. New York: Alfred A. Knopf, 1990.

Sanders, Harry M. "City Hall Market Home to Many Jewish Vendors," *Discovery: The Journal of the Jewish Historical Society of Southern Alberta* vol. 10, no. 2 (Spring 2000): 1-2.

Shute, Allan and Margaret Fortier. *Riverdale: From Fraser Flats to Edmonton Oasis*. Riverdale: Tree Frog Press, 1992.

Vick, Roger. "Alberta Plantsman, Robert Simonet," *Kinnikinnick* vol.2, no. 8 (November 1979): 202-204.

———. "Klondyke Gardens: The Early Years," *Kinnikinnick* vol. 6, no. 5 (February 1989): 127-32.

Waddell, Ross M. *The Exchange District: An Illustrated Guide to Winnipeg's Historic Commercial District*. Winnipeg: Winnipeg Heritage Corporation, n.d.

Zucker, Paul. *Town and Square: From the Agora to the Village Green*. New York: Columbia University Press, 1959.

Further Reading

Arthur, Eric. *Toronto, No Mean City.* 3d ed. Revised by Stephen A. Otto. Toronto: University of Toronto Press, 1986.

Artibise, Alan F. J. *Prairie Urban Development, 1870-1930.* The Canadian Historical Association Booklets No. 34. Ottawa: 1981.

———. "The Urban West, The Evolution of Prairie Towns and Cities to 1930." In *The Canadian City: Essays in Urban and Social History.* Revised and enlarged edition. Edited by Gilbert A. Stelter and Alan F. J. Artibise, 138-64. Ottawa: Carleton University Press, 1984.

Betke, Carl. "The Original City of Edmonton: A Derivative Prairie Urban Community." In *The Canadian City: Essays in Urban and Social History.* Revised and enlarged edition. Edited by Gilbert A. Stelter and Alan F. J. Artibise, 392-430. Ottawa: Carleton University Press, 1984.

Careless, J. M. S. *The Rise of Cities in Canada Before 1914.* Canadian Historical Association Booklets No. 32. Ottawa: Canadian Historical Association, 1978.

Cronon, William. *Nature's Metropolis: Chicago and the Great West.* New York and London: W. W. Norton, 1991.

Davis, Dorothy. *Fairs, Shops, and Supermarkets: A History of English Shopping.* Toronto: University of Toronto Press, 1966.

Dawson, Brian J. with Patricia M. Dawson. *Moon Cakes in Gold Mountain: From China to the Canadian Plains.* Calgary: Detselig, 1991.

Gouglas, Sean. "Produce and Protection: Covent Garden Market, the Socioeconomic Elite, and the Downtown Core in London, Ontario, 1843-1915," *Urban History Review* vol. 25, no. 1 (October 1996): 3-18.

Harris, John R. "Economics: Invisible, Productive, and Problem Cities." In *Cities of the Mind: Images and Themes of the City in the Social Sciences*, edited by Lloyd Rodwin and Robert M. Hollister, 37-54. New York and London: Plenum Press, 1984.

Hough, Michael. *Out of Place: Restoring Identity to the Regional Landscape.* New Haven & London: Yale University Press, 1990.

Jacobs, Jane. *The Economy of Cities.* New York: Random House, 1969.

———. *Cities and the Wealth of Nations: Principles of Economic Life.* New York: Random House, 1984.

———. *The Nature of Economies.* Toronto: Random House Canada, 2000.

Lane, Robert E. *The Market Experience.* New York: Cambridge University Press, 1991.

Matthews, W. Thomas. "Local Government and the Regulation of the Public Market in Upper Canada, 1800-1860: The Moral Economy of the Poor?" *Ontario History* vol. 29, no. 4 (December 1987): 297-326.

Merrett, Kathryn Chase. "The City Market." In *Edmonton: The Life of a City,* edited by Bob Hesketh and Frances Swyripa, 203-211. Edmonton: NeWest Press, 1995.

Morris, A. E. J. *History of Urban Form: Before the Industrial Revolutions.* 3d. ed. New York: Longman Scientific and Technical, 1994.

Nader, George A. *Theoretical, Historical and Planning Perspectives.* Cities of Canada, vol. 1. Canada: Macmillan of Canada, 1975.

———. *Profiles of Fifteen Metropolitan Centres.* Cities of Canada, vol. 2. Canada: Macmillan of Canada, 1976.

Palmer, Howard. *Ethnicity and Politics in Canada Since Confederation.* Canadian Historical Association Booklets No. 17. Ottawa, Canadian Historical Association, 1991.

Person, Dennis and Carin Routledge. *Edmonton, Portrait of a City.* Edmonton: Reidmore, 1981.

Rybczynski, Witold. *City Life.* Toronto: Harper Perennial, 1996.

Schmiechen, James and Kenneth Carls. *The British Market Hall: A Social and Architectural History.* New Haven & London: Yale University Press, 1999.

Sennett, Richard, ed. *Classic Essays on the Culture of Cities.* New York: Appleton-Century-Crofts, 1969.

———. *The Conscience of the Eye: The Design and Social Life of Cities.* New York: Alfred A. Knopf, 1990.

Shorett, Alice and Murray Morgan. *The Pike Place Market: People, Politics, and Produce.* Seattle, Washington: Pacific Search Press, 1982.

Smith, P. J., ed. *Edmonton: The Emerging Metropolitan Pattern.* Western Geographical Series, vol. 15. Victoria: Department of Geography, University of Victoria, 1978.

Watkins, M. H. and H. M. Grant, eds. *Canadian Economic History: Classic and Contemporary Approaches.* Ottawa: Carleton University Press, 1993.

Webster, T. B. L. *Everyday Life in Classical Athens.* London: B. T. Batsford, 1969.

Wetherell, Donald G. and Irene R. A. Kmet. *Town Life: Main Street and the Evolution of Small Town Alberta, 1880-1947.* Edmonton: University of Alberta Press, 1995.

Wirth, Louis. "Urbanism as a Way of Life." In *Classic Essays in the Culture of Cities,* edited by Richard Sennett, 143-64. New York: Appleton-Century-Crofts, 1969.

3R Greenhouses, 163

Agriculture and urban identity, 19-24, 129-30

Alberta farmers' market program, 148, 153-4, 186-7

Alberta Market Gardeners' Association, 186

Alberta Poultry Breeders Association, 124. *See also* Market building (1916): public events in

AMA (Alberta Motor Association), 116, 118

Ardrossan Greenhouses, 110-1, 149

Armstrong, Mayor G., 40-1

Bagley and McManus. *See* Market Square: non-market uses on

Ball, Dr. G. H. (MOH), 136

Belmont Gardens, 149

Belvedere Gardens, 73-4

Birchdale Greenhouses, 163

Brennan, Pat, 104

Bre-Win's Meat Market, 84-6, 94. *See also* Vendors: Bre-Win, Joe; Vendors: Bre-Win, Howard

Browne, George Jr., 14-5

Burgess, Cecil, 105-6

Bury, Mayor A.U.G., 68, 71, 74

Campbell, Stan, 127

Cardy, W. J., 79

Chandler Kennedy Architects, 167-8

Chinatown re-development, 148, 155-7, 166

City Beautiful movement, 9, 35

City Hall (1957), 119

City of Edmonton General Plan (1967), 155

Civic Block, 6, 13, 41, 52-4

Civic centre
    Burgess and Dewar plans for, 104-6
    C. L. Gibbs's influence on, 38, 82-3
    Civic Centre Development Plan for, 128-9, 133
    Detwiler Plan for, 113-4
    Market Square as site for, 15, 19, 26, 35, 47, 51
    Morell and Nichols plan for, 9-10, 35, 38-40
    role of market in, 91, 119, 130-1
    Webb and Knapp plan for, 128-9
Civic Improvement League, 65

Clarke, Mrs. Joseph A., 79

Consumers' League, 45, 47, 49, 60

Cristall, Abe, 33

Dewar, M. C. (Max), city architect, 103-6, 119

Dockstader, Reg, 66

Dominion Square. *See* Market Square

Downtown City Market Association, 166

Dunn, Janine, 177

EDDC (Edmonton Downtown Development Corporation), 162, 166-9, 188

Edmonton and District Market Gardeners and Florists' Association, 66, 73, 77, 79, 83, 86

Edmonton Chamber of Commerce, 79-80, 119, 130-1, 171

Edmonton Horticultural and Vacant Lots Garden Association, 78-9, 83, 124-5, 178

Edmonton Horticultural Society, 66

Edmonton Poultry Association, 78. *See also* Market building (1916): public events in

Edmonton Tree Planting Association, 79. *See also* Market building: public events in

Egg-candling, 74-6, 117, 143, 202n.79. *See also* Market, Edmonton City: eggs sold at

Ennismore, R. H., 75-6, 117

Evergreen Gardens, 149, 163

Eyot Creek Farms, 159-61, 163

Federal Building. *See* Market Square: federal government's interest in

Fire Hall no. 1, 13, 19, 21(fig.)

Gariepy, J. H., 25-6, 33

Garside, Thomas, city solicitor, 89. *See also* Market Square: legal status of

Gibbs, C. L. (Lionel). *See* Market Square: C. L. Gibbs's influence on

Great Depression, 1, 68, 83-8

Grierson, Ernest, 30-3, 35-6

Harris, Ken, 141, 153-4

Hawrelak, Mayor William, 137-8

Haymarket. *See* Markets: 101st Street Market,
    Edmonton

Heiminck, Isabella, 26, 89

Heiminck, Philip, 4-5, 11, 25-30, 33, 117

Hinse Poultry Farms, 149, 163, 169, 183-6. *See also*
    Vendors: Hinse, Denis; Vendors: Hinse, Flore

HLA Consultants, 157, 166-7

Hole, Lois, 178

Hunger March (1932), 80-1

Hyndman, Mrs. Lou Sr., 182

Ingram, C. J. (Clarence), 95-104, 115-16

IODE (Imperial Order Daughters of the Empire),
    8-9, 35, 65, 137

Jeffers, Allan Merrick, city architect, 5, 14, 40-5,
    53-4

Kassian Kennedy Architecture, Interior Design and
    Planning, 168

Keeler, Bea and J. R. (Roy), 125

Kelly and Ennes, 36-7

Kendall, Edgar, 56-61, 66-8, 70-6, 78, 84, 86, 89,
    91-5

Kerr, Illingworth, 16

Kipling, Grace (née Hinse), 143, 145(fig.). *See also*
    Egg-candling

Klondyke Gardens, 34. *See also* Vendors:
    Frederiksen, Frederik

Knott, Mayor Daniel, 81-8

Kuhlmann's Market Gardens and Greenhouses,
    150-2, 163

McIntyre, N. J., 117, 121-7

McLeod, K. A. (Kenny), 6, 36, 54

McLeod Building, 54

McMann, Allan and Ella, 55(fig.)

McMann, John (Jack), 55

Managers
    Campbell, S. (Stan), 127
    Grierson, Ernest, 30-3, 35-6
    Harris, Ken, 141, 153-4
    Ingram, C. J. (Clarence), 95-104, 115-6
    Kelly and Ennes, 36-7
    Kendall, Edgar, 56-61, 66-8, 70-6, 78, 84, 86, 89,
        91-5
    McIntyre, N. J., 117, 121-7
    Robertson, D. C., 36, 40, 43
    Sumka, Jerry, 141, 162, 169
    Tremblay, Michael (Mike), 127-8, 146, 148, 154

Market, Edmonton City
    by-laws concerning, 29, 34, 36, 42, 68-9, 101
    charity stall at, 66, 76-7, 99, 108, 122, 137-9
    Civic Employment Bureau and, 95-6, 122, 126
    discrimination and, 71
    eggs sold at, 74-6, 111, 143
    finances of, 16-17, 32, 64, 86-7, 152-3, 209n.60
    Great Depression and, 1, 68, 83-8
    retail stores and, 7, 49, 59-60, 69-70, 88,
        108, 121, 136-7, 216n.48. *See also* Market,
        Edmonton City: finances of
    site search for, 19, 25-6, 107
    staffing of, 31, 67-8, 86, 95, 126-7, 152. *See also*
        Managers
    stall rents at, 32, 60-1, 69, 84, 100, 117, 121,
        147, 153
    usage of, 60-3, 70, 88, 121-2, 148
    vendor selection criteria for, 70-2
    World War II and, 98-103, 119, 127, 147, 155

Market building (1916)
    appearance and features of, 7(fig.), 50(fig.),
        51(fig.), 59-60, 100(fig.)
    capital cost of, 51, 199n.33
    enlargements of, 63, 83-8
    non-market uses of, 99-101, 122
    physical deterioration of, 103, 124-6
    public events in, 76, 78-80, 124-5
    renovations to, 96, 103, 117

Market building (new, 1965)
    cost and financing of, 135-6
    design and appearance of, 135-7, 141-2
    urban context of, 147-8, 157, 161-2
    vendors complaints about, 139-42
Market clerk. *See* Managers
Market Square
    activities on, 7, 56-9, 93, 99-100, 115-9
    appearance and features of, 7(fig.), 30, 41(fig.),
        56-9, 61(fig.), 80(fig.), 126
    cars on, 115, 118-9, 121
    federal government's interest in, 88-9, 91-3,
        102-4, 106-7, 109, 114, 208n.56
    horses on, 9, 56-7, 62, 118, 31
    legal status of, 29, 89, 91, 103
    non-market uses on, 116-8
    selling on, 61, 120-1
    parades and demonstrations on, 61(fig.), 80-2,
        116
    urban context of, 33, 52-4
    weigh scales on, 30-2, 93, 117, 119
Market superintendent. *See* Managers
Markets
    101st Street Market, Edmonton, 2(fig.), 5, 42-6,
        67
    agora, 5-7
    Calgary, Alberta, 173-4
    Coventry, England, 131-2
    European (general), 8
    Hamilton, Ontario, 12
    Irvine, Alberta, 174
    London, Ontario, 131
    Macleod, Alberta, 174
    Old Strathcona Farmers' Market, Edmonton,
        187-8
    private market in Empire Auditorium,
        Edmonton, 4-5
    St. John, New Brunswick, 12
    South Side Market, Edmonton, 40, 67, 220n.25
    Toronto, 12-3
    Winnipeg, 13-5

Martland, John, city architect, 64, 86-8, 102-3
Mo-Na Mushrooms, 163-65
Morell and Nichols. *See* Civic Centre: Morell and
    Nichols plan for
Morin, François, 77

Nelligan, Father Leo, 77-8

Old Towne Market Plan, 161-2, 166
O'Neill, Jim, 188

Pay'N Save building (formerly Edmonton Motors
    building, 94(fig.), 129, 132(fig.), 137
Pearson, Joyce, 189
Post Office, Edmonton Main, 52-3
Prince Rupert Fish Market, 63-4, 121, 142-3,
    157-8, 163. *See also* Vendors: Heeks, Roy;
    Vendors: Mandlis, Harry; Vendors: Lampa, Val

Relief vouchers, 84
Retail Butchers and Merchants of Edmonton, 69
Retail Merchants' Association, 42
Robertson, D. C., 36, 40, 43
Ross, Donald, 22-4
Rummage sale. *See* Market building (1916): public
    events in

St. Joseph's Cathedral, 77-8
South Cooking Lake Greenhouses, 149, 163
Stallholders. *See* Vendors
Sumka, Jerry, 141, 162, 169
Svekla, Mary, 3
Swanson Lumber Company. *See* Market building
    (1916): non-market uses of

Telfer, Walter, assistant to city architect, 136-41
Thiel's Greenhouses, 149, 163, 178-81
Town Hall and Market Committee, 9, 19, 25
Town planning, 9
Tremblay, Michael (Mike), 127-8, 146, 148, 154

United Farm Women of Alberta, 76
United Farmers of Alberta, 37, 47
Urban renewal and the 'new' city market, 147-8,
    154-7, 161

Vacant Lots Garden Club, 65-6
Vendors
    Andreanna, Dominic, 158, 163
    Arends (née Granstrom), Rita, 72. *See also*
        Virginia Park Greenhouses
    Ash, Melvin, 140
    Baader, Max, 71
    Bannard, H. A., 72
    Belinsky, Alexandra, 145(fig.), 146
    Bennett, Garth, 112
    Berger, François (Frank) and Louise (née
        Marletaz), 73-4
    Bilodeau, Flore (later Flore Hinse). *See* Hinse,
        Flore
    Blochlinger, Émile and Mrs. Émile, 142, 149
    Bong, Patrick, 163
    Brassard, Marie-Anne (née Magnan), 146, 183
    Bre-Win, Betty (née Oppelt, wife of Joe Bre-
        Win), 101-2, 121, 142, 145(fig.), 158-9
    Bre-Win, Howard (father of Joe Bre-Win), 84-6,
        88, 108
    Bre-Win, Joe (son of Howard Bre-Win), 67, 78,
        85-6, 94-5, 121, 142, 157-9
    Chamaschuk, Pearl, 163
    Chapman, John, 74
    Close, Arthur and Geneva (née Hardy), 88, 93-4
    De Klerk, Carolyn and Dick, 159-61
    Dimitrov, Mrs. George, 147
    Edgar, Laurette (née Hinse, daughter of Flore
        and René Hinse), 163
    Elliott, William (Bill), 104-5, 121, 142, 157
    Farkas, Frank (son of Konrad and Minnie
        Farkas), 123, 141
    Farkas, Konrad and Minnie, 123, 183
    Fayad, Albert and Fatima, 158
    Finnemore, Mrs. N. P., 97

Finnemore, N. P. (Norman), 60-2, 66, 107-8
Francis, Pat, 163
Frederiksen, Frederik, 24, 34
Frenzel, Lisa and Werner, 146-7, 149, 163
Gaudio, Joe, 177
Gielen, Marc, 177
Gordulic, Mary, 144-5
Granstrom, Kathrine (wife of Marius, mother of
    Ray Granstrom and Rita Arends), 33, 72-3,
    145(fig.). *See also* Virginia Park Greenhouses
Granstrom, Marius (husband of Kathrine,
    brother of Pete, father of Ray Granstrom
    and Rita Arends), 72-3. *See also* Virginia Park
    Greenhouses
Granstrom, Pete (brother of Marius Granstrom),
    72. *See also* Virginia Park Greenhouses
Granstrom, Ray (son of Kathrine and Marius
    Granstrom), 72, 145(fig.). *See also* Virginia
    Park Greenhouses
Hauf, Dorothee (née Kuhlmann, sister of Dieter
    Kuhlmann), 151(fig.)
Heeks, Roy, 64-5, 142, 157
Henri (also spelled Henry), Jean, 70, 75
Hinse, Denis (son of Flore and René Hinse),
    120, 123, 143, 158, 182-6
Hinse, Flore (wife of René), 59(fig.), 62, 70,
    145-6, 163, 182-4, 186(fig.)
Hinse, Gerry (son of Denis Hinse), 185
Hinse, René (husband of Flore), 59(fig.), 182,
    186(fig.)
Holzbauer, Otto, 163-5
Hurlbut, Dorothy (née Oppelt, daughter of Mary
    and Peter Oppelt), 109-11, 120, 149
Hurlbut, Jim, 109-11, 149
Jensen, N. J., 108
Jones, James, 63
Jones, Mrs. James, 63, 65, 121
Juchli, Augustine (née Accarias, wife of Charles
    Juchli), 63
Juchli, Charles (husband of Augustine Juchli),
    62-3

Juchli, Peter (brother of Charles Juchli), 62, 71

Klimke, Wanda, 120

Krukowski, Ron, 136-7

Kublik, Robert (Bob), 163

Kuhlmann family: Dieter and Elizabeth (Liz) and daughters Anita (later McDonald) and Angela (later Kruk), 150-2

Lampa, Val, 157-8

Lupul, Peter, 8, 111-3, 121, 142, 158

Madaski, Cheryl and Joe, 163

Malcolm, Mary, 104, 114-5, 121, 158-9

Malcolm, Wilfrid Laurier (Laurie), 104, 114-5

Mandlis, Harry, 63-4

Milne, Joe, 88

Motruk, S., 142

Neal, Ronald, 79

Noble, Lois, 163

Oppelt, Betty (later Bre-Win). *See* Vendors: Bre-Win, Betty

Oppelt, Dorothy (later Hurlbut). *See* Vendors: Hurlbut, Dorothy

Oppelt, Margaret (later Tremblay). *See* Vendors: Tremblay, Margaret

Oppelt, Mary (wife of Peter), 61-2, 101-2, 108, 142, 157, 179

Oppelt, Peter (husband of Mary), 61-2

Oppelt, Walter (son of Peter and Mary Oppelt), 8, 120

Peck, Norman, 108, 142

Powell, Frieda, 3

Prins, Leslie and Ron, 169(fig.)

Rasimus family, 163

Sernowski, Mary (née Chipil, called Baba), 3, 123, 183

Simonet, Lillian (née Hérard), 177

Simonet, Robert, 88, 175-80

Templeman, Thomas, 108

Thiel family: Analotte and Rudolf (Rudi) and sons Horst and Rudy, 178-81

Tong, Ann, 164-5

Tonsi, Antonio, 71

Tremblay, Margaret (née Oppelt), 120(fig.), 128

Triska, Anna, 3

Van Dorsser family, 163

Veerman family, 163

Visser, Doug and Evelyn, 159, 163

Wagner, Fred, 77

Wallish family, including Robert, 66

Wanke family, 149, 163

Virginia Park Greenhouses, 33, 72-3, 149, 163

Visser, Jennie and Clarence, 159

Warner, J. R., 130, 138-9

Warwick, Elaine, 187

Winspear, W. W., 130-1, 171-3, 175